Better Homes
& Gardens®

Annual
Recipes 2018

Meredith. Consumer Marketing
Des Moines, Iowa

SHRIMP IN GARLIC-PEPPER SAUCE
Recipe on page 235

TORTILLA ESPAÑOLA
Recipe on page 235

from the editor

At *Better Homes & Gardens* ® magazine our goal is to inspire experimentation with new ingredients and flavors that, though they may be unfamiliar now, will soon be a time-honored tradition on your menus.

What's your go-to cuisine when you're cooking on an ordinary weeknight? Mine is decidedly somewhere in the Mediterranean: one-pan bakes with vegetables, chicken, herbs, garlic, lemons, and olive oil. Maybe a lamb burger or a casserole of eggplant and tomatoes. Pasta, of course. I don't know why I gravitate to these bright flavors. (I didn't grow up with them. Our version of Mediterranean was pizza or spaghetti with meat sauce.) I rely on them mostly for health reasons and the quick and easy cooking methods; even so, sometimes I get bored and realize I need to mix things up.

That's why lately I've been trying to expand my culinary horizons a bit by using classic Asian flavors like ginger, soy sauce, sesame, and rice wine. Or by blending spices—cumin, allspice, red pepper, and cinnamon—for complex Middle Eastern flavors. I've also jumped on the grain-bowl bus by learning to cook quinoa, Kamut, and wheat berries. But I'm always looking for new ideas.

If you are too, you've come to the right book. We are so excited about all of the fabulous foods the world has to offer, we want to entice you to try something new with the recipes and beautiful photos in this book—a collection of all the recipes that appeared in *Better Homes & Gardens* magazine throughout the year. We hope as you page through it, something will catch your eye and draw you to the kitchen— whether it's entirely unfamiliar or an intriguing new take on an old favorite.

Stephen Orr, Editor in Chief
Better Homes & Gardens magazine

Better Homes & Gardens.

Annual Recipes 2018

Our seal assures you that every recipe in *Better Homes & Gardens. Annual Recipes 2018* has been tested in the Better Homes & Gardens. Test Kitchen. This means that each recipe is practical and reliable, and it meets our high standards of taste appeal. We guarantee your satisfaction with this book for as long as you own it.

All of us at Meredith Consumer Marketing are dedicated to providing you with information and ideas to enhance your home. We welcome your comments and suggestions. Write to us at: Meredith Consumer Marketing, 1716 Locust St., Des Moines, IA 50309-3023.

Pictured on front cover:
Pumpkin Bread Trifle, recipe on page 254.

MEREDITH CONSUMER MARKETING
Director of Direct Marketing-Books: Daniel Fagan
Marketing Operations Manager: Max Daily
Assistant Marketing Manager: Kylie Dazzo
Business Manager: Diane Umland
Senior Production Manager: Al Rodruck

WATERBURY PUBLICATIONS, INC.
Editorial Director: Lisa Kingsley
Associate Editor: Tricia Bergman
Creative Director: Ken Carlson
Associate Design Director: Doug Samuelson
Production Assistant: Mindy Samuelson
Contributing Copy Editors: Terri Fredrickson, Peg Smith
Contributing Indexer: Mary Williams

BETTER HOMES & GARDENS® MAGAZINE
Editor in Chief: Stephen Orr
Editors: Nancy Wall Hopkins, Jan Miller

MEREDITH CORPORATION
Executive Chairman: Stephen M. Lacy

In Memoriam: E.T. Meredith III (1933–2003)

VINEYARD BEET AND STRAWBERRY SALAD
Recipe on page 100

**CHILLED CORN SOUP
WITH CRISPY CORN
AND PANKO TOPPER**
Recipe on page 183

BALANCE Striving for balance in life transcends to the foods we eat and the recipes we choose to prepare and serve. In addition to choosing recipes for delicious flavor and appetizing appeal, we look for approachable methods, seasonably fresh as well as occasionally trendy ingredients, and dishes so easy, reliable, and favorable that we turn to them again and again. You'll find that the recipes in *Better Homes & Gardens Annual Recipes 2018* achieve parity between good taste and convenience, between familiar comfort foods and intriguing new tastes and textures, and between quick-to-the-table weeknight meals and special occasion dinners (or holiday brunches). With this vast collection of kitchen-tested recipes, life becomes deliciously more balanced.

LOOK FOR

MONTHLY FEATURES BHG food specialists, cookbook authors, artisan farmers, and popular chefs reveal their talents for all things food. One chef calls on edible flowers—even roses—in recipes both sweet and savory, confirming that flowers are more than simply beautiful and fragrant. Another expert inspires backyard BBQs while sharing recipes for a tasty marinade that results in the juiciest burger. Or learn how to grill pork tenderloin along with fresh peaches. From a garlic farmer, experience making fragrant garlic spreads and jams. Taste seasonal salads, sides, and desserts—all taking advantage of bumper crops: peaches in a rice salad, corn in a chilled soup, peach-berry hot honey crisp, and much more. Then, as fall enters the scene, get creative with sweet and nutty delicata squash, stir up a batch of spooky Halloween treats, and start planning your Thanksgiving feast.

HOW TO COOK Cooking can be—and should be—enjoyable! Step into your kitchen and be guided by food pros, while learning new tips, tricks, and techniques. In January, follow easy steps to make golden buttermilk pancakes—elevating an ordinary breakfast (or anytime) fare to fluffy perfection. If making a comforting pot pie is on your agenda, master the skills to turn out a flaky crust and perfectly seasoned filling (the lesson provides options for a large casserole or individual ramekins). In June, just in time for spring and summer, learn the art and science of versatile herby sauces to heighten flavors of familiar dishes.

NEW WAYS This inspiring collection of recipes brings new approaches to common ingredients. April showcases cauliflower in low-carb and gluten-free recipes—a mouthwatering pizza with cauliflower crust, colorful Mediterranean tabbouleh, and a roasted head of the cruciferous vegetable dressed in caraway seeds and mustard. June highlights tuna in an updated casserole with cheesy potato tots, an eggy-crunchy ramen salad, and a creamy tuna salad with Cajun kick. Then in August, mild-flavor spinach—that plays so well with other flavors—teams up with eggs, tomatoes, bacon, and cheese in a dutch baby, adds flavor and color to soup, and quickly transforms into spaetzle.

FAST & FRESH For weeknight dinners, turn to this feature for soon-to-be family favorites. Our formula is simple: fresh produce combined with a few pantry staples plus strategies to get meals to the table quickly and confidently. Savor these convenient dishes: Sheet-Pan Chicken with Lemons and Green Olives, Creamy Mushroom and Bacon Pasta, Steak and Black Bean Burritos, and many more.

**PINK PEPPERCORN AND
ROSE TEA CAKES**
Recipe on page 139

contents

74

228

277

**BERRY AND STONE
FRUIT RICOTTA
PIZZAS**
Recipe on page 59

PAN-SEARED
SALMON WITH
KUMQUATS
Recipe on page 21

january

Start the day with a stack of fluffy pancakes, then, for dinner, put your slow cooker to work. Taste how citrus adds remarkable flavor and dimension to salmon, chicken, salads, and desserts.

16

17

24

how to cook
BUTTERMILK PANCAKES

Bedhead, slippers, and a tall stack of fluffy, golden flapjacks. This is why weekend mornings are savored.

Cooking pancakes is about as simple as recipes go, while a few key details make the difference between a mediocre stack and fluffy perfection. Buttermilk gives the cakes a slightly tangy flavor and makes them extra moist; a combination of baking soda and baking powder gives them the right amount of puff. For brown on the outside, tender on the inside pancakes, make sure the skillet is hot enough before adding batter. The test: Flick a drop of water onto the surface. If the drop sputters and dances across the griddle, it's the right temp. (If it evaporates, the griddle is too hot.) Whatever you do, avoid smashing the cakes with your spatula, which deflates and toughens the cakes.

BASIC BUTTERMILK PANCAKES

TOTAL TIME 25 minutes

1¾	cups all-purpose flour or whole wheat flour
2	Tbsp. sugar
2	tsp. baking powder
½	tsp. baking soda
¼	tsp. salt
1	egg, lightly beaten
1½	cups buttermilk or sour milk*
3	Tbsp. vegetable oil

1. Sift flour, sugar, baking powder, baking soda, and salt into a large bowl. (This step ensures equal distribution of the leaveners: baking powder and soda.) In another bowl combine egg, buttermilk, and oil.

2. Add the egg mixture all at once to the flour mixture. Stir just until moistened. Batter should be slightly lumpy; overmixing results in tough pancakes.

3. Pour ¼ cup batter onto a hot, lightly greased griddle. Cook over medium heat 1 to 2 minutes each side or until golden brown. Flip when top is bubbly and edges look slightly dry. Makes 10 servings.

PER SERVING *184 cal, 5 g fat, 21 mg chol, 265 mg sodium, 20 g carb, 1 g fiber, 12 g sugars, 4 g pro*

*Tip Place 1½ Tbsp. lemon juice in a glass measuring cup then add enough milk to equal 1½ cups. Let stand 5 minutes before using.

PB-BANANA CRUNCH

BUCKWHEAT, FIG, AND PROSCIUTTO

CHOCOLATE AND VANILLA

LEMON-RICOTTA WITH ROASTED STRAWBERRIES

CORNMEAL WITH BLUEBERRIES AND FETA

CINNAMON-PEAR

FLAVOR CHANGE-UPS

PB-BANANA CRUNCH Stir in a handful of Cap'n Crunch cereal. Top with banana slices, melted peanut butter, and more cereal.

BUCKWHEAT, FIG, AND PROSCIUTTO Swap buckwheat flour for ½ cup of the 1¾ cups flour. Stir in 2 tsp. chopped fresh sage. Top with figs, prosciutto, and balsamic glaze.

CHOCOLATE AND VANILLA Stir in 1 tsp. vanilla bean paste and ½ cup chopped dark chocolate. Top with whipped cream and chopped chocolate.

LEMON-RICOTTA WITH ROASTED STRAWBERRIES Swap ¼ cup ricotta cheese for ¼ cup of the buttermilk. Stir in 1 Tbsp. lemon zest. Top with roasted strawberries.

CORNMEAL WITH BLUEBERRIES AND FETA Swap ½ cup cornmeal for ½ cup of the flour. Stir in ½ cup fresh corn kernels. Top with blueberries, crumbled feta, more corn, and honey.

CINNAMON-PEAR Swap packed brown sugar for granulated. Stir in ¼ tsp. cinnamon. Top with sautéed pears and maple syrup.

FAST & FRESH

Less than 25 minutes of prep then the slow cooker does the rest.

HABANERO BEEF TACOS

Habanero chiles aren't the hottest pepper (that distinction goes to the Carolina Reaper), but they are on the fiery end of the scale.

HANDS-ON TIME 25 minutes
TOTAL TIME 8 hours 25 minutes (low) or 4 hours 25 minutes (high)

- 2 cups coarsely chopped tomatoes
- ½ cup chopped onion
- 3 poblano peppers,* stemmed, seeded, and chopped
- 1 to 2 habanero chile peppers,* stemmed and seeded, if desired
- ¾ cup reduced-sodium beef broth
- 2 Tbsp. tomato paste
- 2 tsp. ground cumin
- 2 lb. boneless beef chuck pot roast, trimmed and cut into 1½-inch pieces
- 8 to 12 6- to 8-inch flour tortillas
  Red onion slivers, fresh cilantro leaves, sliced radishes, sour cream, and/or crumbled queso fresco (optional)

1. In a blender combine tomatoes, onion, peppers, broth, tomato paste, and cumin. Cover; blend until smooth.
2. Place beef in a 3½- or 4-qt. slow cooker. Pour pepper mixture over beef. Cover; cook on low 8 to 10 hours or on high 4 to 5 hours.
3. Using a slotted spoon, remove beef from cooker. Skim fat from cooking liquid. Serve beef on tortillas. Drizzle with cooking liquid. If desired, top with red onion, cilantro, radishes, sour cream, and/or queso fresco.
 Makes 4 servings.
PER SERVING *527 cal, 23 g fat, 100 mg chol, 998 mg sodium, 45 g carb, 4 g fiber, 7 g sugars, 35 g pro*
*Tip Chile peppers contain oils that can irritate your skin and eyes. Wear plastic or rubber gloves when working with them.

TUSCAN TORTELLINI SOUP

Try refrigerated tortellini or ravioli stuffed with other ingredients like spinach-cheese or Italian sausage.

HANDS-ON TIME 20 minutes
TOTAL TIME 6 hours 20 minutes (low) or 3 hours 20 minutes (high) + 30 minutes (high)

3	14.5-oz. cans reduced-sodium chicken broth
1	28-oz. can diced tomatoes with basil, garlic, and oregano
1	fennel bulb, trimmed, quartered, cored, and sliced
1	cup chopped onion
1	8-oz. bunch kale, stemmed and chopped (8 cups)
1	9-oz. pkg. cheese-filled tortellini
2	Tbsp. chopped fresh oregano
1	to 2 Tbsp. heavy cream
½	cup grated Parmesan cheese

1. In a 6-qt. slow cooker stir together broth, tomatoes with juices, fennel, and onion. Cover; cook on low 6 hours or on high 3 hours.

2. If cooking on low, turn to high. Stir in kale, tortellini, and oregano. Cover; cook on high 30 minutes more or until tortellini are tender. Stir in cream. Serve with Parmesan cheese. Makes 8 servings.

PER SERVING *294 cal, 7 g fat, 25 mg chol, 1,222 mg sodium, 46 g carb, 7 g fiber, 12 g sugars, 16 g pro.*

SAUSAGE AND SWEET PEPPER HASH

For a little heat, add chopped jalapeño with the sweet peppers.

HANDS-ON TIME 20 minutes
TOTAL TIME 6 hours 20 minutes (low) or 3 hours 20 minutes (high) + 15 minutes (high)

1   **12-oz. pkg. smoked chicken sausage with apple, cut into ½-inch pieces**
1½   **cups sliced onions**
1   **Tbsp. vegetable oil**
    Nonstick cooking spray
2   **tsp. snipped fresh thyme**
1½   **lb. red potatoes, quartered and cut into ½-inch pieces**
½   **tsp. black pepper**
¼   **cup reduced-sodium chicken broth**
1½   **cups chopped yellow, orange, and/or red sweet peppers**
½   **cup shredded Swiss cheese (2 oz.)**
2   **tsp. snipped fresh tarragon**
4   **fried eggs (optional)**

1. In a large nonstick skillet cook sausage and onions in hot oil over medium heat 5 minutes or until browned.

2. Coat a 3½- or 4-qt. slow cooker with nonstick cooking spray. In prepared cooker combine sausage mixture, potatoes, thyme, and black pepper. Pour broth over all.

3. Cover; cook on low 6 hours or on high 3 hours. Stir in sweet peppers. Sprinkle with cheese.

4. If cooking on low, turn to high. Cover; cook 15 minutes more. Using a slotted spoon, transfer hash to serving dishes. Sprinkle with tarragon and additional black pepper. If desired, top each serving with an egg. Makes 4 servings.

PER SERVING *335 cal, 9 g fat, 60 mg chol, 551 mg sodium, 46 g carb, 5 g fiber, 16 g sugars, 19 g pro.*

ORANGE CRUSH

With more types of citrus in the market than ever, you have several choices to try their sweet, puckery bite in savory dishes as well as in desserts.

PAN-SEARED SALMON WITH KUMQUATS

The kumquat compote pairs well with the richness of seared salmon. Intensely sour with a sweet and bitter finish, raw kumquats are an acquired taste—cooking mellows them nicely. Serve the salmon skin sides up if you like it crispy.

HANDS-ON TIME 35 minutes
TOTAL TIME 1 hour

2½ cups kumquats, halved
2 Tbsp. sea salt
4 6-oz. fresh salmon fillets, skin on
1 large navel orange
2 cups water
5 Tbsp. olive oil
½ cup thinly sliced shallots
  Freshly ground black pepper
2 tsp. grated fresh horseradish or prepared horseradish
2 tsp. packed brown sugar
⅔ cup dry white wine
¼ cup fresh basil leaves, torn
½ head radicchio, shredded

1. In a medium bowl sprinkle kumquat halves with 1 Tbsp. of the salt; let stand 25 minutes. Rinse under cold water; drain. Pat dry; set aside.
2. Meanwhile, to brine salmon: Place fillets in a shallow dish. Over a bowl zest and juice orange; stir in the water and 1 Tbsp. salt until dissolved. Pour over salmon; let brine at room temperature 15 minutes.
3. In a 12-inch nonstick skillet heat 3 Tbsp. olive oil over medium heat. Add kumquats and shallots. Cook 8 minutes or until starting to brown, stirring occasionally. Transfer to a small bowl; set aside. Wipe skillet clean.
4. Remove salmon from brine; pat dry. Season with additional salt and freshly ground black pepper.
5. In the same skillet heat 2 Tbsp. oil 1 to 2 minutes over medium heat. Add salmon, skin sides down (oil will sizzle). Press with a spatula to prevent skin from curling. Cook 8 minutes without moving fish or until skin is browned and crispy and fillets are opaque. Using tongs, carefully turn fillets over; sear 1 minute. Transfer to a cutting board or plate, skin sides up. Tent with foil.

6. Drain fat from skillet; return to heat. Increase heat to medium-high. Add kumquat-shallot mixture, horseradish, and brown sugar; cook 1 minute. Carefully add wine; cook 2 to 3 minutes or until it reaches a saucelike consistency. Remove from heat. Stir in half the basil.
7. Serve salmon over shredded radicchio and kumquat compote. Top with remaining basil. Makes 4 servings.
PER SERVING *621 cal, 41 g fat, 94 mg chol, 865 mg sodium, 20 g carb, 6 g fiber, 12 g sugars, 37 g pro.*

ALTHOUGH ORANGE VARIETIES SHARE A FAMILY RESEMBLANCE, EACH VARIETY HAS ITS OWN PERSONALITY. MANDARINS AND CLEMENTINES ARE SWEET WITH THIN SKINS; BLOOD ORANGES AND CARA CARAS HAVE DARKER FLESH AND HINTS OF BERRY IN THE JUICE. SWAP IN THE KIND YOU'RE SWEET ON OR WHICHEVER ONE HAPPENS TO BE AT YOUR MARKET.

**ORANGE-ROASTED
CHICKEN**
Recipe on page 24

CITRUS COUSCOUS
SALAD
Recipe on page 24

ORANGE-ROASTED CHICKEN

Photo on page 22.

Layers of crisp bacon and clementines basted with a maple-sherry vinaigrette will have friends who routinely remove the skin reconsidering when they see this gorgeous bird.

HANDS-ON TIME 15 minutes
TOTAL TIME 1 hour 45 minutes

7   clementines or other oranges
1   3½- to 4-lb. whole chicken
1   tsp. salt
½   tsp. black pepper
4   strips bacon
12   fresh sage leaves
⅓   cup pure maple syrup
¼   cup dry sherry
1   Tbsp. extra-virgin olive oil
3   cloves garlic, minced

1. Preheat oven to 450°F. Halve all seven clementines. Thinly slice four halves into half-moons; set all aside.
2. Rinse chicken body cavity; pat dry. Season inside and outside of chicken with salt and pepper. Place one clementine half in cavity. Twist wing tips under back; tie drumsticks together using 100-percent-cotton kitchen string. Place breast side up in a 13×9-inch baking pan or dish.
3. Lay bacon lengthwise on chicken breast; tuck six sage leaves and all clementine slices under bacon.
4. For vinaigrette: Over a small bowl juice four clementine halves. Whisk in maple syrup, sherry, oil, and garlic; set aside.
5. Place remaining five clementine halves around chicken. Chop remaining sage leaves; sprinkle over clementines. Roast chicken 20 minutes. Spoon half the vinaigrette over chicken. Reduce heat to 350°F; cover chicken with foil. Roast 50 to 60 minutes, spooning remaining vinaigrette over chicken every 15 minutes. Remove; set aside foil. Roast 10 minutes more or until a meat thermometer inserted into thigh registers at least 170°F. Cover with foil; let stand 10 minutes. To serve, squeeze one roasted clementine half over chicken. Makes 4 to 6 servings.
PER SERVING *603 cal, 19 g fat, 204 mg chol, 882 mg sodium, 33 g carb, 2 g fiber, 27 g sugars, 64 g pro.*

CITRUS COUSCOUS SALAD

Photo on page 23.

HANDS-ON TIME 30 minutes
TOTAL TIME 1 hour

6   large Cara Cara, navel, or other oranges
4   Tbsp. extra-virgin olive oil
1   cup Israeli couscous
1¼   cups reduced-sodium chicken broth or vegetable broth
½   tsp. salt
3   cloves garlic, minced
1   Tbsp. chopped fresh thyme
1   cup very thinly sliced red onion
¼   cup blanched hazelnuts, toasted* and coarsely chopped
¼   cup coarsely chopped pitted Castelvetrano or Manzanilla olives
2   Tbsp. red wine vinegar
⅛   tsp. black pepper
     Crushed red pepper (optional)

1. Using a vegetable peeler remove strips of zest from one orange.
2. In a medium saucepan heat 1 Tbsp. olive oil over medium heat. Add couscous; cook 2 minutes or until lightly toasted, stirring often. Add two orange strips, broth, and ¼ tsp. salt. Bring to boiling over medium-high heat; reduce heat. Cover; cook 12 to 15 minutes or until couscous is tender and liquid is absorbed. Let cool; discard strips.
3. Meanwhile, using a paring knife, remove peel and pith from all oranges. Working over a bowl to catch juices, cut out segments from membranes. (Or slice into wheels.)
4. For citrus oil: Chop enough remaining orange strips to get 1 Tbsp. In a 10-inch skillet combine chopped strips, 3 Tbsp. olive oil, the garlic, and thyme. Heat over low heat 5 minutes or until warm.
5. On a platter combine orange segments and juices, couscous, onion, hazelnuts, and olives. Drizzle with vinegar. Spoon citrus oil over top. Sprinkle with ¼ tsp. salt and black pepper, and, if desired, crushed red pepper. Makes 6 servings.
PER SERVING *308 cal, 14 g fat, 306 mg sodium, 41 g carb, 4 g fiber, 14 g sugars, 7 g pro.*

*Tip To toast hazelnuts, spread in a shallow baking pan. Bake in a 350°F oven 8 to 10 minutes or until nuts are lightly toasted. Cool slightly; place on a clean kitchen towel. Rub nuts with towel to remove loose skins.

ROASTED CARROTS AND ORANGES

Oven roasting carrots and oranges intensifies the sweetness of navel oranges to hold up to a smoky-hot dressing made with paprika and chipotle pepper.

HANDS-ON TIME 20 minutes
TOTAL TIME 1 hour

5   navel or other oranges
2   lb. multicolor carrots with 1- to 2-inch tops, peeled and halved lengthwise if large
3   Tbsp. extra-virgin olive oil
½   tsp. salt
5   pitted dates
¼   cup water
1   Tbsp. apple cider vinegar
½   tsp. paprika
½   tsp. ground chipotle chile pepper
½   tsp. salt
½   tsp. black pepper

1. Preheat oven to 425°F. Thinly slice two and a half oranges. Zest one orange; set zest aside. Juice zested orange and remaining one and a half oranges (about ⅔ cup juice). Set aside ⅓ cup for dressing.
2. Line a large roasting pan with foil. In a large bowl combine orange slices and ⅓ cup juice, the carrots, 1 Tbsp. olive oil, and salt; toss to coat. Transfer to pan. Roast 20 minutes. Gently turn carrots and oranges. Roast 20 minutes more or just until carrots are tender and light brown.
3. Meanwhile, for dressing: In a small food processor or blender combine dates and the water. Cover; pulse until nearly smooth. Add orange zest and reserved ⅓ cup juice, remaining 2 Tbsp. olive oil, the vinegar, paprika, chipotle chile pepper, salt, and black pepper; set aside. Cover; process to combine. To serve, drizzle carrots and oranges with half the dressing; pass remaining. Makes 4 to 6 servings.
PER SERVING *258 cal, 11 g fat, , 571 mg sodium, 41 g carb, 9 g fiber, 26 g sugars, 3 g pro.*

ROASTED CARROTS
AND ORANGES

BLOOD ORANGE AND BEET UPSIDE-DOWN TART

Tangy goat cheese contrasts the sweetness of this beautiful tart.

HANDS-ON TIME 30 minutes
TOTAL TIME 2 hours 20 minutes

- 2 small golden beets, trimmed, peeled, and sliced ⅛ inch thick
- ½ cup freshly squeezed orange juice
- 3 medium blood oranges (or other variety), peeled, seeded, and sliced ¼ inch thick
- 3 Tbsp. honey
- 2 Tbsp. olive oil
- 1 Tbsp. unsalted butter
- ½ tsp. salt
- ½ tsp. black pepper
- ½ 17.3-oz. pkg. puff pastry (1 sheet), thawed
- ½ cup fresh pea sprouts or watercress leaves
- ¼ cup coarsely chopped toasted* walnuts
  Crumbled goat cheese

1. Preheat oven to 400°F. Place beets and orange juice in a 10-inch ovenproof skillet. Bring to boiling over medium-high heat. Reduce heat to low. Cover; cook 12 minutes or until beets are tender, adding orange slices the last 2 minutes. Using a slotted spoon, transfer beets and orange slices to a plate; set aside to cool.
2. Add honey, olive oil, butter, salt, and pepper to cooking liquid in skillet. Bring to boiling; cook 1 minute or until syrupy. Pour into an 8-inch square baking pan. Arrange cooled orange slices and beets in syrup, overlapping as needed. Top with puff pastry sheet, tucking pastry edges between beet-orange mixture and pan. Bake 30 minutes or until pastry is puffed and golden. Transfer to a wire rack; let cool 10 minutes.

3. Invert onto a large plate. Rearrange any beet or orange slices left in pan. Cool completely. To serve, top with pea sprouts, walnuts, and crumbled goat cheese. Makes 9 squares.
PER SQUARE *290 cal, 18 g fat, 7 mg chol, 166 mg sodium, 30 g carb, 2 g fiber, 13 g sugars, 5 g pro.*
*Tip Toast small amounts of nuts or seeds in a dry skillet over medium heat 3 to 5 minutes, stirring frequently. For larger amounts, preheat oven to 350°F. Spread them in a shallow baking pan. Bake 5 to 10 minutes or until light brown, shaking pan once or twice.

EASY APPETIZER OR LIGHT DINNER? YOU DECIDE. BAKE THIS TART PASTRY SIDE UP FOR THE CRISPIEST CRUST, THEN FLIP TO REVEAL HONEY-DRENCHED GOLDEN BEETS AND BLOOD ORANGES.

TWO CARAMEL LAYERS (CRACKLY ON TOP AND SYRUPY ON THE BOTTOM) SURROUND A MANDARIN-STUDDED AND WHISKEY-SPIKED CUSTARD IN THIS IRRESISTIBLE MASH-UP OF CRÈME BRÛLÉE AND CRÈME CARAMEL.

BOOZY ORANGE CRÈME BRÛLÉE

A culinary torch ensures crisp, evenly burnt sugar on the cold custard. If you want to brown the top in your broiler, bake the dessert in a ceramic pie plate.

HANDS-ON TIME 25 minutes
TOTAL TIME 4 hours 30 minutes, includes chilling

1½	cups granulated sugar
1	cup cold water
2	mandarin or other oranges
4	to 5 kumquats
1¼	cups heavy cream
1½	cups milk
2	Tbsp. whiskey
6	eggs
1	Tbsp. vanilla
3	Tbsp. granulated or Demerara sugar

1. Center rack in oven; preheat to 350°F. Place a 9-inch deep-dish pie plate (use ceramic if you will broil topping in Step 7) in a large roasting pan; set aside.

2. For caramel: In a small saucepan combine ¾ cup sugar and the cold water over medium-low heat. Heat 5 minutes or until sugar is dissolved, stirring constantly. Increase heat; bring to boiling. Cook without stirring 25 to 30 minutes or until golden. Remove from heat; cool 2 minutes. Pour into pie plate; set aside.

3. Meanwhile, zest one mandarin; set zest aside. (Reserve mandarin for another use.) Slice remaining mandarin and all kumquats to ⅛-inch thickness; set aside.

4. In a medium saucepan combine cream, milk, whiskey, and zest over medium heat. Heat 8 to 10 minutes or until bubbles form at sides of saucepan, stirring occasionally; remove from heat.

5. In a medium bowl whisk eggs and ¾ cup sugar until pale and creamy, about 30 seconds. Whisk half the cream mixture into egg mixture. Slowly pour egg mixture into remaining cream mixture, whisking constantly. Whisk in vanilla. Slowly pour into pie plate.

6. Pour boiling water into roasting pan around pie plate to a depth of 1 inch. Bake about 60 minutes or until set, topping with reserved citrus slices the last 20 minutes of baking. Let cool on a wire rack 30 minutes. Cover; chill at least 2 hours or overnight.

7. Sprinkle top with 3 Tbsp. sugar. Using a kitchen torch, caramelize sugar by evenly moving the tip of the flame across the top. It will crisp as it cools. Or broil 5 inches from the heat, rotating pan until sugar is evenly caramelized. Makes 6 to 8 servings.

PER SERVING *504 cal, 24 g fat, 247 mg chol, 117 mg sodium, 60 g carb, 1 g fiber, 59 g sugars, 10 g pro.*

Recipes begin on page 36

february

Eat outside the box—courtesy of Amy Guittard—with chocolate featured in desserts and more. Plus, discover weeknight main dishes that are as healthful as they are delicious.

43

44

46

CHOCOLATE & FLOWERS

When a chocolate expert and a floral designer gather their girlfriends for a tea party, two things are certain.

"Taste has a memory, and few foods evoke as many memories for people as chocolate," says Amy Guittard, whose family has been making Guittard chocolate for 150 years in San Francisco. "Whether it was your first taste of a chocolate chip cookie or your first sip of hot cocoa, chances are you have a bit of nostalgia associated with my most favorite ingredient. Chocolate, for me, is about celebration."

That's why Amy and her pal, floral designer Natalie Bowen Brookshire, chose chocolate as the theme for their modern take on an age-old tradition: afternoon tea. Today, they are hosting a gathering of their girlfriends for a grown-up tea party that's more fun than fussy.

"In February there's so much talk about romance, but we also have an opportunity to nurture relationships that aren't romantic—our friendships," Natalie says.

The two women bring their expertise to the table, quite literally. Amy, an avid baker who penned the *Guittard Chocolate Cookbook,* creates a simple menu of finger foods sharing a common ingredient: chocolate. "There are so many varieties: single origin and blends; bittersweet, milk, and white," Amy says. "I love finding ways to incorporate them in recipes, both sweet and savory."

She adds shaved chocolate to the top of her chicken salad sandwiches (it adds surprising depth to an otherwise expected dish, Amy says) and updates

the traditional PB&J with a chocolate-cashew spread and smashed berries. Her not-too-sweet signature tart marries Earl Grey tea and dark chocolate.

"Our beverage incorporates chocolate flavor, too," says Natalie, who makes a light tisane by steeping handfuls of fresh chocolate mint (a variety with a faint chocolate scent) picked from her garden. "I've been making this since I was a child, sipping it with my mom and grandmother," she says. "Our tea parties weren't fancy, but we made them special with the presentation. There were always flowers on the table, and I was usually responsible for putting them there."

This gathering is no exception. Natalie adds life to the table with simple, artful arrangements. "Various shades of lavender and pink, from quite pale to very bold, create a unified look," Natalie says. She brings extra flowers for the gathering's group activity: making posies to take home. "I love engaging in something creative with my friends, where we put our phones away and relish an afternoon doing something different," Natalie says.

Amy agrees. "I think we need to slow down more and consider the most important ingredient of our friendships, which is spending quality time together."

**APRICOT-
CHOCOLATE
TOASTS**
Recipe on page 40

**CHOCOLATE-
PECAN SCONES**
Recipe on page 37

**EARL GREY
CHOCOLATE TART**
Recipe on page 40

**SALTED
CHOCOLATE
BAGUETTES**
Recipe on page 40

**RASPBERRY
SHORTCAKES
AND WHITE
CHOCOLATE CREAM**
Recipe on page 37

**CHICKEN SALAD
SANDWICHES WITH
MILK CHOCOLATE**
Recipe on page 36

**CASHEW-
CHOCOLATE-BERRY
SANDWICHES**
Recipe on page 36

"THERE ARE SO MANY VARIETIES: SINGLE ORIGIN AND BLENDS; BITTERSWEET, MILK, AND WHITE," AMY SAYS. "I LOVE FINDING WAYS TO INCORPORATE THEM IN RECIPES, BOTH SWEET AND SAVORY."

THE POWER OF CHOCOLATE

"Chocolate has this incredible power to turn an ordinary moment into a celebration," says Amy Guittard of the Guittard Chocolate Company. But you have to use the correct kind for the best results. Each recipe lists a preferred cacao percentage—the amount of chocolate, by weight, from cacao beans—and type (dark, bittersweet, etc.). However, cacao percentages and type names vary among manufacturers. Make sure to use a similar percentage; when one is not listed, use the type called for.

CHOCOLATE MATH

1 cup chips = 6 oz.
1 cup wafers = 6 oz.

Check specific weight on packaging for accurate conversions.

CASHEW-CHOCOLATE-BERRY SANDWICHES

Photo on page 35.

Baking wafers are flat chocolate discs ideal for melting. Find them in the baking section by chocolate chips.

HANDS-ON TIME 20 minutes
TOTAL TIME 1 hour 20 minutes

3   cups fresh raspberries, blueberries, and blackberries
1   24-oz. loaf brioche or other rich yeast bread
1   recipe Chocolate-Cashew Spread

1. In a medium bowl smash berries with a fork, leaving some whole; set aside.
2. Trim off rounded top of loaf so it's flat. Slice loaf horizontally into three ½-inch-thick slices. Spread smashed berries on bottom slice. Top with middle slice; spread with 1½ cups Chocolate-Cashew Spread. Top with remaining slice. Cover in plastic wrap; chill 1 hour. Trim crust off sides and ends. Cut crosswise to 1-inch thickness. Makes 14 sandwiches.

Chocolate-Cashew Spread Place 4½ oz., about ¾ cup, milk chocolate baking wafers (38% cacao) in a double boiler. Place double boiler over hot, not boiling, water; upper pan should not touch water. Stir constantly just until melted (104°F). In a food processor process the melted chocolate, 1⅓ cups cashew butter, 6 Tbsp. unsalted butter, ¼ tsp. salt, and ¼ tsp. vanilla bean paste until smooth. Chill in an airtight container up to 1 month. Makes 2 cups.

PER SANDWICH *329 cal, 23 g fat, 64 mg chol, 235 mg sodium, 28 g carb, 2 g fiber, 9 g sugars, 6 g pro.*

CHICKEN SALAD SANDWICHES WITH MILK CHOCOLATE

Photo on page 35.

"The bold richness of our dark milk chocolate—with strong dairy notes—complements the chicken in an unexpected way," Amy says.

TOTAL TIME 30 minutes

¼   cup olive oil mayonnaise
3   Tbsp. cider vinegar
3   Tbsp. olive oil
2   Tbsp. bourbon
2   tsp. Dijon-style mustard
2   cups shredded cooked chicken
¼   cup chopped dried tart red cherries
¼   cup finely chopped red onion
2   Tbsp. chopped Italian parsley
2   Tbsp. finely chopped green onion
    Salt and black pepper
8   1-inch-thick slices whole grain bread, French bread, or baguette
    Toppings, such as chopped tart dried cherries, red onion, fresh Italian parsley, and/or microgreens
    Milk chocolate bar (45% cacao)

1. For chicken filling: In a large bowl whisk together mayonnaise, vinegar, olive oil, bourbon, and mustard. Fold in chicken, cherries, red onion, parsley, and green onion. Season to taste with salt and black pepper. Cover; chill.
2. Preheat oven to 375°F. Hollow out the center out of each bread slice, being careful to not go through the bottom. Arrange on a baking sheet. Bake 8 to 10 minutes or until toasted, turning once; Remove; cool.
3. Fill hollow portion of bread with chicken filling. Top with desired toppings. Using a zester, shave chocolate over sandwiches. Makes 8 sandwiches.

PER SANDWICH *289 cal, 9 g fat, 31 mg chol, 341 mg sodium, 33 g carb, 2 g fiber, 10 g sugars, 15 g pro.*

RASPBERRY SHORTCAKES AND WHITE CHOCOLATE CREAM

Photo on page 35.

HANDS-ON TIME 20 minutes
TOTAL TIME 50 minutes

- 1½ cups all-purpose flour
- ⅓ cup sugar
- ¼ cup freeze-dried raspberries, finely crushed
- 2½ tsp. baking powder
- ¼ tsp. salt
- ¼ cup cold butter, cut up
- 1 egg
- ¼ cup heavy cream
- 2 Tbsp. raspberry jam
- 2 Tbsp. whole milk
- 1 recipe White Chocolate Cream
  Fresh raspberries
  Pink peppercorns, crushed

1. Preheat oven to 375°F. Line a baking sheet with parchment paper; set aside. In a medium bowl stir together flour, sugar, crushed raspberries, baking powder, and salt. Using a pastry blender, cut in butter until mixture resembles coarse crumbs. In a small bowl combine egg, cream, jam, and milk. Add to flour mixture all at once, stirring just until moistened.
2. On a lightly floured surface, pat dough to ½-inch thickness; cut dough with a floured 2-inch round cutter. Repeat with scraps. Place rounds on prepared baking sheet. Bake 8 to 10 minutes or until golden. Cool on a wire rack. Sandwich two shortcakes with White Chocolate Cream; top with additional White Chocolate Cream, fresh raspberries, and pink peppercorns. Makes 15 shortcakes.
White Chocolate Cream In a medium saucepan combine 1 cup heavy cream, 6 sprigs fresh lavender, and ¼ tsp. salt. Stir over medium heat until mixture just begins to simmer. Remove from heat. Cover; let steep 5 minutes. Place 3 oz., about ½ cup, white chocolate wafers (31% cacao) in a medium bowl. Strain cream over chocolate; discard lavender. Let stand 2 minutes without stirring. Whisk until smooth. Chill, covered, at least 4 hours or overnight. Beat with an electric mixer on medium speed 5 minutes or until soft peaks form. Makes 1½ cups.
PER SHORTCAKE *119 cal, 5 g fat, 25 mg chol, 152 mg sodium, 17 g carb, 6 g sugars, 2 g pro.*

CHOCOLATE-PECAN SCONES

Photo on page 34.

HANDS-ON TIME 15 minutes
TOTAL TIME 30 minutes

- 1¾ cups all-purpose flour
- ⅓ cup granulated sugar
- 2½ tsp. baking powder
- ½ tsp. salt
- ¼ tsp. baking soda
- 6 Tbsp. cold unsalted butter, cut up
- 2 eggs
- ½ cup buttermilk
- 6 oz. milk chocolate baking chips (31% cacao), about 1 cup
- ½ cup chopped pecans, toasted (tip, page 27)
- ½ cup chopped dried pears or apples
- 1 Tbsp. turbinado sugar (raw sugar) or coarse granulated sugar
- 1 recipe Pear Butter

1. Preheat oven to 375°F. Line a baking sheet with parchment paper; set aside. In a medium bowl stir together flour, granulated sugar, baking powder, salt, and baking soda. Cut in butter until mixture resembles coarse crumbs.
2. In a small bowl combine one egg and the buttermilk. Add all at once to flour mixture. Stir just until moistened. Add chocolate baking chips, pecans, and dried pears; mix just until combined.
3. Turn dough out onto a lightly floured surface. Knead dough by folding and gently pressing for six to eight strokes or until nearly smooth. Transfer to prepared baking sheet. Pat into an 8-inch circle. Using a floured knife, cut into 12 wedges; do not separate.
4. In a small bowl combine remaining egg and 1 Tbsp. water. Brush dough with egg mixture; sprinkle with turbinado sugar. Bake 15 to 18 minutes or until golden brown. Cut apart wedges and serve warm with Pear Butter. Makes 12 scones.
Pear Butter Peel and core 2 lb. Bartlett pears; cut into 1-inch chunks. Place in a large saucepan with ½ cup water. Bring to boiling; reduce heat. Simmer, covered, 20 minutes or until fruit is soft. Add ¼ cup Grand Marnier, 2 to 4 Tbsp. packed dark brown sugar, ¼ tsp. cinnamon, and ⅛ tsp. nutmeg. Bring to boiling; reduce heat to medium. Boil gently, uncovered, 25 minutes or until thick, stirring occasionally. Cool to room temperature. Chill in an airtight container up to 1 week. Makes 2 cups.
PER SCONE *366 cal, 16 g fat, 52 mg chol, 257 mg sodium, 52 g carb, 4 g fiber, 31 g sugars, 4 g pro.*

ROSÉ-POMEGRANATE COCKTAIL

Photo on page 39.

Amy's gal pal Jen Pelka serves this at her Champagne bar, The Riddler.

TOTAL TIME 10 minutes

- 1 750 ml. bottle sparkling rosé, chilled
- 3 Tbsp. pomegranate juice, chilled
  Purchased simple syrup
  Lemon slices
  Pomegranate seeds

In a pitcher combine rosé, pomegranate juice, and simple syrup to taste. Serve in glasses with lemon slices and pomegranate seeds. Makes about 4 cups.
PER 4-OZ. SERVING *104 cal, 9 mg sodium, 11 g carb, 1 g fiber, 8 g sugars, 1 g pro.*

**ROSÉ-
POMEGRANATE
COCKTAIL**
Recipe on page 37

EARL GREY CHOCOLATE TART

Photo on page 34.

HANDS-ON TIME 30 minutes
TOTAL TIME 2 hours 20 minutes

PASTRY CRUST
½   cup unsalted butter, softened
⅓   cup sugar
½   tsp. salt
1   egg
1   egg yolk
2¼   cups all-purpose flour

EARL GREY FILLING
4½   oz. chopped semisweet chocolate
     bar (64% cacao), about ¾ cup
12   Tbsp. unsalted butter
⅓   cup sugar
⅓   cup strong Earl Grey tea*
¼   tsp. salt
2   eggs, lightly beaten
1   tsp. orange zest

1. Preheat oven to 325°F. For crust: In a large bowl beat butter with an electric mixer on medium speed 30 seconds. Add sugar and salt; beat until smooth and creamy. Add egg and egg yolk, one at a time, beating well after each addition. Beat in a third of the flour until just combined, scraping sides of bowl as needed. Beat in remaining flour until just combined. (Mixture may be crumbly.)
2. Gather mixture into a ball. Press evenly into bottom and up sides of a 10-inch tart pan with removable bottom.
3. Bake 15 minutes or until pastry is light brown. Set aside on a wire rack. If crust puffed, gently press down with a spoon while still warm.

4. Meanwhile, for filling: Place chocolate in a bowl; set aside. In a medium saucepan combine butter, sugar, tea, and salt. Bring just to boiling, stirring to melt butter. Pour over chocolate. Let stand 2 minutes without stirring. Whisk until smooth. Whisk in eggs and orange zest until smooth. Pour into baked tart shell. Bake 15 minutes or just until filling is set (doesn't jiggle). Cool in pan on wire rack 30 minutes. Chill at least 1 hour before serving. Makes 12 slices.
*Note For a strong brew that isn't bitter, steep two Earl Grey tea bags in ⅓ cup boiling water 3 minutes. Remove bags; squeeze gently.
PER SLICE *373 cal, 24 g fat, 113 mg chol, 135 mg sodium, 36 g carb, 1 g fiber, 17 g sugars, 5 g pro.*

SALTED CHOCOLATE BAGUETTES

Photo on page 35.

HANDS-ON TIME 15 minutes
TOTAL TIME 1 hour 15 minutes

3   oz. bittersweet chocolate baking
     wafers (74% cacao), about ½ cup
½   cup heavy cream
2   Tbsp. olive oil, plus more for
     brushing and drizzle
15   ¼-inch slices French baguette
     Flaked sea salt (such as Maldon)
     Freshly ground black pepper

1. For ganache: Place chocolate in a small bowl. In a small saucepan bring cream to simmering (bubbles will form around edges); pour cream over chocolate in bowl. Let stand 2 minutes without stirring; whisk until smooth. Whisk in oil. Chill, covered, 30 to 60 minutes or until firm enough to spread.

2. Preheat oven to 375°F. Brush one side of each bread slice with oil. Arrange on a baking sheet. Bake 8 minutes or until golden. Cool.
3. Spread 1 Tbsp. ganache on each toast. Drizzle with additional oil. Sprinkle with salt and pepper. Makes 15 slices.
PER SLICE *129 cal, 9 g fat, 9 mg chol, 161 mg sodium, 10 g carb, 1 g fiber, 2 g sugars, 2 g pro.*

APRICOT-CHOCOLATE TOASTS

Photo on page 34.

HANDS-ON TIME 10 minutes
TOTAL TIME 30 minutes

6   ½-inch slices sourdough bread,
     halved
¼   cup butter, melted
4   to 6 oz. goat cheese, sliced
48   bittersweet chocolate baking
     wafers (74% cacao)
½   cup apricot preserves, warmed
     Marigold petals or other edible
     flowers (optional)

Preheat oven to 375°F. Brush bread slices with melted butter. Arrange on a baking sheet. Bake 12 minutes or until toasted, turning once. Top each with cheese and four wafers. Bake 1 minute or until wafers melt. Top with preserves and, if desired, flowers. Makes 12 toasts.
PER TOAST *206 cal, 9 g fat, 18 mg chol, 247 mg sodium, 25 g carb, 1 g fiber, 8 g sugars, 6 g pro.*

EARL GREY
CHOCOLATE TART

CHOCOLATE, DATE,
AND ALMOND BARS

CHOCOLATE, DATE, AND ALMOND BARS

HANDS-ON TIME 20 minutes
TOTAL TIME 2 hours 20 minutes

- 2 cups crisp rice cereal
- 1⅓ cups quick-cooking rolled oats
- 1¼ cups whole pitted dried dates, chopped
- 1 cup sliced almonds, toasted (tip, page 27)
- 3 oz. extra-dark chocolate baking chips (63% cacao), about ½ cup
- ⅛ tsp. salt
- ⅔ cup packed dark brown sugar
- ½ cup light-color corn syrup
- ⅓ cup almond butter
- ½ tsp. vanilla bean paste

1. Line an 8-inch square or 9-inch square baking pan with parchment paper or foil; set aside.
2. In a large bowl combine cereal, oats, dates, almonds, chocolate baking chips, and salt; set aside.
3. In a small saucepan combine brown sugar, corn syrup, almond butter, and vanilla bean paste. Heat and stir over medium heat 3 to 5 minutes or until mixture is smooth and warm. Pour over cereal mixture. Stir to combine.
4. Transfer mixture to prepared pan, pressing firmly and evenly; let cool. Use parchment to remove from pan; cut into 16 squares.
PER SQUARE *254 cal, 9 g fat, 71 mg sodium, 41 g carb, 4 g fiber, 30 g sugars, 4 g pro.*

AMY SENDS HER GUESTS HOME WITH CHOCOLATE, DATE, AND ALMOND BARS—A FAVORITE SNACK. SHE ALSO MAKES LITTLE ROUND CHOCOLATE BITES WITH NUTS.

MENDIANTS

MENDIANTS

HANDS-ON TIME 15 minutes
TOTAL TIME 35 minutes

- 8 oz. semisweet chocolate wafers, milk chocolate wafers, or chopped bittersweet or milk chocolate
  Toppings, such as crushed pink peppercorns, chopped nuts, and/or sugared edible flowers

1. Line a baking sheet or tray with parchment paper. Place ¾ cup (5 oz.) of the chocolate in a small microwave-safe bowl. Melt on high 45 to 60 seconds, stirring every 15 seconds, until melted and an instant-read thermometer registers 113°F for semisweet chocolate and 104°F for milk chocolate. (f necessary, continue to heat at 5- to 10-second intervals until correct temperature is reached.) Stir in remaining chocolate. Stir vigorously 2 minutes or until completely smooth. If small pieces of chocolate remain, heat at 5-second intervals, stirring after each interval, until smooth. The temperature should be 88°F for semisweet chocolate and 85°F for milk chocolate.
2. Spoon chocolate in 1-inch mounds onto prepared baking sheet. Sprinkle with toppings. Allow to stand until set (about 20 minutes). Store in an airtight container at room temperature up to 1 week. Makes 36 servings.
PER SERVING *31 cal, 3 g fat, 6 mg sodium, 3 g carb, 2 g sugars.*

LOVE LETTERS

Send a note sweet enough to eat. Slip stamped conversation heart cookies into purchased packages, made special with simply crafted embellishments. They're a thoughtful and delicious way to say "I love you."

CONVERSATION HEART COOKIES

HANDS-ON TIME 20 minutes
TOTAL TIME 1 hour 30 minutes

1⅓	cups butter, softened
⅔	cup sugar
1	tsp. baking powder
½	tsp. salt
2	eggs
2	tsp. vanilla
⅛	to ¼ tsp. liquid red food coloring
3	cups all-purpose flour

1. Preheat oven to 375°F. In a large bowl beat butter with an electric mixer on medium speed 30 seconds. Add sugar, baking powder, and salt; beat until combined. Beat in eggs, vanilla, and food coloring until combined. (Use ⅛ tsp. for peach, ¼ tsp, for pink, or more as desired.) Beat in as much of the flour as you can; stir in remaining flour. Divide dough in half; wrap each half in plastic wrap. Chill 30 to 60 minutes or until easy to handle.
2. On a lightly floured surface, roll out one dough half to ¼-inch thickness. Using a 2 ¼- to 3 ¼-inch heart-shape cutter, cut out cookies. Arrange 2 inches apart on ungreased baking sheets. Use small stamps to press words into cutouts as desired. Reroll and repeat with scraps. Bake 7 minutes or until edges are firm. Remove; cool on a wire rack. Repeat with remaining dough. Makes 48 servings.
PER SERVING *88 cal, 5 g fat, 21 mg chol, 78 mg sodium, 9 g carb, 3 g sugars, 1 g pro.*
Chocolate Conversation Heart Cookies
Prepare as above, except reduce flour to 2 ½ cups. Add ½ cup unsweetened cocoa powder and 2 oz. melted unsweetened chocolate along with the eggs. Omit food coloring.
PER SERVING *93 cal, 6 g fat, 79 mg sodium, 9 g carb, 1 g fiber, 3 g sugars, 1 g pro.*

FAST & FRESH

Easy, healthful recipes for a better dinner tonight.

CHICKEN WITH ESCAROLE AND WARM MUSTARD DRESSING

Escarole, a sturdy green with slightly bitter yet bright flavor, holds up to this warm mustard dressing. If you prefer, substitute romaine.

TOTAL TIME 25 minutes

- 1   12-oz. head escarole, trimmed and cut into 1-inch pieces (4 cups)
- 1   medium fennel bulb, halved, cored, and thinly sliced
- 1   lb. boneless, skinless chicken breasts, halved horizontally and pounded to ⅛-inch thickness
- ½   tsp. salt
- ½   tsp. black pepper
- 6   Tbsp. olive oil
- 2   Tbsp. finely chopped shallot
- 1   Tbsp. white wine vinegar
- 1   Tbsp. Dijon-style mustard

1. In a large bowl combine escarole and fennel; set aside. Season chicken with salt and pepper. In an extra-large skillet heat 4 Tbsp. olive oil over medium-high heat. Cook chicken, half at a time, 4 minutes until browned and no longer pink, turning once. Transfer to a plate; cover with foil to keep warm.

2. For dressing: Add shallot to skillet. Cook and stir 30 seconds. Add vinegar; stir until evaporated, scraping up any browned bits. Pour ½ cup water into skillet; cook, uncovered, 2 minutes or until reduced by about half. Remove from heat. Whisk in mustard and 2 Tbsp. olive oil. Pour 3 Tbsp. dressing over escarole and fennel; toss lightly. Season with salt and black pepper.

3. Stir any accumulated juices from chicken into dressing in skillet. Serve over chicken. Makes 4 servings.

PER SERVING *294 cal, 17 g fat, 83 mg chol, 488 mg sodium, 8 g carb, 5 g fiber, 3 g sugars, 27 g pro.*

**GOLDEN
TURMERIC FISH**

CREAMY MUSHROOM AND BACON PASTA

Creminis (sometimes called baby bellas) are immature portobellos and slightly firmer and fuller in flavor than button mushrooms. Substitute a mix of wild mushrooms for even more earthy flavor.

TOTAL TIME 25 minutes

- 4   slices thick-cut bacon
- 16   oz. cremini mushrooms, quartered
- 2   cloves garlic, minced
- ¼   tsp. salt
- ¼   tsp. black pepper
- 12   oz. dried orecchiette pasta
- ½   cup heavy cream
- ½   cup reduced-sodium chicken broth
- 2   Tbsp. red wine vinegar
- ¼   cup chopped fresh chives

1. In a 12-inch skillet cook bacon over medium heat until browned and crisp. Transfer to a paper-towel-lined plate, reserving drippings. Add mushrooms, garlic, salt, and pepper to skillet. Cook and stir 8 to 10 minutes or until mushrooms are tender and browned, stirring occasionally. Meanwhile, cook pasta according to package directions. Drain.
2. Add cream and broth to skillet with mushrooms. Cook 1 to 2 minutes or until bubbly and slightly thickened. Crumble bacon; add to skillet. Stir in pasta, vinegar, and chives; heat through. Makes 4 servings.
PER SERVING *592 cal, 28 g fat, 59 mg chol, 474 mg sodium, 69 g carb, 4 g fiber, 7 g sugars, 20 g pro.*

GOLDEN TURMERIC FISH

Coconut oil, solid at room temperature, liquefies when it's warm. It doesn't matter whether it's solid or liquid when it's stirred into the spices.

TOTAL TIME 30 minutes

- 2   Tbsp. coconut oil
- 2   Tbsp. fresh lime juice
- 1   Tbsp. grated fresh ginger
- 1   tsp. ground coriander
- ½   tsp. ground turmeric
- ⅛   tsp. cayenne pepper
- 4   5- to 6-oz. red snapper fillets
- ½   tsp. salt
- ¼   tsp. black pepper
     Purchased mango chutney
     Chopped fresh cilantro

1. Preheat broiler. In a small bowl combine coconut oil, lime juice, ginger, coriander, turmeric, and cayenne pepper. Season fish with salt and black pepper. Spread skinless sides of fish with spice mixture.
2. Place fish on a greased broiler pan. Broil 4 inches from heat 8 to 10 minutes or until fish flakes easily. Serve topped with chutney and cilantro. Makes 4 servings.
PER SERVING *268 cal, 9 g fat, 52 mg chol, 382 mg sodium, 16 g carb, 9 g sugars, 29 g pro.*

CREAMY MUSHROOM
AND BACON PASTA

HEIRLOOM TOMATO
AND BURRATA
SALAD
Recipe on page 60

march

Dinner is easier then ever with these versatile recipes, including comforting pot pie. And if cooking with edible flowers is new to you, these recipes will show you the way.

how to cook
POT PIE

The beauty of a tried-and-true dish like pot pie is that you know it will be well-received. A combo of chicken and root vegetables is the classic filling, but improvise with other proteins and vegetables.

CHICKEN POT PIE

HANDS-ON TIME 30 minutes
TOTAL TIME 1 hour 30 minutes

- 2 Tbsp. butter
- 4 oz. pancetta, chopped
- 8 oz. mushrooms, such as cremini or button, sliced
- 1 cup chopped leeks (3 medium)
- 2 cloves garlic, minced
- 2 tsp. snipped fresh thyme
- ½ tsp. salt
- ⅓ cup all-purpose flour
- 1 14.5-oz. can reduced-sodium chicken broth
- ¼ cup plus 1 Tbsp. heavy cream, half-and-half, or whole milk
- 2 tsp. lemon zest
- 1½ lb. skinless, boneless chicken thighs, cut into 1-inch pieces
- ¼ tsp. black pepper
- 1 recipe Pastry for Single-Crust Pie (page 54)
- 2 Tbsp. snipped fresh thyme

1. Preheat oven to 400°F. For filling: In a Dutch oven melt butter over medium heat. Add pancetta. Cook and stir 5 minutes or until pancetta starts to brown. Add mushrooms and leeks; cook and stir until mushrooms are soft and starting to brown, about 5 minutes. Add garlic, 2 tsp. thyme, and ¼ tsp. of the salt. Cook and stir 30 seconds. Add flour; cook and stir 1 minute. Stir in broth, ¼ cup cream, and lemon zest, scraping up any browned bits. Cook and stir until thickened and bubbly, 3 to 5 minutes.

2. Add chicken. Season with remaining ¼ tsp. salt and ¼ tsp. black pepper. Simmer, covered, 8 minutes; chicken will be slightly underdone. Transfer to a 2-qt. round or oval baking dish or 9-inch deep-dish ceramic pie plate.

3. Prepare Pastry for Single-Crust Pie, adding 2 Tbsp. thyme to flour and salt mixture. Roll pastry between two pieces of parchment paper from center to edges into a circle or oval 1 inch larger than baking dish. Carefully fit pastry over filling. Fold under pastry edges even with dish edges. Press to seal (or crimp as desired). Cut a few slits in pastry top; brush with 1 Tbsp. cream.

4. Bake 35 to 40 minutes or until pastry is golden and center is bubbly. Let stand 15 to 30 minutes before serving. Makes 6 servings.

PER SERVING *621 cal, 39 g fat, 165 mg chol, 968 mg sodium, 34 g carb, 2 g fiber, 2 g sugars, 32 g pro.*

A COMBINATION OF BROTH AND CREAM THICKENS THE FILLING THAT IS BRIGHTENED WITH LEMON ZEST. HOMEMADE PIECRUST ADDS EXTRA APPEAL.

SERVE THESE MINI POT PIES ALONG WITH A SIMPLE SIDE SALAD AT YOUR NEXT DINNER PARTY. A LITTLE PARMESAN IN THE CRUST INSPIRES AUDIBLE MMMMS.

MINI ITALIAN WHITE BEAN AND KALE POT PIES

This recipe also works in a 9-inch deep-dish pie plate or a 2-quart rectangular baking dish. For a 2-quart dish, use the Pastry for Rectangular Baking Dish recipe on page 54, increase the Parmesan to 3 Tbsp., and bake 35 to 40 minutes.

HANDS-ON TIME 30 minutes
TOTAL TIME 1 hour 30 minutes

- 2 Tbsp. butter
- 1 fennel bulb, quartered, cored, and thinly sliced
- 1 cup chopped onion (1 medium)
- 3 cloves garlic, minced
- 1 tsp. fresh snipped oregano
- ½ tsp. salt
- ¼ tsp. crushed red pepper
- 1 medium bunch kale, stemmed and chopped (8 cups)
- ⅓ cup all-purpose flour
- 1 14.5-oz. can vegetable broth
- ¼ cup plus 1 Tbsp. heavy cream, half-and-half, or whole milk
- 1 15-oz. can cannellini beans, rinsed and drained
- ⅓ cup oil-packed dried tomatoes, drained and chopped
- 1 recipe Pastry for Single-Crust Pie (page 54)
- 2 Tbsp. Parmesan cheese

1. Preheat oven to 400°F. Arrange six 10- to 12-oz. ramekins in a shallow baking pan lined with foil. For filling: In a Dutch oven melt butter over medium heat. Add fennel and onion; cook and stir 5 minutes or until tender. Add garlic, oregano, salt, and crushed red pepper. Cook and stir 30 seconds. Add kale; cook until wilted, 3 to 5 minutes more. Add flour; cook and stir 1 minute. Stir in broth and ¼ cup cream, scraping up any browned bits. Cook and stir until thickened and bubbly. Stir in beans and tomatoes. Divide filling among ramekins.

2. Prepare Pastry for Single-Crust Pie, adding 2 Tbsp. Parmesan cheese to flour and salt mixture. Divide pastry into six portions. Roll each pastry between sheets of parchment paper, from center to edges, into a circle ½ inch larger than ramekins. Top filling with pastry. Fold under pastry so it is even with ramekin edges; press to seal (or crimp as desired). Cut a few slits in pastry top; brush with 1 Tbsp. cream.

3. Bake 30 to 35 minutes or until pastry is golden and centers are bubbly. Let stand 15 minutes before serving. Makes 6 servings.
PER SERVING *502 cal, 27 g fat, 46 mg chol, 954 mg sodium, 55 g carb, 9 g fiber, 6 g sugars, 13 g pro.*

FOR THE FLAKIEST CRUST, USE BOTH SHORTENING AND BUTTER. SHORTENING MELTS SLOWER THAN BUTTER, CREATING LAYERS THAT PUFF APART; BUTTER HAS RICH FLAVOR.

PASTRY FOR SINGLE-CRUST PIE

TOTAL TIME 15 minutes

- 1½ cups all-purpose flour
- ½ tsp. salt
- ¼ cup shortening
- ¼ cup butter, cut into pieces
- ¼ to ⅓ cup cold water

1. In a medium bowl stir together flour and salt. Using a pastry blender, cut in shortening and butter until pieces are pea size.

2. Sprinkle 1 Tbsp. water over part of flour mixture; toss with a fork. Push moistened pastry to side of bowl. Repeat, using 1 Tbsp. water at a time, until flour mixture is moist. Gather into a ball, kneading gently until ball holds together. Flatten slightly. If making ahead, wrap in plastic wrap and chill up to 3 days or freeze up to 3 months. Makes 8 servings.

PER SERVING *191 cal, 12 g fat, 15 mg chol, 187 mg sodium, 18 g carb, 1 g fiber, 2 g pro.*

Pastry for Rectangular Baking Dish
Prepare as directed above, except use 2¼ cups flour, 1 tsp. salt, ⅓ cup shortening, ¼ cup butter, and ⅓ to ½ cup cold water.

1 AIM FOR PEA SIZE Fats tenderize to create flakiness. Cut in the fat until pieces are pea size; these sizable chunks melt and make pockets of air in the crust.

2 KEEP IT COLD Make sure water is ice-cold, which will keep fat pieces cold while mixing. If the fat melts into the flour, the crust will have a sandy texture.

3 DON'T OVERWORK Stop adding water when the mixture is just moistened; gather into a ball. Avoid overworking the dough or it will become tough.

4 DUST WITH FLOUR Dust the surface with just enough flour to prevent sticking (any more can make the dough tough). Roll dough out to 1 inch beyond dish edge.

FAST & FRESH

Easy, healthful recipes for a better dinner tonight.

FLATBREAD WITH BALSAMIC GREENS AND PROSCIUTTO

Hearty, pleasantly bitter greens soften and mellow when sautéed with balsamic vinegar.

HANDS-ON TIME 30 minutes
TOTAL TIME 45 minutes

- 1 lb. purchased or homemade pizza dough, room temperature
- 1 Tbsp. finely chopped fresh rosemary
- 3 Tbsp. olive oil
- 1 large red onion, cut in ½-inch wedges (2 cups)
- ¼ tsp. black pepper
- 6 cups kale and/or radicchio, stemmed and torn
- 3 Tbsp. balsamic vinegar
- 4 oz. fontina cheese or Gouda cheese, shredded
- 4 to 6 paper-thin slices prosciutto

1. Set a rack in center of oven; preheat to 450°F. Divide dough in half. On a floured surface, roll out each dough half to a 12×6-inch rectangle. Transfer both to a lightly oiled baking sheet. Sprinkle with rosemary; drizzle with 1 Tbsp. olive oil. Bake 10 to 12 minutes or until golden.
2. Meanwhile, in a 12-inch skillet heat 2 Tbsp. olive oil over medium heat. Add onion and pepper. Cook 10 minutes or until tender and light brown, stirring occasionally. Add greens and vinegar; toss to coat. Cook 3 to 5 minutes or until greens are wilted and liquid has evaporated.
3. Divide cooked greens between flatbreads; top with cheese. Bake 5 minutes or until cheese is melted. Top with sliced prosciutto before serving. Makes 4 servings.
PER SERVING *575 cal, 24 g fat, 36 mg chol, 913 mg sodium, 67 g carb, 6 g fiber, 11 g sugars, 24 g pro.*

ROASTED SALMON AND GREEN BEANS

Cooked salmon separates from its skin easily. To serve without skin, hold down the skin with one spatula while lifting the fillet with a second spatula.

HANDS-ON TIME 15 minutes
TOTAL TIME 30 minutes

4	4- to 6-oz. salmon fillets with skin
1	small shallot minced (about 2 Tbsp.)
1	large lemon, zested and halved
½	tsp. salt
6	Tbsp. olive oil
¾	lb. green beans, trimmed
½	cup loosely packed fresh basil leaves, chopped

1. Preheat oven to 375°F. Place salmon, skin sides down, in a shallow baking pan.
2. In a small bowl combine shallot, lemon zest, and salt; stir in olive oil. Spoon about 2 tsp. mixture over top of each fillet; set remaining mixture aside.
3. Roast salmon 10 to 15 minutes or until fish flakes when tested with a fork. Meanwhile, steam beans 5 minutes or until crisp-tender. Transfer to a platter. Toss with reserved shallot mixture and half the basil; season to taste with salt. Remove skin from salmon and place fillets on green beans. Squeeze lemon over fish; top with remaining basil. Makes 4 servings.
PER SERVING *374 cal, 28 g fat, 62 mg chol, 196 mg sodium, 8 g carb, 3 g fiber, 4 g sugars, 24 g pro.*

SQUASH AND CURRIED NOODLE SOUP

Turmeric (also present in curry powder) imparts pungent flavor and vibrant yellow to the broth.

TOTAL TIME 30 minutes

2	lb. butternut squash, peeled and cut into 1-inch cubes (5 cups)
8	oz. lo mein noodles
1	Tbsp. vegetable oil
1½	tsp. curry powder
½	tsp. ground turmeric
4	cups reduced-sodium chicken broth or vegetable broth
1	13- to 14-oz. can unsweetened coconut milk
1	6-oz. pkg. baby spinach
2	limes

1. Bring a large pot of salted water to boiling. Add butternut squash; reduce heat to medium. Simmer, covered, 5 minutes. Add noodles. Simmer, uncovered, 4 to 6 minutes or until noodles are al dente; drain. Set aside.
2. In the same pot heat oil over medium-high heat. Add spices; cook and stir 1 minute. Carefully add broth and coconut milk; bring to boiling. Stir in cooked noodles and squash; return to boiling. Stir in spinach. Season to taste with salt. Remove pot from heat. Stir in juice of one lime. Cut remaining lime into wedges to serve with soup. Makes 6 servings.
PER SERVING *324 cal, 13 g fat, 680 mg sodium, 44 g carb, 4 g fiber, 3 g sugars, 7 g pro.*

ROASTED SALMON AND
GREEN BEANS

BERRY AND STONE
FRUIT RICOTTA
PIZZAS

FLORAL FEAST

Don't underestimate the power of flowers. Sure, they're pretty, but looks aren't everything. Edible petals add sweet, spicy, herbal, and peppery flavors to these dishes.

BERRY AND STONE FRUIT RICOTTA PIZZAS

HANDS-ON TIME 25 minutes
TOTAL TIME 2 hours 35 minutes

1   recipe Pizza Dough
2   Tbsp. cornmeal
1   15-oz. carton ricotta cheese
1   tsp. lemon zest
½   tsp. snipped fresh thyme, plus sprigs
    for topping
2   oz. thinly sliced prosciutto
4   peaches (or other stone fruit, such
    as plums or apricots), pitted and cut
    into wedges; and/or 4 cups fresh
    raspberries and/or blackberries
2   Tbsp. olive oil
    Flowers from perennial phlox
    and/or dianthus
    Honey (optional)

1. Prepare Pizza Dough. Set a pizza stone or baking sheet in oven; preheat to 475°F. Working in batches, roll or stretch two dough balls into 8-inch circles. Sprinkle a cookie sheet (without sides) with 1 Tbsp. of the cornmeal. (Cornmeal eases sliding the dough onto the pizza stone.) Place dough rounds on sheet; set aside.

2. In a medium bowl combine ricotta, lemon zest, and snipped thyme. Spread half over the two dough rounds, then top with half the prosciutto and fruit. Drizzle with 1 Tbsp. of the olive oil. Transfer rounds to pizza stone in oven. Bake 15 minutes or until crust is golden.

3. Repeat with remaining dough and toppings. To serve, top with thyme sprigs and flowers. If desired, drizzle with honey. Makes 4 pizzas.

Pizza Dough In an extra-large bowl combine 1¾ cups lukewarm water (105°F to 115°F) and 1½ tsp. active dry yeast; let stand 5 minutes or until yeast is foamy. Stir in 4½ cups all-purpose flour and 2 tsp. salt. Dough will be shaggy. Turn dough out onto a lightly floured surface. Knead until smooth and elastic, about 3 minutes. Place in a well-greased bowl, turning to grease surface of dough. Cover with plastic; let rise at room temperature until double in size, 1½ hours. Punch dough down. Divide into quarters; shape into balls. Cover; let rest 10 minutes. Makes about 2 lb.

PER HALF PIZZA *437 cal, 12 g fat, 30 mg chol, 751 mg sodium, 65 g carb, 4 g fiber, 7 g sugars, 17 g pro.*

Make Ahead Dough may be refrigerated in an airtight container up to 2 days.

APPETIZER? DESSERT? ACTUALLY, THESE COULD BE BOTH AT YOUR NEXT COCKTAIL PARTY. SALTY PROSCIUTTO AND SWEET SUMMER FRUITS TOP A MAKE-AHEAD PIZZA DOUGH. AFTER BAKING, DRESS THEM UP WITH A SCATTERING OF SPICY PHLOX AND CLOVE-SCENTED DIANTHUS.

IT MIGHT BE A SURPRISE TO IMPROVE ON A BELOVED CLASSIC LIKE CAPRESE SALAD, BUT THIS RECIPE DOES JUST THAT.

GARDEN TO PLATE

These popular edible flowers show up more and more at gourmet groceries and farmers markets. They're easy to grow in your garden too.

NASTURTIUMS Flowers and leaves start sweet then finish with a bold, peppery flavor like watercress or radishes. Try blending petals with a soft cheese, such as goat or Boursin.

ROSES Fruity and fragrant, the darker the petals, the more pronounced the flavor.

MARIGOLDS Ranging in flavor based on variety, signet marigolds taste citrusy; calendulas have a smoky, honeylike sweetness; and common garden marigolds may be pungent and bitter.

VIOLAS Use sweet, mild violets, pansies, and Johnny-jump-ups in abundance on frosted cakes or pressed onto shortbread for cheerful color and pattern.

BORAGE This star-shape blue flower lends refreshing cucumberlike flavor to lemonades, chilled soups, and yogurt-base dips.

PHLOX Pink and purple perennial phlox have a slightly spicy taste. (Annual and creeping phlox are not edible.)

Note Never eat flowers treated with pesticides or fungicides, whether grown commercially or at home.

HEIRLOOM TOMATO AND BURRATA SALAD

Prized for their complex flavors and varied hues, heirloom tomatoes are increasingly available year-round in specialty food stores and are worth growing in your garden. Dozens of varieties are available; some of the most popular are Brandywine, Striped German, Cherokee Purple, and Amish Paste.

TOTAL TIME 15 minutes

2	to 3 large heirloom tomatoes (about 3 lb.), cored and cut into large wedges
3	4-oz. balls Burrata cheese
1	to 2 tsp. sea salt flakes
¼	cup extra-virgin olive oil
2	Tbsp. red wine or sherry vinegar
	Freshly ground black pepper
	Flowers from oregano or cilantro

Arrange tomato wedges in a large serving platter or bowl. Top with whole Burrata. Season to taste with salt. Drizzle with oil and vinegar. Sprinkle with freshly ground black pepper. Snip flowers over salad. Makes 6 servings.
PER SERVING *284 cal, 22 g fat, 40 mg chol, 489 mg sodium, 11 g carb, 3 g fiber, 8 g sugars, 12 g pro.*

CORN CHOWDER TAKES ON THE VIBE OF AN INDIAN DAL WHEN YOU STIR IN LENTILS, CURRY, TURMERIC, AND GINGER. CUCUMBER BLOSSOMS (THE LARGER GOLDEN PETALS) HAVE A MILD ZUCCHINI TASTE. WHITE LACY GARLIC CHIVE FLOWERS AND GOLDEN MUSTARD FLOWERS EACH HINT AT THEIR NAMESAKE.

Tossing a few petals of edible flowers into sweet and savory recipes is on trend. Although certain varieties were selected for each recipe (e.g., nasturtiums on Spice-Roasted Vegetables), feel free to experiment. Just make sure the flowers are edible—not all are meant for consumption.

CORN-LENTIL CHOWDER

This chowder takes advantage of the entire vegetable. While the broth simmers, the cobs enhance the sweet corn flavor and release starches that help to thicken the broth.

HANDS-ON TIME 25 minutes
TOTAL TIME 1 hour 20 minutes

2	Tbsp. olive oil
1½	cups finely chopped yellow onion
1	Tbsp. curry powder
½	tsp. ground turmeric
1	32-oz. carton reduced-sodium chicken broth
2	cups water
1	Tbsp. peeled and grated ginger
5	ears fresh corn, husked, silks removed, and kernels cut off (set aside cobs), or 3 cups frozen corn
1½	cups dry yellow lentils, rinsed
1½	tsp. salt
¼	tsp. black pepper
1	Tbsp. chili or olive oil
	Flowers from cucumber blossoms, golden mustard, and/or garlic chives
	Sour cream (optional)

1. In a large pot heat olive oil over medium-low heat. Add onion; cook until slightly softened, about 3 minutes. Add curry powder and turmeric; cook 1 minute. Add broth, the water, ginger, and, if using, corn cobs. Bring to boiling; reduce heat. Simmer, covered, 20 minutes.

2. Remove cobs from broth; cool slightly. Using back of a paring knife, scrape cobs over pot to remove as much liquid as possible; discard cobs.

3. Stir in lentils. Bring to boiling; reduce heat. Simmer, covered, 15 minutes or until lentils are tender. Season with salt and pepper. Stir in 2 cups corn; cook 10 minutes more, stirring occasionally.

4. Using an immersion blender or food processor, blend soup until smooth. Just before serving, in a small saucepan heat chili oil over medium heat. Add remaining 1 cup corn to oil. Cook until corn is golden, 3 to 4 minutes. To serve, top soup with toasted corn, flowers, and, if desired, sour cream. Makes 6 servings.

PER SERVING *325 cal, 8 g fat, 928 mg sodium, 50 g carb, 8 g fiber, 8 g sugars, 17 g pro.*

THE NEXT TIME YOU HAVE A FARMERS MARKET HAUL OF VEGGIES TO DEVOUR, GIVE THEM A WARM CORIANDER-AND-CUMIN RUB THEN ROAST THEM IN THE OVEN. LEMONY SIGNET MARIGOLDS BRIGHTEN THE SMOKY, NEARLY CHARRED VEGETABLES, AND NASTURTIUMS ADD AN ASSERTIVE PEPPERY BITE.

SPICE-ROASTED VEGETABLES

For a complete meal, serve these vegetables over cooked Israeli couscous. Top with a dollop of Greek yogurt mixed with harissa paste for a spicy yet cooling flavor.

HANDS-ON TIME 30 minutes
TOTAL TIME 1 hour 10 minutes

- 1½ tsp. coriander seeds
- 1 tsp. cumin seeds
- ½ tsp. caraway seeds
- ¼ cup olive oil
- ½ tsp. sweet paprika
- 4 to 4½ lb. mixed vegetables (such as small leeks, halved lengthwise and rinsed; small beets,* peeled and quartered; carrots, peeled; shishito peppers; small or regular eggplant,** cut into eighths) Flowers from nasturtiums and/or signet or calendula marigolds

1. Preheat oven to 425°F. In a small skillet heat coriander, cumin, and caraway seeds over low heat 2 minutes or until fragrant, stirring occasionally. Remove from heat; let cool slightly. Transfer to a spice grinder or mortar and pestle; grind to a powder.

2. Place ground spices in a small bowl; combine with olive oil and paprika. Place vegetables in an extra-large shallow baking pan; toss with oil mixture. Season with salt and black pepper.

3. Roast 40 minutes or until tender and charred, turning once or twice. Serve topped with flowers. Makes 6 servings.
PER SERVING *214 cal, 10 g fat, 132 mg sodium, 31 g carb, 8 g fiber, 14 g sugars, 4 g pro.*
*Tip If using red beets, season separately with oil mixture and place in a separate baking pan to prevent bleeding onto other vegetables. Or shape a small pan from aluminum foil and place seasoned beets in the pan next to the other veggies.
**Tip If using eggplant, add to baking pan during last 30 minutes of roasting.

THE DOS AND DON'TS OF EDIBLE FLOWERS

DO store in the original clamshell packaging or in a lidded container lined with a damp paper towel.

DO taste them before you add them. Some edible flowers are an acquired taste.

DO test to see if they wilt or brown in vinegar if the recipe calls for a vinegar-base dressing. Or toss them in at the last possible minute.

DO use them as soon as possible. Fresh flowers mold and wilt quickly. Snip them from your garden right before using.

DON'T eat flowers treated with pesticides or fungicides, whether grown at home or commercially.

Tip Edible flowers are available year-round from online sources such as Gourmet Sweet Botanicals and seasonally at farmers markets and some gourmet stores. To grow your own, Johnny's Selected Seeds sells a wide collection.

HUMMINGBIRD
CUPCAKES
Recipe on page 82

april

Hello spring! Start anew with recipes for totable dishes, creative—and delicious—ways to use cauliflower, easy weeknight meals, and sweet bites of light-as-air-cake.

76

79

88

HOP TO IT

Eggs to hunt! Bunnies to chase! And this help-yourself buffet is designed to be tasty and totable. With a grab-and-eat savory pie, totally rad(ish) sides, and cute decorations, this party makes it hip to hop.

EASTER RAINBOW SALAD

Arrange stripes of golden beets, pink-and-white watermelon radishes, and strawberries on a bed of Bibb lettuce to resemble a giant Easter egg.

TOTAL TIME 30 minutes

- ⅓ cup white balsamic vinegar or balsamic vinegar
- 2 Tbsp. honey
- 1 Tbsp. lemon juice
- ½ tsp. salt
- ⅓ cup olive oil
- 3 Tbsp. finely chopped pistachios, plus more for topping
- 3 Tbsp. finely chopped green onion
- 3 Tbsp. finely chopped fresh dill
- 1 head Bibb lettuce or Boston lettuce, leaves separated
- 2 golden beets, roasted,* halved, and thinly sliced
- 8 oz. whole fresh strawberries, hulled and sliced (about 2 cups)
- 2 watermelon radishes, peeled and thinly sliced
- 2 oz. ricotta salata cheese, finely shredded or feta cheese

1. For vinaigrette: In a small bowl whisk together vinegar, honey, lemon juice, and salt. Gradually whisk in olive oil. Stir in pistachios, green onion, and dill; set aside.
2. For salad: Arrange lettuce leaves on a large platter. Top with rows of roasted beets, strawberries, and radishes. Sprinkle with cheese and additional pistachios. Serve with dressing on the side. Makes 8 servings.

*To Roast Beets Preheat oven to 375°F. Place whole beets on a sheet of heavy-duty foil on a baking sheet; fold foil to enclose beets. Bake 1 hour or until tender; cool. Remove skin. Beets will keep up to 3 days covered in the refrigerator.
PER SERVING *262 cal, 21 g fat, 6 mg chol, 229 mg sodium, 18 g carb, 3 g fiber, 14 g sugars, 3 g pro.*

THIS PIE FEEDS A CROWD. YOU WILL NEED TO MAKE TWO BATCHES OF DOUGH; ONE RECIPE AT A TIME IS JUST RIGHT FOR A STANDARD FOOD PROCESSOR. EASTER MAINSTAYS HAM AND PEAS TEAM WITH RED PEPPERS AND LEEKS IN THIS SAVORY PIE.

HAM-AND-CHEESE SLAB PIE

A healthy dose of Gruyère cheese in the filling and a crust fortified with cream cheese keep slices intact for this handheld pie.

HANDS-ON TIME 1 hour 10 minutes
TOTAL TIME 3 hours 15 minutes

2	recipes Pastry Dough
2	Tbsp. unsalted butter
2	Tbsp. vegetable oil or olive oil
4	cups chopped leeks, white and light green parts only (3 to 4 leeks)
2	cloves garlic, minced
½	cup reduced-sodium chicken broth
1	tsp. Dijon-style mustard
1	lb. cooked smoked ham, cut into ¼-inch cubes (about 3 cups)
2	cups chopped red sweet peppers
1	cup frozen peas
2	Tbsp. chopped fresh marjoram, oregano, and/or thyme
2	Tbsp. chopped Italian parsley
½	tsp. salt
6	oz. Gruyère cheese, shredded (about 1½ cups)
⅓	cup all-purpose flour
1	egg

1. On a floured surface, roll one batch of Pastry Dough to a 17×12-inch rectangle, to about ⅛-inch thickness. Fold into quarters; unfold into a 15×10-inch baking pan. Ease into sides and corners. Trim to ½ inch beyond pan edges. Cover and chill trimmings.

2. For filling: In a 3-qt. saucepan heat butter and vegetable oil over medium-high heat. Add leeks and garlic. Cook and stir 3 to 4 minutes or until tender. Add chicken broth and mustard; bring to boiling. Reduce heat; simmer, uncovered, 1 minute. Remove from heat. Stir in ham, sweet peppers, peas, herbs, parsley, and salt. Cool 10 minutes. Stir in Gruyère cheese and flour. Transfer filling to pastry-lined baking pan.

3. Preheat oven to 375°F. On a floured surface, roll second batch of Pastry Dough to a 17×12-inch rectangle, about ⅛-inch thickness. Trim to a 15×10-inch rectangle, keeping trimmings as similar in width as possible; chill trimmings. Cut pastry into quarters; unfold over filling.* Fold edges of bottom pastry over top; pinch to seal.

4. Decorate edges by twisting reserved trimmings and laying along each edge. If desired, decorate the top with any remaining reserved trimmings. Beat egg with 1 Tbsp. water; brush over top.

5. Bake 45 to 55 minutes or until filling is bubbly and crust is golden brown. Let cool 10 minutes; cut into 10 rectangles. If desired, wrap each portion in waxed paper or bakery tissue; tie with kitchen twine. Serve warm or at room temperature. (It can sit at room temp for up to 2 hours then needs to be reheated 15 minutes at 350°F.) Makes 10 servings.

Pastry Dough In a food processor add 2¼ cups all-purpose flour; ½ cup unsalted butter, cubed; ¼ tsp. salt; and ½ tsp. black pepper. Pulse until pea-size pieces. Add one 8-oz. pkg. cream cheese, cut up; process until dough comes together. Place in a resealable gallon-size plastic bag; gently shape into a rectangle. Seal; chill 1 hour or until ready to use. Repeat for second batch.

* To look like the photo, in Step 3 cut the 15×10-inch rectangle into ten 5×3-inch rectangles. In Step 4, use trimmings to decorate each rectangle as desired. Using a floured wide spatula or bench scraper, transfer each rectangle onto the filling so they form neat rows. Fold bottom edges over top; brush with egg wash. Continue with Step 5.

PER SERVING *499 cal, 30 g fat, 115 mg chol, 1,016 mg sodium, 37 g carb, 3 g fiber, 6 g sugars, 20 g pro.*

Make Ahead The pie can be assembled and refrigerated unbaked 1 day in advance. Or bake ahead, refrigerate, and reheat in a 350°F oven 20 minutes.

POLKA-DOT EGG BAKES
Recipe on page 74

THESE SOFT SUGAR COOKIES HAVE TWICE THE ALMOND FLAVOR: FROM EXTRACT AND SLICED ALMONDS IN THE DOUGH (FOR A LITTLE CRUNCH).

POLKA-DOT EGG BAKES

Photo on page 73.

Dotted with yellow grape tomatoes and baked in a muffin tin, these individual egg casseroles are extra light—thanks to beaten egg whites folded in.

HANDS-ON TIME 25 minutes
TOTAL TIME 50 minutes

2	tsp. olive oil
2	shallots, cut into thin wedges (½ cup)
8	eggs, separated
½	cup milk
¼	tsp. crushed red pepper
1	cup shredded Monterey Jack cheese (4 oz.)
¼	cup finely shredded Parmesan cheese
¼	cup chopped fresh Italian parsley, plus more for topping
½	cup sliced orange, yellow, or red grape tomatoes (about 12)

1. Preheat oven to 375°F. Grease twelve 2½-inch muffin cups; set aside. In a small skillet or saucepan heat olive oil over medium-high heat. Add shallots; cook 3 minutes or just until tender. Remove from heat; let cool.

2. In a large bowl whisk egg whites to soft peaks. In a second large bowl whisk together egg yolks, milk, and crushed red pepper. Stir in cooked shallots, cheeses, and parsley. Gently fold egg whites into yolk mixture.

3. Spoon ¼ cup egg mixture into each prepared muffin cup (cups will be nearly full). Top each with a few tomato slices and additional parsley. Bake 18 to 20 minutes or until puffed, set, and golden brown. Cool 5 minutes on a wire rack.

(Egg bakes will fall as they cool.) Loosen sides; remove from cups. Serve warm or at room temperature. (They can stand at room temp up to 2 hours then need to be reheated 12 to 15 minutes at 325°F.) Makes 12 egg bakes.

PER EGG BAKE *108 cal, 7 g fat, 134 mg chol, 139 mg sodium, 2 g carb, 1 g sugars, 8 g pro.*

ALMOND COOKIE CARROTS

HANDS-ON TIME 45 minutes
TOTAL TIME 3 hours

ALMOND COOKIE DOUGH

2	cups all-purpose flour
1½	tsp. baking powder
½	tsp. salt
⅔	cup butter, softened
⅔	cup granulated sugar
2	eggs
2	Tbsp. sour cream
1	tsp. vanilla
¼	tsp. almond extract
⅔	cup sliced almonds, toasted

ALMOND FROSTING

1	cup butter, softened
⅛	tsp. salt
3½	cups powdered sugar
3	Tbsp. milk
¼	tsp. almond extract
	Orange paste food coloring, or yellow and red liquid food coloring*
	Sliced almonds

1. In a small bowl combine flour, baking powder, and salt; set aside. In a large bowl beat butter and granulated sugar with a mixer on medium 1 minute or until well combined. Add eggs, sour cream, vanilla, and almond extract; beat until combined. Gradually add flour mixture; beat until combined. Beat in sliced almonds. Cover; chill dough 2 to 3 hours or until firm enough to handle.

2. Preheat oven to 400°F. Line two cookie sheets with parchment paper; set aside.

3. On a lightly floured surface, roll dough to about ¼-inch thickness. Using a floured knife, cut into 2- to 4-inch-long carrot shapes, dipping knife in flour between cuts as necessary. Arrange 2 inches apart on prepared cookie sheets. Bake 6 minutes or until edges are golden. Let cookies cool on a wire rack.

4. For frosting: In a large bowl beat butter and salt with a mixer on medium 30 seconds. Add powdered sugar, ½ cup at a time, beating well after each addition. Gradually add milk until smooth. Add almond extract; beat until smooth. Tint frosting to desired shade of orange. Using a star tip or other shape, pipe frosting over cookies. Top with almond slices for carrot stems. Makes 24 to 30 cookies.

PER 2-INCH COOKIE *248 cal, 14 g fat, 46 mg chol, 185 mg sodium, 29 g carb, 1 g fiber, 21 g sugars, 2 g pro.*

*Tip If using liquid food coloring, use a 3:1 ratio of yellow to red to make the frosting orange.

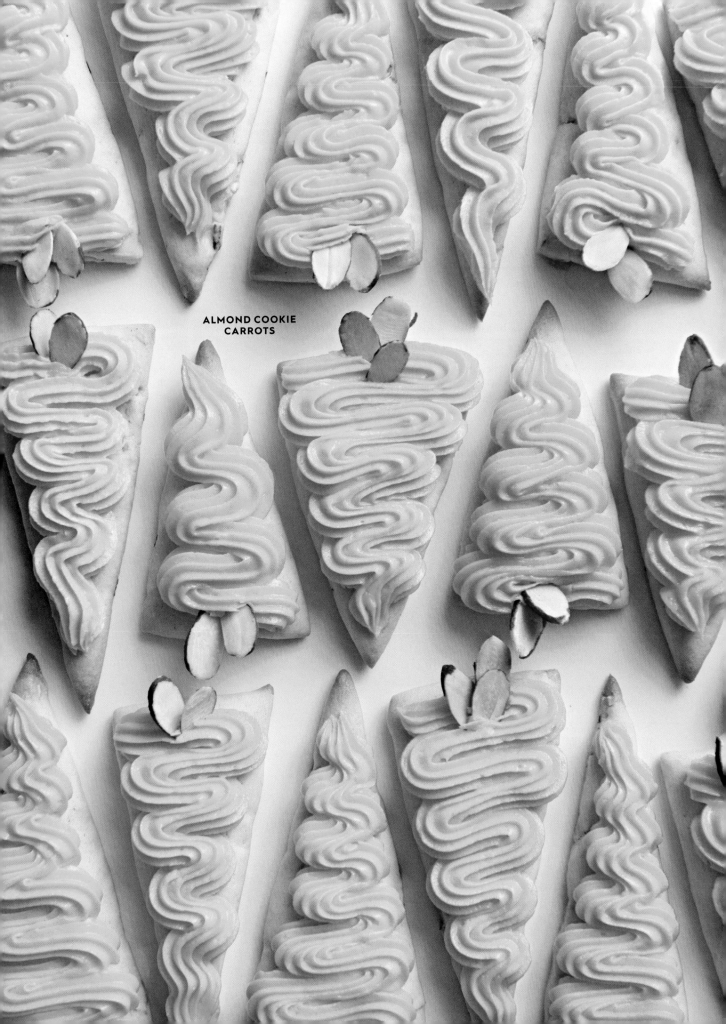

ALMOND COOKIE
CARROTS

VEGGIE AND DIP CUPS

Serve carrots and asparagus with a dollop of lemony chive-yogurt dip in juice glasses for guests to carry while nibbling.

TOTAL TIME 25 minutes

- 4 cloves garlic, coarsely chopped
- ½ tsp. whole black peppercorns
- 2 bunches baby carrots with tops (about 1 lb.)
- 1 lb. thick asparagus spears, trimmed
- 1½ cups whole milk Greek yogurt
- ⅓ cup chopped fresh chives
- 1 Tbsp. olive oil
- 1 lemon (1 Tbsp. zest; 2 tsp. juice)
- 1 tsp. minced garlic

1. For the vegetables: Prepare an ice bath by filling a large bowl halfway with ice and water. Fill a 12-inch deep skillet halfway up sides with water; add chopped garlic, peppercorns, and ½ tsp. salt. Bring to boiling; reduce heat. Simmer, covered, 10 minutes. Add carrots; cook 1 minute. Using a slotted spoon, transfer carrots to ice bath to stop cooking; drain. Repeat blanching process with asparagus.
2. For the dip: In a medium bowl stir together yogurt, chives, olive oil, lemon zest and juice, minced garlic, ½ tsp. salt, and ½ tsp. black pepper. Serve dip with carrots and asparagus. Makes 8 servings.
PER SERVING *118 cal, 6 g fat, 8 mg chol, 344 mg sodium, 12 g carb, 3 g fiber, 6 g sugars, 5 g pro.*

VEGGIE AND DIP CUPS

SUPER JUICE SPRITZER

The colorful ingredient in this super juice spritzer is carrot juice.

HANDS-ON TIME 10 minutes
TOTAL TIME 4 hours 10 minutes

- 2 cups passion fruit juice
- 1½ cups carrot juice
- 1½ cups pineapple juice
- 1 cup peach or mango nectar, or orange juice
- 3 cups sparkling water or club soda, chilled

In a large pitcher combine juices and peach nectar. Cover; chill 4 to 24 hours. Just before serving, stir in sparkling water; serve over ice. Makes 8 servings.
PER SERVING *91 cal, 48 mg sodium, 23 g carb, 1 g fiber, 19 g sugars, 1 g pro.*

SUPER JUICE SPRITZER

new ways with CAULIFLOWER

The star power of cauliflower is far from dimming—maybe because it has become the darling in low-carb and gluten-free recipes along with its chameleon-like ability to morph into rice, pizza crust, and more.

Use white, purple, green, and orange varieties interchangeably in recipes.

CAULIFLOWER
TABBOULEH

CARAWAY
WHOLE-ROASTED
CAULIFLOWER

CAULIFLOWER-
POTATO PIZZA
WITH CAULIFLOWER
CRUST

CAULIFLOWER TABBOULEH

This cauliflower rice tabbouleh is a good companion with any grilled protein or Mediterranean meal.

HANDS-ON TIME 20 minutes
TOTAL TIME 1 hour 20 minutes

- 3 Tbsp. extra-virgin olive oil
- 1½ lb. head cauliflower, finely chopped (5 cups)*
- 1½ tsp. kosher salt
- 1 Tbsp. lemon zest
- ¼ cup lemon juice
- ½ tsp. sugar
- ½ cup sliced green onions
- 1 cup snipped fresh herbs, such as mint, parsley, and/or dill weed
- 1 cup cherry tomatoes, halved
- 1 cup chopped cucumber
- ½ cup sunflower kernels

1. In a 12-inch skillet heat olive oil over medium-high heat. Add cauliflower and 1 tsp. salt. Cook 5 minutes or until crisp-tender, stirring occasionally; let cool.
2. In a large bowl stir together lemon zest and juice, sugar, and remaining ½ tsp. salt. Add cauliflower, sliced green onions, fresh mint, parsley, and/or dill weed, cherry tomatoes, and cucumber. Let stand 1 hour, stirring occasionally. Stir in sunflower kernels before serving. Makes 4 servings.
* Or substitute two 10-oz. pkg. frozen riced cauliflower, thawed.
PER SERVING *241 cal, 19 g fat, 576 mg sodium, 16 g carb, 6 g fiber, 6 g sugars, 7 g pro.*

CARAWAY WHOLE-ROASTED CAULIFLOWER

Give cauliflower center stage by roasting it whole. For an appetizer, slice into pieces and serve with dried fruit, pickles, mustard, and rye toasts.

HANDS-ON TIME 30 minutes
TOTAL TIME 1 hour 15 minutes

- 2 Tbsp. extra-virgin olive oil
- 1 Tbsp. stone-ground mustard
- 2 tsp. caraway seeds, toasted and crushed (tip, page 27)
- 1 tsp. kosher salt
- 1 2- to 2½-lb. head cauliflower, trimmed
- ½ cup sliced red onion
- ⅓ cup red wine vinegar
- 1 tsp. sugar
- ½ tsp. kosher salt
- ¼ cup snipped dried apricots
  Stone-ground mustard (optional)
  Rye bread (optional)

1. Preheat oven to 425° F. In a small bowl whisk together olive oil, mustard, caraway seeds, and salt; spread over cauliflower. Add ¼ cup water to an 8- to 10-inch cast-iron or other oven-going skillet. Place cauliflower in skillet; cover. Bake 30 minutes.
2. Meanwhile, in a small bowl combine onion, vinegar, sugar, and salt; stir occasionally.
3. Uncover cauliflower and increase oven temperature to 450° F. Continue roasting, uncovered, 30 minutes or until golden brown and tender. Serve with prepared pickled red onion, dried apricots, and, if desired, additional mustard and rye bread. Makes 4 servings
PER SERVING *115 cal, 7 g fat, 390 mg sodium, 12 g carb, 3 g fiber, 7 g sugars, 2 g pro.*

CAULIFLOWER-POTATO PIZZA WITH CAULIFLOWER CRUST

Try pizza toppings on this light cauliflower crust. Key to its sturdy texture: squeezing out excess water.

HANDS-ON TIME 25 minutes
TOTAL TIME 1 hour 20 minutes

- 1 2- to 2½-lb. head cauliflower, trimmed and cut into small florets (about 5 cups)
- 1 egg
- ¼ cup finely shredded Italian cheese blend (2 oz.)
- ¼ cup grated Parmesan cheese (2 oz.)
- ¼ cup panko bread crumbs
- ½ tsp. dried Italian seasoning, crushed
- ¼ tsp. salt
- 2 small Yukon gold potatoes (4 oz. total), thinly sliced (about 1 cup)
- 2 Tbsp. extra-virgin olive oil
- 1 Tbsp. snipped fresh rosemary

1. Place 4 cups cauliflower in a food processor; cover. Pulse 6 to 10 times or until rice size. Place a pizza stone or baking sheet in oven. Preheat oven to 400°F.
2. Place riced cauliflower and 2 Tbsp. water in a 2-qt. microwave-safe bowl. Microwave on high, covered, 4 minutes or until tender, stirring once or twice. Let cool. Transfer to a 100-percent-cotton flour-sack towel. Squeeze until all liquid is removed (critical for a crisp crust).
3. Transfer cauliflower to a medium bowl. Add egg, cheeses, panko, Italian seasoning, and salt; stir to combine. Pat cauliflower mixture into a 12-inch circle on parchment paper. Using a cookie sheet and leaving crust on the parchment paper, transfer crust to preheated pizza stone. Bake 20 minutes or until crust begins to brown.
4. Meanwhile, in a large bowl toss together potatoes, remaining cauliflower, olive oil, and rosemary. Using baking sheet, remove crust from oven. Spread potato mixture over crust. Slide crust back onto pizza stone.
5. Bake 25 minutes more or until potatoes are tender and crust is crisp and golden brown around edges. If desired, top with additional Parmesan, olive oil, rosemary, and salt. Makes 4 servings.
EACH SERVING *185 ca., 11 g fat, 56 mg chol, 362 mg sodium, 14 g carb, 3 g fiber, 3 g sugars, 8 g pro.*

EACH COLORFUL VARIETY HAS ITS OWN NUTRITIONAL BENEFITS. EACH HAS AMPLE SOURCES OF VITAMIN C. ORANGE HAS A HIGH AMOUNT OF BETA-CAROTENE, PURPLE IS RICH IN ANTIOXIDANTS, AND GREEN HAS AN EXTRA DOSE OF VITAMIN A.

A PIECE OF CAKE

Lemon-poppy seed meets lavender, carrot pairs with zucchini, and hummingbird loves white chocolate. Three traditional cakes court new flavors for spring. Keep them casual with a quick frost or decorate for special occasions with these clever tips.

LEMON-LAVENDER-POPPY SEED CAKE

HANDS-ON TIME 20 minutes
TOTAL TIME 3 hours, includes cooling

3	cups all-purpose flour
1	Tbsp. poppy seeds
2½	tsp. baking powder
1	tsp. salt
2	cups sugar
3	Tbsp. dried lavender buds*
1	cup butter, softened
3	eggs
1	tsp. vanilla
1½	cups milk
1	lemon (2 tsp. zest; 3 Tbsp. juice)
1	recipe Lemon Buttercream Frosting **

1. Preheat oven to 350°F. Grease and flour a 13×9-inch baking pan. In a medium bowl combine flour, poppy seeds, baking powder, and salt. Place sugar and lavender in a blender or food processor; blend or process until combined.

2. In an extra-large bowl beat butter with a mixer on medium 30 seconds. Add sugar mixture, ¼ cup at a time, beating well after each addition. Scrape sides of bowl; beat 2 minutes more. Add eggs one at a time, beating well after each addition. Beat in vanilla. Alternately add flour mixture and milk beating on low after each addition until well combined. Stir in lemon zest and juice. Spread batter evenly in prepared pan.

3. Bake 35 to 40 minutes or until top springs back when lightly touched. Cool in pan on a wire rack 10 minutes. Remove from pan. Cool completely on wire rack.

4. Frost and decorate using Lemon Buttercream Frosting. (See decorating how-tos, right.) Makes 12 servings.

Lemon Buttercream Frosting In a large bowl beat ½ cup softened butter with mixer on high 30 seconds. Reduce speed; gradually add 6 cups powdered sugar, beating continuously. Beat in 2 tsp. lemon zest and 4 Tbsp. lemon juice. Beat in 2 cups additional powdered sugar. Beat in enough heavy cream (4 to 6 Tbsp.) to make spreading consistency. To tint frosting purple, use a 2:1 ratio of red to blue liquid food coloring. (If you halve the frosting, use 6 drops red and 3 drops blue.)

PER SERVING *722 cal, 25 g fat, 111 mg chol, 500 mg sodium, 120 g carb, 1 g fiber, 94 g sugars, 6 g pro.*

*Tip Find dried culinary lavender buds in gourmet food stores or online.

**Tip If you aren't decorating the cake, halve the frosting recipe.

FROST IT
Use a foolproof dot-and-drag technique for petals.

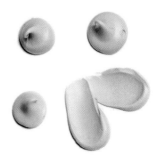

FORM THE PETALS Pipe dots in a circle using a piping bag with a large round tip. Use an offset spatula to pull frosting toward center; add a second layer if you like.

ADD A CANDY Place a lemon drop or several small candies or sprinkles in the center.

THIS CAKE WILL BE A HIT AT A SPRINGTIME BRIDAL OR BABY SHOWER. LAVENDER BRIGHTENS CLASSIC LEMON-POPPY SEED WITH FLORAL FLAVOR.

THE ICONIC THREE-LAYER SOUTHERN BANANA-PINEAPPLE SPICE CAKE IS REINVENTED AS EASIER-TO-HANDLE CUPCAKES. A RICH WHITE CHOCOLATE FROSTING UPS THE DECADENCE.

HUMMINGBIRD CUPCAKES

HANDS-ON TIME 20 minutes, excludes decorating
TOTAL TIME 1 hour 50 minutes, includes cooling

2	cups all-purpose flour
1	cup sugar
1½	tsp. baking powder
½	tsp. salt
½	tsp. ground cinnamon
¼	tsp. baking soda
¼	tsp. ground cloves
⅔	cup mashed ripe bananas (2 medium)
1	20-oz. can crushed pineapple in juice, drained
2	eggs, lightly beaten
½	cup vegetable oil (such as corn)
1	tsp. vanilla
½	cup chopped toasted walnuts (tip, page 27)
1	recipe White Chocolate-Cream Cheese Frosting*

1. Preheat oven to 350°F. Line eighteen 2½-inch muffin cups with paper bake cups; set aside.
2. In a large bowl stir together flour, sugar, baking powder, salt, cinnamon, baking soda, and cloves.
3. In a medium bowl stir together bananas, pineapple, eggs, oil, and vanilla. Add banana mixture to flour mixture; stir to combine. Fold in walnuts. Divide batter evenly among muffin cups; fill about three-quarters full.

4. Bake 20 minutes or until tops spring back when lightly touched. Cool in pans on wire racks 5 minutes. Remove from pans. Let cool completely on racks.
5. Frost and decorate using White Chocolate-Cream Cheese Frosting (see decorating how-tos, page 81 and right). Makes 18 cupcakes.
White Chocolate-Cream Cheese Frosting In an extra-large bowl beat 8 oz. softened cream cheese and ⅔ cup softened butter with a mixer on medium 30 seconds or until smooth. Beat in 8 oz. melted and cooled white baking chocolate and 3 tsp. vanilla. Gradually beat in 4 cups powdered sugar. Beat in 2 Tbsp. milk. Gradually beat in 4 cups additional powdered sugar. If needed, beat in additional milk, 1 tsp. at a time, to make frosting spreading consistency. For pink frosting, tint 2 cups frosting with 2 drops red liquid food coloring. For brown icing, tint ½ cup frosting with 1 oz. melted semisweet chocolate.
PER CUPCAKE 450 cal, 19 g fat, 43 mg chol, 201 mg sodium, 68 g carb, 1 g fiber, 55 g sugars, 4 g pro.
*Tip If you aren't decorating the cake, halve the frosting recipe.

FROST IT
A few simple shapes make this sweet lamb face.

FROST THE TOP AND ADD A WOOLLY TRIM Use a piping bag and star tip to make a ruffly border around the edge. If you don't have a star tip, make curly loops using a small open tip or plastic bag. For the ears, pipe pink icing onto a mini marshmallow cut in half and press into the frosting. Use a small round tip to pipe on the eyes and nose.

FROST IT
For bunny ears, use the dot-and-drag frosting technique (page 81) with a pink layer on top of a white one.

MAKE THE FACE Pipe a circle using a large round tip for face; add eyes, nose, and mouth using a small round tip. Press in white sprinkle whiskers.

HUMMINGBIRD
CUPCAKES

ZUCCHINI-
CARROT
CAKE

A FAN OF ZUCCHINI BREAD AND CARROT CAKE? THIS SUBTLY SPICED CAKE WITH HONEY-SWEETENED CREAM CHEESE FROSTING PROVES THE TWO FAVORITES ARE EVEN BETTER TOGETHER.

ZUCCHINI-CARROT CAKE

HANDS-ON TIME 20 minutes, excludes decorating
TOTAL TIME 2 hours, includes cooling

1½	**cups all-purpose flour**
1	**tsp. baking powder**
1	**tsp. ground cinnamon**
½	**tsp. salt**
¼	**tsp. baking soda**
¼	**tsp. ground nutmeg**
¾	**cup sugar**
½	**cup vegetable oil**
¼	**cup evaporated milk**
1	**tsp. lemon juice**
1	**tsp. vanilla**
2	**eggs**
½	**cup finely shredded carrots**
½	**cup finely shredded zucchini**
⅓	**cup finely chopped pecans**
1	**recipe Honey-Cream Cheese Frosting***
½	**7-oz. pkg. marzipan** **Orange paste food coloring** **Chopped pistachios (for grass)**

1. Preheat oven to 350°F. Grease and flour a 9×1½-inch round cake pan. In a medium bowl stir together flour, baking powder, cinnamon, salt, baking soda, and nutmeg; set aside.
2. In a large bowl stir together sugar, oil, milk, lemon juice, and vanilla. Stir in eggs until combined. Stir in flour mixture, carrots, zucchini, and pecans. Spread batter evenly in prepared pan.
3. Bake 35 to 40 minutes or until a toothpick inserted near center comes out clean. Cool in pan on a wire rack 10 minutes. Remove from pan. Cool completely on wire rack.
4. Frost and decorate using Honey Cream-Cheese Frosting. (See decorating how-tos, right.)
5. For carrots: Wearing gloves, dip marzipan in food coloring to reach desired color (we dipped it twice); knead in color. Roll into a 7-inch-long rope; cut into 1-inch lengths. Makes 8 servings.
Honey-Cream Cheese Frosting In a large bowl combine 4 oz. softened cream cheese and ¼ cup softened butter. Beat with a mixer on medium until smooth. Gradually add 2 cups powdered sugar and 2 Tbsp. honey; beat until combined. Add 1 cup additional powdered sugar and 1 Tbsp. milk, beating until smooth.
***Tip** If you aren't decorating the cake, halve the frosting recipe.
PER SERVING *682 cal, 35 g fat, 79 mg chol, 378 mg sodium, 87 g carb, 2 g fiber, 67 g sugars, 8 g pro.*

FROST IT
Marzipan—a sweet almond paste sold in many grocery store baking sections—can be tinted with food coloring and formed into shapes.

TINT MARZIPAN Knead orange food coloring (paste works best) into marzipan. To keep hands dye-free, coat them with powdered sugar or wear plastic gloves.

SHAPE CARROTS Roll colored marzipan into carrot shapes and create ridges with a toothpick. Finish with a mint sprig in the top.

BAGEL BRUNCH

Buy a stack of bagels, set out a spread of toppings, brew some coffee, and gather friends for a laid-back chat.

BAGEL BAR

Fill your bagel bar with both sweet and savory toppings, including a few stir-together flavored cream cheese spreads.

TOTAL TIME 15 minutes

8   oz. cream cheese, softened
    Stir-Ins (below)
    Sliced deli meats and smoked salmon
    Thinly sliced fruits and vegetables, such as apples, cucumbers, tomatoes, and/or red onion
    Drained capers
    Everything bagel seasoning
    Fresh herbs, such as dill weed and basil
    Orange juice and coffee

1. For flavored cream cheese, in a medium bowl combine cream cheese and one Stir-In. Beat on medium with a mixer just until combined. Transfer to an airtight container. Chill at least 1 hour.
2. On a large platter arrange flavored cream cheese, deli meats, smoked salmon, fruits, vegetables, capers, bagel seasoning, and fresh herbs. Serve with orange juice and coffee.

Onion-Chive Stir-In In a small bowl combine ¼ cup finely chopped green onions, 2 Tbsp. snipped fresh chives, ½ tsp. onion powder, and ¼ tsp. garlic powder. Makes 18 servings.
PER 1 TBSP. *44 cal., 4 g fat, 14 mg chol, 46 mg sodium, 1 g carb, 0 g fiber, 0 g sugar, 1 g pro.*

Maple-Spiced Pumpkin Stir-In In a small bowl combine ¼ cup canned pumpkin, 2 Tbsp. maple syrup, and ½ tsp. pumpkin pie spice. Makes 21 servings.
PER 1 TBSP. *43 cal, 4 g fat, 11 mg chol, 40 mg sodium, 2 g carb, 2 g sugars, 1 g pro.*

Cinnamon-Berry Stir-In In a small bowl combine ½ cup finely chopped raspberries, strawberries, and/or blueberries; 2 Tbsp. honey; and ½ tsp. ground cinnamon. Use a fork to smash berries. Makes 24 servings.
PER 1 TBSP. *39 cal, 3 g fat, 10 mg chol, 35 mg sodium, 2 g carb, 2 g sugars, 1 g pro.*

Garden Veggie Stir-In In a small bowl combine ¼ cup finely shredded carrot, 2 Tbsp. finely chopped sweet red pepper, 2 Tbsp. finely chopped green onions, ½ tsp. onion powder, ½ tsp. paprika, ¼ tsp. garlic powder, and ¼ tsp. kosher salt. Makes 18 servings.
PER 1 TBSP. *45 cal, 4 g fat, 14 mg chol, 75 mg sodium, 1 g carb, 1 g sugars, 1 g pro.*

FAST & FRESH

Easy, healthful recipes for a better dinner tonight.

STEAK AND POTATO TOASTS

Grated fresh horseradish yields a brighter, sharper flavor than the bottled version. Look for firm roots free of wrinkles and soft spots. Peel off the tough brown skin with a paring knife and grate just before using. Chill root wrapped in a damp paper towel in a plastic bag up to 10 days.

TOTAL TIME 40 minutes

- 1 lb. boneless beef sirloin
   Salt and black pepper
- ½ cup crème fraîche or sour cream
- 4 tsp. fresh horseradish, finely grated (or 2 Tbsp. bottled)
- 2 tsp. red wine vinegar
   Olive oil
- 1 lb. russet potatoes, thinly sliced
- 4 slices seeded rye bread, toasted
- ¼ cup fresh Italian parsley

1. Generously season steak with salt and pepper. In a small bowl stir together crème fraîche, horseradish, and vinegar; season lightly with salt and pepper.

2. In an extra-large heavy skillet heat 1 Tbsp. olive oil over medium-high heat; add steak. Cook 12 to 14 minutes or until desired doneness (145°F for medium), turning once. Let rest, covered with foil, on cutting board 10 minutes.

3. Wipe skillet clean, then heat 2 tsp. olive oil over medium heat. Working in batches to avoid crowding pan, cook potatoes in a single layer just until browned and tender, about 2 minutes each side. Repeat two more batches using an additional 2 tsp. olive oil each time. Season with salt and pepper.

4. Spread toast with crème fraîche mixture. Slice steak across the grain; top toast with potatoes, steak, and parsley. Makes 4 servings.

PER SERVING *523 cal, 27 g fat, 103 mg chol, 661 mg sodium, 37 g carb, 4 g fiber, 2 g sugars, 31 g pro.*

**GINGER PORK
WITH CUCUMBER
AND HERBS**

SHEET-PAN CHICKEN WITH LEMONS AND GREEN OLIVES

Manzanillas—briny Spanish olives with firm texture and slightly smoky taste—pair well with the smokiness of paprika-rubbed chicken. For more subtle flavor, turn to bright green Italian Castelvetranos, which have meaty, buttery flesh.

HANDS-ON TIME 10 minutes
TOTAL TIME 55 minutes

2   Tbsp. extra-virgin olive oil
8   chicken thighs bone-in with skin
    (2½ to 3 lb. total)
    Salt
¾   tsp. smoked paprika
2   lemons, quartered
2   shallots, quartered
1   cup green olives (with or without
    pits), rinsed
2   Tbsp. butter

1. Preheat oven to 400°F. Coat a 15×10-inch baking pan with 2 Tbsp. olive oil. Add chicken to pan, turning to coat both sides with oil. Season chicken with salt and ½ tsp. paprika. Place lemons and shallots in pan around chicken. Roast 30 to 40 minutes or until skin is browned and chicken is done (175°F).
2. Remove pan from oven. Squeeze lemon juice over chicken. Transfer chicken to a platter; cover with foil to keep warm. Transfer liquid from pan to a glass measure. Skim off fat; return liquid to pan. Stir in olives, butter, and remaining ¼ tsp. paprika. Roast 5 minutes to warm olives and melt butter. Spoon sauce, olives, and shallots over chicken. Serve with mashed potatoes or couscous. Makes 4 servings.
PER SERVING *606 cal, 51 g fat, 164 mg chol, 937 mg sodium, 5 g carb, 2 g fiber, 2 g sugars, 32 g pro.*

GINGER PORK WITH CUCUMBER AND HERBS

The tastiest part of this recipe is the crisped chunks of ground pork in the soy-garlic-ginger base.

TOTAL TIME 25 minutes

6   green onions, finely chopped
3   Tbsp. soy sauce reduced-sodium
2   tsp. packed brown sugar
½   tsp. crushed red pepper (optional)
1   Tbsp. vegetable oil
1   clove garlic, minced
1   Tbsp. fresh ginger minced
1   lb. ground pork
1   medium cucumber, peeled and
    chopped into ½-inch cubes
½   cup fresh herb leaves (mint, cilantro,
    and/or basil)

Hot cooked rice
Lime wedges and/or sriracha

1. In a medium bowl stir together half the green onions, the soy sauce, sugar, and, if desired, crushed red pepper; set aside.
2. In a large skillet heat oil over medium-high heat. Add garlic and ginger; cook until fragrant, about 30 seconds. Add pork; press flat to make one large patty. Cook, without stirring, until pork is crisp on bottom, about 4 minutes. Break up pork and stir in soy sauce mixture. Cook and stir until pork is cooked through and crumbly, 2 to 3 minutes more. Top pork with remaining green onions, cucumber, and herbs. Serve over rice with lime wedges and sriracha. Makes 4 servings.
PER SERVING *500 cal, 23 g fat, 77 mg chol, 505 mg sodium, 46 g carb, 4 g fiber, 6 g sugars, 26 g pro.*

SHEET-PAN CHICKEN
WITH LEMONS AND
GREEN OLIVES

VINEYARD BEET
AND STRAWBERRY
SALAD
Recipe on page 100

may

Fresh vegetables deserve a special place at the table. This recipe collection shows off their flavor—and how to pair them with wine. Plus dishes from the pro's for inspiration to try something new.

96

104

113

VEGGIES & VINES

We all know the rules: white wine with fish, red with meat. But what goes with beets? The answer is easy to find in wine country.

In late spring and summer, meals begin to reflect the produce filling gardens and farmers markets. Vegetables, rather than meat, dominate plates with bright flavors and vibrant colors. The shift in focus can make hosts wonder what wine to pour at dinner. What is the best taste match for an earthy beet, a peppery radish, or a cool cucumber?

"There's always been so much focus on pairing wines with meat, poultry, and fish that when vegetables dominate the meal, people get stumped on what wines to serve," says Tracey Shepos Cenami, one of the chefs at Kendall-Jackson Winery in Sonoma County, CA. "We start with the wines everybody craves and find vegetables that pair well with them," Cenami says. At Kendall-Jackson, wine pairings revolve around the produce grown in the estate's organic garden—a living laboratory for gardener Tucker Taylor and chefs Justin Wangler and Cenami. Together, they work to demystify this matchmaking game and pick wines that bring out the diversity of flavors in vegetables.

Consider rosés. The summertime favorite's red-fruit notes and melon undertones beg for salads that star berries or watermelon, with welcome contrast with acidic tomatoes or earthy baby potatoes. Bright, floral Pinot Gris brings out subtle flavors of cucumbers and celery. A big fruity Cabernet Sauvignon is an obvious pick for steak and also enhances edible flowers and greens—like arugula or pesto sauces.

"This is more art than science," Taylor says. "I love composing green salad mixes from whatever is ready in the garden. It could be all kinds of baby lettuces, spinach, and endive. Any simple salad comes alive when you sprinkle on tender herbs like dill and tarragon and taste it with a sip of grassy white wine like Sauvignon Blanc."

There's a reason the chefs keep mentioning salads. "The thing about vegetables is that you barely have to cook them, so it just makes sense to toss them together," Wangler says. "Overcooked vegetables often lose their flavors, but raw or barely cooked vegetables hold onto them. And you want to hold onto every flavor so you can experience the magic of matching them with wines."

LEMONY VEGGIE
BRUSCHETTA
Recipe on page 96

PICK A PAIRING

"A simple guideline when pairing wine and vegetables is to mimic the color of the vegetables with the color of the wine," says Kendall-Jackson estate chef Tracey Shepos Cenami.

BLUSH & DRY A dry rosé pairs beautifully with salads containing strawberries. The summer favorite also marries well with earthy beets and spicy radishes because of the flavor contrasts.

LIGHT & BRIGHT Serve Pinot Gris or Sauvignon Blanc with vegetables like squash and asparagus or dishes featuring citrus flavors. Grassy herbs (tarragon, parsley, and dill) go with dry whites.

BIG & RED Spicy black pepper notes in a Cabernet Sauvignon underscore the pepperiness of Nasturtium Pesto and watercress. The dark fruit flavors in Cabs complement blackberries, plums, and Swiss chard.

THE RUSTIC GRILLED SQUASH AND ONION FLATBREAD: ITS FOOLPROOF DOUGH GRILLS MORE CRISPY THAN CHEWY TO HOLD LOTS OF THE GARDEN VEGGIES.

SQUASH AND ONION FLATBREAD

Pair with a Sauvignon Blanc that has grapefruit, fig, and star fruit flavors.

HANDS-ON TIME 45 minutes
TOTAL TIME 2 hours 15 minutes

⅓ cup warm water (105°F to 115°F)
3½ tsp. olive oil, plus more for drizzling
½ tsp. active dry yeast
⅛ tsp. sugar
1 cup bread flour*
½ tsp. salt
8 oz. assorted baby summer squash with flowers attached, trimmed, and halved (quartered if large)
6 red or green spring onions, trimmed and quartered
8 oz. Burrata or fresh mozzarella cheese, drained and chopped
Edible flowers, such as fennel or golden mustard
Sea salt flakes

1. For flatbread dough: In a bowl stir together the water, 1½ tsp. oil, the yeast, and sugar. Let stand 5 minutes. Stir in flour and salt. Turn dough out onto a lightly floured surface. Knead 1 to 2 minutes or until smooth and elastic. Place in a greased bowl; turn to grease surface of dough. Cover; let rise at room temperature 1 hour or until double in size. Turn dough out onto a floured surface; halve. Cover; let rest 20 minutes.
2. Meanwhile, preheat oven to 375°F. Place squash and onions in a shallow baking pan. Toss with remaining 2 tsp. olive oil. Season with salt. Roast 6 to 8 minutes or until crisp-tender.
3. Roll or stretch each dough portion to a 10×7-inch oval. For a gas grill, grill on rack of covered grill directly over high heat 1 to 2 minutes or until golden, turning once. Reduce heat to medium. Top each flatbread with squash-onion mixture and Burrata. Grill 2 minutes more or until crisp and grill marks form. Sprinkle with flowers and sea salt; drizzle with additional oil. Makes 8 servings.

PER SERVING *164 cal, 10 g fat, 20 mg chol, 246 mg sodium, 14 g carb, 8 g pro.*
*Note The high protein of bread flour gives bread distinctive chew; all-purpose flour will work as well.

LEMONY VEGGIE BRUSCHETTA

Photo on page 94.

Pair with a dry rosé that has strawberry and pink grapefruit flavors.

TOTAL TIME 30 minutes

6 oz. fresh green beans and/or yellow wax beans, trimmed
¼ cup sugar
1 lemon (1½ tsp. zest; ¼ cup juice)
1 8-oz. carton mascarpone cheese or whipped goat cheese
16 ½-inch slices country-style bread, toasted
1 cup thinly sliced green onions and/or radishes
Fresh mint leaves
Sea salt flakes

1. Prepare an ice bath with cold water and ice cubes in a large bowl. Cook beans in boiling salted water 1 minute; transfer to ice bath. Remove; pat dry. Cut into ½-inch pieces.
2. In a small saucepan combine sugar, ¼ cup water, and the lemon zest and juice. Bring to boiling over medium heat; reduce heat. Simmer, uncovered, 6 to 8 minutes or until syrupy; cool.
3. Spread mascarpone on toasted bread slices. Top with green beans, green onions and/or radishes, mint, and sea salt flakes; drizzle with syrup. Makes 8 servings.
PER SERVING *217 cal, 12 g fat, 40 mg chol, 163 mg sodium, 21 g carb, 7 g sugars, 3 g pro.*

GRILLED RIBEYE STEAKS WITH NASTURTIUM PESTO

Photo on page 98.

Pair with a berry-forward Cabernet Sauvignon that has hints of mocha and nutmeg.

HANDS-ON TIME 10 minutes
TOTAL TIME 1 hour

3 12- to 14-oz. boneless beef ribeye steaks, about 1 inch thick
½ cup extra-virgin olive oil, plus more for rubbing on steaks
1 oz. baby nasturtium leaves* or arugula leaves (1½ cups)
¾ oz. pea shoots or baby greens (1 cup)
2 fresh basil leaves
1 small clove garlic, peeled
1 lemon (1 tsp. zest; 2 Tbsp. juice)
¼ tsp. salt
⅛ tsp. black pepper
½ oz. nasturtium petals* (¾ cup)
Purslane or baby greens (optional)

1. Allow steaks to stand at room temperature 30 minutes. Meanwhile, for nasturtium pesto: In a food processor or blender combine ½ cup olive oil, the nasturtium leaves, pea shoots, basil, garlic, lemon zest and juice, salt, and pepper. Process until smooth.
2. Pat steaks dry. Rub with additional olive oil; season both sides generously with kosher salt and black pepper.
3. Grill steaks on greased rack of covered grill directly over medium-high heat 8 to 10 minutes or until desired doneness (145°F for medium rare). Cover with foil; let stand 10 minutes. Meanwhile, stir half the nasturtium petals into nasturtium pesto; sprinkle with remaining petals. Thinly slice steak. If desired, serve over purslane. Pass with nasturtium pesto. Makes 8 servings.
PER SERVING *430 cal, 37 g fat, 87 mg chol, 209 mg sodium, 2 g carb, 5 g fiber, 25 g pro.*
*Tip Find nasturtium leaves and petals, which add color and a peppery bite, at gourmetsweetbotanicals.com.

SQUASH AND
ONION FLATBREAD

GRILLED RIBEYE
STEAKS WITH
NASTURTIUM
PESTO
Recipe on page 96

CUCUMBER-CELERY SALAD
Recipe on page 100

VINEYARD BEET AND STRAWBERRY SALAD
Recipe on page 100

CUCUMBER-CELERY SALAD

Photo on page 99.

Pair with a floral Pinot Gris that has pear-tangerine flavors.

HANDS-ON TIME 20 minutes
TOTAL TIME 35 minutes

1½ lb. cucumber, chopped*
½ tsp. kosher salt
1 lb. celery, sliced
5 fresh apricots, cut into wedges
1 to 2 avocados, halved, seeded, peeled, and cut into large chunks
½ cup salted Marcona or regular almonds, toasted (tip, page 27) and chopped
2 lemons (1 tsp. zest; ⅓ cup juice)
⅓ cup Meyer lemon olive oil or extra-virgin olive oil
  Dill sprigs
  Sea salt flakes

1. In a bowl toss cucumber with salt. Let stand 15 minutes; drain. Add celery, apricots, avocado, and almonds. Place lemon juice in a bowl. Add oil gradually, whisking constantly until emulsified.
2. Drizzle over salad; toss lightly to coat. Top with lemon zest, dill, and sea salt flakes. Makes 8 servings.
PER SERVING *194 cal, 16 g fat, 192 mg sodium, 11 g carb, 4 g fiber, 5 g sugars, 4 g pro.*
Make Ahead Make salad up to 2 hours ahead; add the avocado right before serving. The dressing can be made up to 3 days ahead.
*Tip Chef Justin Wangler loves Armenian cucumbers in this salad. "They grow long and curvy like melons and are sweet, tender, and less watery than average ones," he says. Seedless English cucumbers work too.

FARMER T'S HERB AND FLOWER SALAD

Pair with a Sauvignon Blanc that has tropical fruit flavors and layers of fig and honeysuckle.

TOTAL TIME 25 minutes

6 cups mixed baby greens
1 cup fresh tarragon leaves
1 cup fresh dill
1 cup fresh chervil or Italian parsley

1 cup edible flowers, such as nasturtium, calendula petals, and Lanai blue verbena
½ cup white verjus*
1½ tsp. Dijon-style mustard
1½ tsp. white wine vinegar
1½ tsp. sugar
¾ cup extra-virgin olive oil
½ tsp. kosher salt
⅛ tsp. ground white pepper
2 Tbsp. chopped fresh tarragon, dill sprigs, and/or thyme

1. In a bowl toss together baby greens, herbs, and edible flowers.
2. For verjus vinaigrette: In a medium bowl whisk together verjus, mustard, vinegar, and sugar. Gradually add oil, whisking constantly until emulsified. Add salt and the white pepper. Add chopped tarragon; pass with salad. Makes 8 servings.
*Tip You can substitute ⅓ cup white grape juice and 2 Tbsp. white wine vinegar for the white verjus.
PER SERVING *195 cal, 20 g fat, 107 mg sodium, 3 g carb, 1 g fiber, 2 g sugars, 1 g pro.*

VINEYARD BEET AND STRAWBERRY SALAD

Photo on page 99.

Pair with a rosé that has bright fruit flavors and a hint of watermelon.

HANDS-ON TIME 30 minutes
TOTAL TIME 1 hour 10 minutes

2 lb. red, golden, and/or candy-stripe baby beets, trimmed
3 Tbsp. canola oil
1 tsp. kosher salt
1 lb. small fresh strawberries, hulled
3 Tbsp. red verjus*
2 Tbsp. red wine vinegar
1 Tbsp. pomegranate molasses**
¼ tsp. salt
½ cup extra-virgin olive oil
6 small red or purple radishes, sliced
1 recipe Fried Leeks

1. Preheat oven to 350°F. In a roasting pan combine beets, 1 cup water, the canola oil, and kosher salt. Cover pan with foil. Roast 40 to 45 minutes or until tender; drain. Let cool. Peel and quarter.
2. For dressing: In a blender combine ¼ cup strawberries, the verjus, vinegar, pomegranate molasses, and salt. Cover; process until smooth. Gradually add oil, blending until emulsified.

3. Cut up remaining strawberries; arrange with beets and radishes in a serving bowl. To serve, drizzle with dressing; top with leeks. Makes 8 servings.
Fried Leeks Trim and halve one leek lengthwise; slice lengthwise. Rinse; pat dry. In a skillet heat 1 Tbsp. olive oil over medium heat. Toss leeks with 2 Tbsp. all-purpose flour. Add leeks to skillet; fry until crispy. Drain; season with salt to taste.
PER SERVING *256 cal, 19 g fat, 159 mg sodium, 21 g carb, 5 g fiber, 13 g sugars, 2 g pro.*
*Tip Verjus, French for green juice, is made from the pressings of unripe grapes and is milder and sweeter than vinegar. Find it at kj.com, or sub 2 Tbsp. grape juice and 1 Tbsp. red wine vinegar.
**Tip Pomegranate molasses is a reduction of the fruit's juices. The chefs use the Carlo brand.

OLIVE OIL CAKE WITH CHARDONNAY SABAYON

Pair with a sweet Chardonnay that has apricot and pear flavors and honeysuckle aromas.

HANDS-ON TIME 45 minutes
TOTAL TIME 2 hours

⅔ cup almond meal or almond flour*
½ cup all-purpose flour
½ tsp. baking powder
⅛ tsp. salt
¼ cup butter, softened
¾ cup sugar
¼ cup olive oil
½ tsp. lemon zest
2 eggs
2 Tbsp. buttermilk
3 Tbsp. honey
  Chardonnay Sabayon
  Roasted Stone Fruit
  Edible flowers (optional)
  Fresh micro herbs (optional)

1. Preheat oven to 350°F. Grease and lightly flour a 9-inch round cake pan.
2. For cake: In a bowl stir together almond meal, flour, baking powder, and salt. In a large bowl beat butter on medium speed 30 seconds. Gradually add sugar, olive oil, and zest, beating until creamy. Add eggs, one at a time, beating on low 30 seconds after each until combined. (Batter will be thick.) Add flour mixture; beat until combined. Stir in buttermilk. Spread in prepared pan.

3. Bake 20 to 25 minutes or until a toothpick comes out clean and surface is golden brown. Cool in pan on a wire rack 10 minutes. Remove from pan; cool completely on wire rack.

4. Meanwhile, make honey glaze: In a small bowl stir together honey and 1 Tbsp. water. Reserve 1 Tbsp. for Roasted Stone Fruit; drizzle remaining over cake. Serve cake with Chardonnay Sabayon and Roasted Stone Fruit. If desired, top with edible flowers and herbs. Makes 8 slices.

Chardonnay Sabayon Place a medium heatproof bowl on top of double boiler, being careful that water doesn't touch bowl. Add four egg yolks, 2 Tbsp. sugar, and 2 Tbsp. Chardonnay. Cook 10 minutes or until thick enough to coat the back of a spoon (160°F), whisking constantly. Remove bowl from double boiler. Beat with a mixer on medium 2 minutes or until cool. In a large bowl beat ½ cup heavy cream and 2 tsp. sugar with mixer on medium until soft peaks form. Gradually fold in yolk mixture until combined. Chill, covered, until ready to serve or up to 1 day.

Roasted Stone Fruit Preheat oven to 450°F. Place four apricots, halved and pitted, in a baking pan. Drizzle with reserved 1 Tbsp. honey glaze; toss to coat. Arrange cut sides down. Roast 5 to 10 minutes or until light brown and soft. Cool in pan on a wire rack.

PER SLICE *422 cal, 26 g fat, 171 mg chol, 143 mg sodium, 42 g carb, 2 g fiber, 34 g sugars, 7 g pro.*

*Tip Almond meal and almond flour are interchangeable, but have subtle differences. Meal is coarsely ground skin-on almonds; flour is finely ground blanched skinless almonds.

CUSTARDY CHARDONNAY SABAYON SAUCE IS A TASTY PAIRING WITH SUBTLY SWEET AND NUTTY OLIVE OIL CAKE.

OLIVE OIL CAKE WITH CHARDONNAY SABAYON

RESETTING *the* TABLE

Meet the cooks, makers, and authors who change the way we eat. Their tips can inspire us to shake up the meal plan and try something new.

SESAME-GINGER BOWL

Simmering a blend of whole grains in coconut milk infuses them with tropical flavor and a rich, creamy texture.

TOTAL TIME 30 minutes

1	13.5- to 14-oz. can unsweetened coconut milk
1½	cups millet, quinoa, and/or bulgur
1	tsp. salt
2	Tbsp. toasted sesame oil
1	Tbsp. tamari sauce or soy sauce
1	Tbsp. rice vinegar
2	tsp. grated fresh ginger
1	clove garlic, minced
1	tsp. honey
3	cups toppings, such as avocado slices, basil leaves, shredded red cabbage, sliced red sweet pepper, and/or sesame seeds
	Lime wedges (optional)

In a saucepan combine 2½ cups water, the coconut milk, grains, and salt. Bring to boiling; reduce heat. Cook, covered, 15 minutes or until liquid is absorbed. Meanwhile, in a screw-top jar combine sesame oil, tamari sauce, vinegar, 1 Tbsp. water, the ginger, garlic, and honey. Cover; shake well. Serve over grains and toppings. If desired, serve with lime wedges. Makes 6 servings.
PER SERVING *393 cal, 23 g fat, 609 mg sodium, 40 g carb, 7 g fiber, 3 g sugars, 8 g pro.*

THE WHOLE GRAIN PIONEER

BOB MOORE, FOUNDER OF BOB'S RED MILL Long before grain bowls acquired their own hashtags, 89-year-old Bob Moore was eating his daily grains. He began milling 40 years ago while on a mission to feed his family wholesome food. His whole grain and alternative flour brand has expanded to 300-plus products, including reemerging ancient varietals and gluten-free (GF) flours. Yet even this Pied Piper of cereals, kernels, and seeds is surprised by the many ways people reimagine quinoa or millet: "I love to see how creative people can be with my grains."

TRY THIS CHICKEN WITH ANY COMBINATION OF SWISS CHARD, MUSTARD GREENS, OR SPINACH. THE GREENS COOK WHILE THE CHICKEN RESTS AND THEY PICK UP FLAVOR AND CARAMELIZED BITS FROM THE DRIPPINGS IN THE SKILLET.

THE WEEKNIGHT-DINNER WARRIOR

MELISSA CLARK, AUTHOR & FOOD WRITER FOR THE *NEW YORK TIMES*
Melissa Clark is on a crusade to retool weeknight dinner mind-sets, one one-dish meal at a time. One-pan meals certainly aren't new, and traditionally they're closely aligned with ease and comfort food, such as cheesy noodle casserole. While Melissa doesn't spurn cheese or noodles, the recipes in her cookbook, *Dinner: Changing the Game* focus on bold flavors and a-ha techniques. And they come together in less than an hour. "I'm all about more flavor and less work," she says.

SWEET GARLIC CHICKEN AND KALE

Using Melissa's innovative splayed preparation, roasted chicken moves from weekends to weeknights. The method delivers juicy white meat and perfectly cooked dark meat—in 40 minutes.

TOTAL TIME 1 hour

1	3½- to 4½-lb. whole chicken
	Salt and black pepper
1	lemon, quartered lengthwise
1	Tbsp. extra-virgin olive oil
5	cloves garlic, smashed and peeled
12	oz. kale or chard, stemmed and leaves torn into bite-size pieces*
¼	cup sliced pitted black olives, such as Kalamata
⅛	tsp. crushed red pepper

1. Splay chicken by cutting skin between legs and body. Pull thighs and wings away until joints pop out of sockets. Season with salt and black pepper. Place two lemon quarters in cavity.
2. Preheat oven to 475°F. Heat an oven-going skillet over high heat 5 to 10 minutes. Add chicken, breast side up, with legs and wings flat out to sides and bottom. Drizzle with oil. Roast in oven 25 to 35 minutes. Add garlic; roast 5 minutes, stirring garlic once. Roast 5 to 15 minutes more or until a meat thermometer inserted in thigh registers 170°F. Transfer chicken to cutting board to rest.
3. Transfer skillet and its juices to stove on medium-high heat. Add kale, olives, and crushed red pepper. Cook 5 minutes or until kale wilts. Slice chicken. To serve, drizzle skillet juices over chicken and kale; squeeze remaining lemon over all. Makes 4 servings.
PER SERVING *620 cal, 43 g fat, 201 mg chol, 893 mg sodium, 5 g carb, 2 g fiber, 1 g sugars, 52 g pro.*
*Tip If using chard, chop stems into ½-inch pieces and add with garlic in Step 2. Add chard leaves with olives in Step 3.

BRAISED PORK "HUMBA" TACOS

CHIPOTLE-VEGGIE TACOS

KOREAN BBQ STEAK TACOS

Large sesame leaves (also called perilla leaves) are a traditional wrap for meat or vegetable fillings in Korean cooking. Find them in Asian groceries or farmers markets. Bill Kim uses a Pickled Cucumbers to brighten the salty funkiness of the ssamjang, a fermented soybean paste.

HANDS-ON TIME 25 minutes
TOTAL TIME 4 hours 25 minutes

½   cup packed brown sugar
½   cup soy sauce
⅔   cup coarsely chopped Asian pear
½   cup coarsely chopped white onion
1   kiwi, peeled and chopped
¼   cup peeled garlic cloves
¼   cup peeled, sliced fresh ginger
¼   cup toasted sesame oil
3   lb. skirt steak or flank steak*
      Ssamjang paste
8   tortillas, warmed, or sesame leaves
1   recipe Pickled Cucumbers

1. For sauce: In a blender add brown sugar, soy sauce, and ¼ cup water. Process until combined. Add pear, onion, kiwi, garlic, and ginger. Process until smooth. Gradually add sesame oil, blending until emulsified.
2. Set a gallon-size resealable plastic bag in a shallow baking pan; add steak and sauce. Chill 4 to 24 hours, turning bag occasionally.
3. Drain meat. Grill steak on rack of a covered grill directly over medium heat 6 minutes, turning once. Let stand, covered, 5 minutes. Slice against grain. To serve, spread ssamjang on tortillas or sesame leaves; top each with steak and Pickled Cucumbers. Makes 8 servings.
Pickled Cucumbers In a bowl combine ½ cup rice vinegar, 2 tsp. sugar, and ½ tsp. salt. Add 2 cups thinly sliced seedless cucumber, ¾ cup sliced white onion, and ¼ cup sliced green onion; toss to coat. Let stand, covered, 30 minutes to 2 hours.
PER SERVING *487 cal, 28 g fat, 111 mg chol, 671 mg sodium, 24 g carb, 3 g fiber, 11 g sugars, 37 g pro.*
*Tip If using flank steak, grill over medium heat 13 to 16 minutes for medium rare, turning once.

THE TACO IS ON A WORLD TOUR. THE STREET-FOOD STAPLE IS A FAMILIAR WAY TO TRY GLOBAL FLAVORS, AND THESE CHEFS PROVE ANYTHING CAN GO ON A TORTILLA.

BRAISED PORK "HUMBA" TACOS

Chef Yana Gilbuena's tacos are a riff on a pork dish served over rice in the Visayas region of the central Philippines. Humba is a Filipino pork dish with Chinese (star anise, oyster sauce) and Mexican (toppings similar to al pastor tacos) influences.

HANDS-ON TIME 30 minutes
TOTAL TIME 2 hours 30 minutes

1   cup pineapple juice
⅓   cup packed brown sugar
2   Tbsp. soy sauce
2   Tbsp. oyster sauce
1   tsp. black pepper
2   Tbsp. canola oil or coconut oil
1   lb. pork belly or boneless pork shoulder, cut into 1-inch cubes
1   medium red onion (chop half; slice half)
4   cloves garlic, finely minced
6   shiitake mushrooms, stemmed and sliced (4 oz.)
4   whole star anise
1   ½-inch-thick slice peeled fresh pineapple
8   corn tortillas, warmed

1. Preheat oven to 425°F. For marinade: In a bowl combine pineapple juice, ½ cup water, brown sugar, soy sauce, oyster sauce, and pepper.
2. In a skillet heat oil over high heat. Add pork belly; cook and stir 8 minutes or until browned. Add chopped red onion and garlic the last 3 minutes. Transfer to a 2-qt. baking dish. Add marinade, mushrooms, and star anise. Cover; roast 1 hour. Reduce heat to 375°F; roast 1 to 1½ hours more or until tender (45 minutes for pork shoulder). Let rest, uncovered, 5 minutes. Skim off fat.
3. Meanwhile, grill pineapple on a greased grill pan or rack of a covered grill 6 minutes or until charred, turning once; dice. Serve pork in tortillas; top with pineapple and sliced red onion. Makes 4 servings.
PER SERVING *846 cal, 62 g fat, 74 mg chol, 769 mg sodium, 58 g carb, 5 g fiber, 31 g sugars, 14 g pro.*

CHIPOTLE-VEGGIE TACOS

Baby potatoes get smashed then crisped in olive oil with onions, zucchini slices, and wilted Swiss chard. Chef Hugo finishes his veggie tacos with peppers in adobo sauce for smoky heat.

HANDS-ON TIME 20 minutes
TOTAL TIME 40 minutes

8   oz. small red potatoes
2   Tbsp. olive oil
½   cup chopped onion
2   cloves garlic, minced
1   medium zucchini, halved lengthwise and sliced ½ inch thick
4   cups stemmed, torn chard
6   corn tortillas, warmed
1   chipotle pepper in adobo, slivered
    Crumbled Cotija or feta cheese

1. In a saucepan cook potatoes, uncovered, in boiling salted water 10 minutes or until tender. Drain; let cool. Press to ½-inch thickness.
2. In a skillet heat oil over medium heat. Add potatoes; cook 10 minutes or until crispy on both sides, turning once. Add onion and garlic; cook and stir 2 minutes. Add zucchini; cook and stir 3 minutes. Add chard; cook, covered, 3 to 5 minutes or until wilted, stirring once. Serve in tortillas topped with chipotle pepper and cheese. If desired, serve with lime wedges. Makes 6 servings.
PER SERVING *147 cal, 6 g fat, 3 mg chol, 224 mg sodium, 21 g carb, 3 g fiber, 3 g sugars, 3 g pro.*

THE WORLD OF TACOS

BILL KIM emigrated from Seoul, South Korea, to Chicago in the late '70s. Each time his family moved between neighborhoods, Bill picked up friends, foods, and culinary influences (Indian, Jewish, Italian). His cultural crash course gave him the ingredients to master the mash-up. "I want to cook food that reflects my heritage of Korea and Chicago, of kimchi and hot dogs."

YANA GILBUENA "A taco is so versatile," says Yana. "Anything can be put in a taco." Her take serves as a gateway to Filipino food. She is so passionate about introducing the duality of Filipino-American cuisine that she does Salo Series, a cross-country tour of pop-up family-style Filipino dinners.

HUGO ORTEGA expresses himself through tortillas. "It all starts with the tortilla," Hugo says. "Wrap anything up, and you've got a bundle of flavor and self-expression." The Mexico City-born chef began his career as a dishwasher at a nightclub in Texas. Now he's the award-winning chef and owner of four of Houston's top restaurants, including Xochi, Hugo's love letter to the state of Oaxaca and its culinary customs.

"VEGETABLES ARE NOT SOMETHING WE HAVE TO EAT, BUT SOMETHING WE GET TO EAT. IT DOESN'T TAKE MUCH TO MAKE VEGGIES THE MOST INTERESTING PART OF DINNER." CARA MANGINI

THE VEGGIE INNOVATOR

CARA MANGINI, CHEF, AUTHOR & RESTAURANT OWNER Vegetable butcher Cara Mangini wants to change the conversation about veggies. "Vegetables are not something we have to eat, but something we get to eat," Cara says. The granddaughter of a butcher, she got her start at New York City's Eataly market, where she applied the tenets of butchery to prep produce using a root-to-leaf mentality while teaching shoppers how to love their veggies. Her book, *The Vegetable Butcher,* naturally, and two restaurants continue the mission: Vegetables are the stars of the plate, not mere side dishes.

ROASTED BROCCOLI WITH RICOTTA AND TOASTED ORZO

Treat hearty veggies like pieces of meat: Chunked into big pieces and served with a side of creamy ricotta and toasty pasta, broccoli is a bold centerpiece in this meatless main.

TOTAL TIME 30 minutes

2	lb. fresh broccoli with stalks
¼	cup extra-virgin olive oil, plus more for drizzling
½	tsp. salt
1	tsp. crushed red pepper
¼	tsp. black pepper
2	Tbsp. unsalted butter
4	large cloves garlic, thinly sliced
½	cup cooked orzo pasta
1	lemon
1	cup whole milk ricotta cheese
3	Tbsp. pine nuts, toasted
2	Tbsp. grated Parmesan cheese
1	Tbsp. chopped fresh Italian parsley

1. Preheat oven to 450°F. Trim ½ inch off ends of broccoli stalks; discard. Cut off 3 inches from stem end of stalks (enough stalk to cut into coins with substantial stalks to roast). Peel and slice 3-inch pieces into thin coins. Halve stalks lengthwise. Arrange stalks, cut sides down, in a baking pan. Drizzle with 2 Tbsp. oil; season with salt, ½ tsp. crushed red pepper, and black pepper. Roast 15 to 20 minutes or until crisp-tender and charred, turning once.
2. Meanwhile, in a large skillet heat remaining 2 Tbsp. olive oil and the butter over medium-high heat. Add garlic; cook 30 seconds, stirring frequently. Add coins; cook and stir 5 to 6 minutes or until tender and brown. Add cooked orzo; cook and stir 2 to 3 minutes or until toasted.
3. Coarsely zest lemon. Halve lemon; juice one half. For ricotta mixture: In a bowl combine ricotta, 1 tsp. zest, and the lemon juice. For pine nut topper: In a bowl combine pine nuts, Parmesan, parsley, remaining zest, and remaining ½ tsp. crushed red pepper.
4. To serve, spread ricotta mixture on a platter. Top with roasted broccoli stalks, coins and orzo mixture, and pine nut topper. Drizzle with additional olive oil and squeeze remaining lemon half over all. Makes 4 servings.
PER SERVING *447 cal, 36 g fat, 49 mg chol, 436 mg sodium, 21 g carb, 4 g fiber, 3 g sugars, 14 g pro.*

"BAKING IS A LOVE LANGUAGE. THE SPIRIT OF THE BAKER COMES THROUGH IN THE TREATS." CHRISTINA TOSI

FLUFFERNUTTER COOKIES

Embrace these imperfect-looking cookies. Mini marshmallows make the edges lacy as they melt during baking. Christina sandwiches strawberry jam between them.

HANDS-ON TIME 30 minutes
TOTAL TIME 1 hour

- 1 cup unsalted butter, softened
- 1¼ cups granulated sugar
- ⅔ cup packed light brown sugar
- 1 egg
- ½ tsp. vanilla
- 1¾ cups all-purpose flour
- 1½ tsp. kosher salt
- ½ tsp. baking powder
- ½ tsp. baking soda
- 2½ cups crisp rice cereal
- 1¼ cups tiny marshmallows
- ⅔ cup peanut butter chips
  Milk chocolate, melted (optional)
  Sprinkles (optional)

1. Preheat oven to 350°F. Line two cookie sheets with parchment paper; set aside.
2. In a bowl beat butter and sugars with a mixer on medium-high 2 minutes or until well combined. Scrape sides of bowl. Beat in egg and vanilla until light and fluffy, 5 minutes. Beat in flour, salt, baking powder, and baking soda on low just until combined, about 1 minute. Stir in cereal, marshmallows, and chips.
3. Drop dough by rounded tablespoons 2 inches apart on cookie sheets. Bake 10 minutes or until golden. Cool on a wire rack 2 minutes. Transfer cookies to wire rack; cool. If desired, drizzle with melted chocolate; top with sprinkles. Store in an airtight container up to 3 days. Makes 34 cookies.
PER COOKIE *157 cal, 7 g fat, 20 mg chol, 102 mg sodium, 22 g carb, 15 g sugars, 2 g pro.*

CEREAL MILK PANNA COTTA

Spooned over tangy passion fruit jam, the silky layer is a mixture of cream and milk infused with fruity cereal, like the sugary milk at the bottom of a cereal bowl.

HANDS-ON TIME 15 minutes
TOTAL TIME 4 hours 35 minutes

- 6 cups fruit-flavor round cereal, plus more for topping
- 3 cups whole milk
- 2 cups heavy cream
- 1 Tbsp. unflavored gelatin
- ¼ cup sugar
- ¾ tsp. kosher salt
- 2 Tbsp. red liquid food coloring (optional)
- 1 cup passion fruit or apricot jam
- 1 lime, zested (optional)

1. For cereal milk, in a bowl combine cereal, milk, and cream. Let stand 20 minutes; strain. In a 1-qt. saucepan whisk together 1 cup of the cereal milk and gelatin; let stand 5 minutes.
2. Heat gelatin mixture over low heat until dissolved, stirring constantly. Remove from heat. Whisk in sugar and salt. Pour into bowl with remaining milk, whisking until combined. If desired, stir in food coloring.
3. Spoon 2 Tbsp. jam into each of eight 6-oz. glasses. Spoon milk mixture over jam. Refrigerate until set, 4 to 24 hours. If desired, sprinkle with additional crushed cereal and lime zest. Makes 8 servings.
PER SERVING *361 cal, 20 g fat, 62 mg chol, 179 mg sodium, 42 g carb, 1 g fiber, 32 g sugars, 5 g pro.*

THE DESSERT REVOLUTIONARY

CHRISTINA TOSI, CHEF, AUTHOR & CEO OF MILK BAR "I can't compete with people's food memories," Christina Tosi says. "That's why my bakery doesn't do a standard chocolate chip cookie." What does the award-winning pastry chef do? "My desserts pay homage to my mother's and grandmother's recipes and celebrate nostalgia." Her creative spins incorporate store-bought ingredients in inventive combos (e.g., her Fluffernutter Cookies studded with crisp rice cereal, mini marshmallows, and peanut butter chips). Since opening Milk Bar in New York City almost nine years ago, her whimsical treats have become classics in their own right.

CEREAL MILK PANNA COTTA

GROWING TRADITIONS

Stir things up in your vegetable garden with Chinese varieties. They grow like their popular cousins, and in the kitchen they open all kinds of new flavor possibilities. Wendy Kiang-Spray shows us how.

As a girl growing up in suburban Maryland, Wendy Kiang-Spray had little interest in her father's tidy garden filled with the vegetable varieties he had also grown in China. "I would plant seeds then forget about them," Wendy remembers. Years later when her daughter wanted to garden, Wendy, now a high school counselor, was surprised to discover her own passion for gardening. "My dad isn't one to talk a lot," Wendy says, "and never about his childhood in China." But when she asked about the greens, beans, and radishes he raised as a boy, the stories started to flow. "I've always been curious about my ancestry," Wendy says. "Growing vegetables opened the door." Her book, *The Chinese Kitchen Garden,* not only preserves her family's stories but also demystifies the curious-looking vegetables so popular in farmers markets and specialty groceries.

PICKLED DAIKON RADISHES AND CARROTS

This carrot-shape white radish starts off tasting crunchy and spicy hot. Once pickled, the heat gives way to a mild, sweet flavor.

HANDS-ON TIME 20 minutes
TOTAL TIME 1 hour 50 minutes

- 2 medium daikon radishes, julienned
- 1 large carrot, julienned
- 1 tsp. salt
- 1¼ cups white vinegar
- ¼ cup granulated sugar
- 1 cup water
  Small hot chile pepper and/or crushed red pepper (optional)

1. Place radishes and carrot in a strainer. Toss with salt. Place strainer in a bowl; let stand 30 minutes.
2. Combine vinegar, sugar, and the water. Stir until sugar is completely dissolved.
3. Rinse vegetables; squeeze dry. Transfer to a glass jar. Add chile pepper, if desired. Pour vinegar solution over vegetables and refrigerate at least 1 hour. Makes 3 cups.
PER 2-TBSP. SERVING *8 cal, 18 mg sodium, 2 g carb, 1 g fiber, 1 g sugars.*

STEAMED AND SAUCED CHINESE EGGPLANT

Photo on page 114.

Also known as Japanese eggplant, this slender, thin-skin variety has fewer seeds and milder, sweeter flavor than the more common dark purple globes.

TOTAL TIME 20 minutes

- 2 whole Chinese eggplant (7 to 9 oz. each), halved crosswise
- 3 Tbsp. reduced-sodium soy sauce
- 1 Tbsp. rice vinegar
- 1 tsp. minced garlic (1 large clove)
- ½ tsp. toasted sesame oil
  Toasted sesame seeds (tip, page 27)

1. Place a steamer basket in a stock-pot. Add water to just below the bottom of the basket. Bring water to boiling. Add eggplant halves to basket. Cover and steam 15 to 20 minutes or until tender, turning pieces over once (stem end pieces will take longer than blossom end pieces). Cut each piece in half lengthwise and place on a serving plate. Make crosshatch cuts in the flesh of each eggplant piece.
2. In a small bowl stir together soy sauce, rice vinegar, garlic, and sesame oil. Drizzle over eggplant. Sprinkle with sesame seeds. Serve warm or at room temp. Makes 4 servings.
PER SERVING *51 cal, 1 g fat, 415 mg sodium, 8 g carb, 3 g fiber, 5 g sugars, 2 g pro.*

MASTER GREENS

Photo on page 115.

Gai lan looks like broccoli rabe and has a slightly bitter taste. The entire plant is edible.

TOTAL TIME 20 minutes

- 1 pound gai lan (Chinese broccoli)
- ¼ cup oyster sauce
- 3 Tbsp. corn or peanut oil
- 5 cloves garlic, chopped

1. Wash greens thoroughly. Bring a 8- to 10-qt. pot of water to boiling over high heat. Add greens. Cover and cook 2 to 3 minutes or just until stems are tender. Using tongs, transfer the greens to a serving plate (greens may be a little wet). Spoon oyster sauce over hot greens on platter; toss to coat.
2. Meanwhile, in a small skillet heat 3 Tbsp. corn oil over medium-high heat. Add garlic. Cook 1 to 2 minutes or just until fragrant. Pour oil and garlic over greens. Makes 4 servings.
PER SERVING *116 cal, 11 g fat, 497 mg sodium, 8 g carb, 7 g fiber, 3 g pro.*

STEAMED AND
SAUCED CHINESE
EGGPLANT
Recipe on page 113

MASTER
GREENS
*Recipe on
page 113*

"MY MOM CALLS THIS HER MASTER GREENS RECIPE BECAUSE IT TASTES GREAT WITH ANY LEAFY GREEN," WENDY SAYS

THE ELONGATED VERSIONS OF GREEN BEANS CAN REACH 3 FEET LONG. WENDY HARVESTS THE SLENDER PODS AT THE 12-INCH MARK FOR THE BEST FLAVOR AND CRISPNESS.

YARD LONG BEANS WITH GROUND PORK

Sturdier than other green beans, long beans stand up to high-heat stir-frying.

TOTAL TIME 35 minutes

- 4 oz. ground pork
- 4 tsp. reduced-sodium soy sauce
- 4 tsp. Shaoxing rice wine or dry sherry
- 1 lb. long beans
- 2 Tbsp. water
- 1 tsp. sugar
- 1 tsp. toasted sesame oil
- 1 cup vegetable oil
- 2½ Tbsp. preserved olive vegetable* or fermented black beans
- 2 cloves garlic, minced
  Hot steamed white rice

1. Place the ground pork in a small bowl and add 1 tsp. soy sauce and 1 tsp. Shaoxing rice wine. Marinate 15 minutes.
2. Meanwhile, rinse long beans and pat dry. Cut off ends and cut into 3-inch lengths.
3. In a small bowl combine remaining soy sauce and rice wine, the water, sugar, and sesame oil. Heat a wok or deep pan over medium heat. Add vegetable oil. When hot** add beans and fry 5 minutes, stirring occasionally. A few pieces may begin to wrinkle. Remove beans with a Chinese strainer or slotted spoon to a platter lined with paper towels.
4. Remove all but 1 Tbsp. oil from wok. Add ground pork to wok and stir-fry until cooked through, about 3 minutes. Add preserved olive vegetable and minced garlic and stir 30 seconds.
5. Add cooked beans and soy sauce mixture and stir until beans are hot and all ingredients are incorporated. Serve over steamed white rice. Makes 4 servings.
PER SERVING *428 cal, 25 g fat, 19 mg chol, 415 mg sodium, 37 g carb, 2 g sugars, 11 g pro.*
*Tip Preserved olive vegetable is a popular Chinese condiment sold in jars in Asian supermarkets. It is made of mustard greens and olives and lends a savory and rich umami flavor.
**Tip Test by holding a bean in the oil; it should bubble around the bean. Deep-frying the beans keeps them tender and bright green and is a traditional way of cooking this dish. A variation is to blanch the long beans in water, then stir-fry in 1 Tbsp. oil. This step can be done ahead of time if desired.

YARD LONG BEANS WITH GROUND PORK

**SUMMER FRUIT CRISP
ICE CREAM BARS**
Recipe on page 128

june

Here comes summer! Be company-ready for a party on the patio with recipes for fruity cocktails, grilled meats, versatile sauces, and fresh salads. Take a love of roses from the garden to the table.

121

135

143

SPARKLING
JULEP

WATERMELON
MARGARITA

COLADA
ELIXIR

a toast to
PATIO DRINKS

Why is the iconic summer drink a fruity concoction with an umbrella perched on the rim? Because it's a getaway in a glass—just the thought of one has the power to transport. When you serve these refreshing cocktails with a twist at your outdoor party, be ready for rave reviews. Paper umbrella, optional.

COLADA ELIXIR

Skip the rum, sub coconut water for cream of coconut, and whirl in bananas to make a healthful virgin piña colada.

TOTAL TIME 15 minutes

- 2 medium bananas, peeled
- 2 cups fresh pineapple chunks
- 1 cup pineapple juice
- 1 cup coconut water
- 1 cup ice
  Freshly squeezed juice of 1 lemon (3 Tbsp.)
  Pineapple wedges

1. Combine all ingredients in a powerful blender and process until smooth.
2. Pour the contents of the blender into glasses, garnish with a pineapple wedge, and serve. Makes 4 servings.

WATERMELON MARGARITA

This poolside favorite is less boozy, thanks to a fresh orange simple syrup that takes the place of triple sec.

HANDS-ON TIME 15 minutes
TOTAL TIME 1 hour 15 minutes, including cooling time

- 1 cup sugar
- 1 cup water
- 3 wide strips orange peel
- 8 cups watermelon cubes
- 1 cup fresh lime juice
- 2 cups white or silver tequila
  Salt, for rimming the glasses
  Ice cubes
- 6 small watermelon wedges, for garnish

1. In a small saucepan bring the sugar, water, and orange peel to boiling over high heat. Reduce heat to low; simmer 3 minutes or until sugar is dissolved. Transfer syrup to a bowl to cool; discard orange peel.
2. In a blender puree the watermelon cubes until smooth. Strain through a fine-mesh strainer placed over a serving pitcher, pressing on the solids. Use 1 cup juice for the drink; reserve the rest for another purpose. Stir in the syrup, lime juice, and tequila.
3. Rim six glasses with salt, fill them with ice, then pour in the margarita. Garnish with watermelon wedges. Makes 6 servings.

SPARKLING JULEP

Sparkling Gamay—a rosé from red Gamay grapes—makes this twist on the mint julep lighter and slightly frutier.

TOTAL TIME 10 minutes

- 10 mint leaves
- ½ oz. Turbinado Syrup
- ¾ oz. Cognac, preferably Pierre Ferrand 1840
- 2 oz. sparkling FRV100 Gamay*, plus ½ oz. for topping off
- 1 cup crushed ice
- 2 to 3 mint sprigs
- 1 small bunch champagne or other tiny grapes
  Powdered sugar

1. Place mint leaves and syrup in a Collins glass; lightly press with a muddler or barspoon. Leave muddler in the glass; add Cognac and 2 oz. sparkling Gamay. Stir with the muddler to mix. Fill the glass a little more than halfway with crushed ice; stir with a barspoon 15 to 20 times. Add more ice to completely fill the glass. Top with the remaining ½ oz. sparkling Gamay.
2. To garnish, press mint sprigs between your fingers to release their aroma and tuck them into a grape cluster. Makes 1 serving.
Turbinado Syrup In a screw-top jar combine ½ cup turbinado sugar and ½ cup water. Screw on lid and shake the jar until sugar is dissolved. Cover and store in refrigerator.
*Tip Or choose another dry sparkling rosé wine.

TUNA-TOT
CASSEROLE

CAJUN TUNA
SALAD

TUNA-RAMEN
SALAD

new ways with
TUNA

If you haven't shopped the tuna aisle lately, take note. New packaging and flavors inspired three recipes that go beyond the brown bag.

CAJUN TUNA SALAD

TOTAL TIME 25 minutes

½ cup mayonnaise
2 Tbsp. lemon juice
1 Tbsp. paprika
2 tsp. ground cumin
2 tsp. mild chili powder
½ tsp. cracked black pepper
¼ tsp. kosher salt
⅛ tsp. cayenne pepper
3 5-oz. cans solid albacore tuna in water, well-drained
½ cup finely chopped celery
½ cup finely chopped red sweet pepper
4 bolillo or hoagie rolls, split and toasted
Bibb lettuce leaves

In a bowl combine mayonnaise, lemon juice, paprika, cumin, chili powder, black pepper, salt, and cayenne pepper. Stir in tuna, celery, and sweet pepper. Serve in rolls with lettuce. Makes 4 servings.
PER SERVING *497 cal, 25 g fat, 40 mg chol, 1,000 mg sodium, 41 g carb, 4 g fiber, 5 g sugars, 27 g pro.*

TUNA-TOT CASSEROLE

HANDS-ON TIME 35 minutes
TOTAL TIME 1 hour 15 minutes

Nonstick cooking spray
2 Tbsp. extra-virgin olive oil
8 oz. sliced fresh cremini mushrooms
12 oz. fresh green beans, trimmed and cut into 1-inch pieces
¾ cup finely chopped onion
3 cloves garlic, minced
2 cups half-and-half
2 Tbsp. Worcestershire sauce
1½ tsp. dried thyme, crushed
2 12-oz. (or 5, 5-oz.) cans solid albacore tuna in water, well-drained
1 cup white cheddar cheese, shredded (4 oz.)
1 32-oz. pkg. frozen fried potato nuggets
3 green onions, sliced

1. Preheat oven to 450°F. Lightly coat a 3-qt. rectangular baking dish with nonstick cooking spray. In an extra-large high-sided skillet, heat oil over medium heat. Add mushrooms, green beans, and onion. Cook, stirring occasionally, 7 to 8 minutes or until beans are nearly tender and liquid has evaporated. Add garlic and cook 1 minute more.
2. Increase heat to medium-high. Add half-and-half. Boil gently, uncovered, 5 minutes or until half-and-half has reduced enough to lightly coat vegetables. Stir in Worcestershire sauce and thyme.
3. Spoon mixture into prepared baking dish. Top with tuna, cheese, and potatoes. Bake, uncovered, 30 to 35 minutes or until potatoes are browned and center is bubbly. Let stand 10 minutes before serving. Sprinkle with green onions. Makes 8 servings.
PER SERVING *462 cal, 26 g fat, 58 mg chol, 933 mg sodium, 37 g carb, 5 g fiber, 7 g sugars, 22 g pro.*

TUNA-RAMEN SALAD

TOTAL TIME 30 minutes

4 to 6 eggs, soft-cooked
2 Tbsp. white miso paste
2 Tbsp. toasted sesame oil
⅓ cup rice vinegar
¼ cup extra-virgin olive oil
3 5-oz. cans solid albacore tuna in water, well-drained
1 Tbsp. toasted sesame seeds (tip, p. 27)
1 cup sugar snap peas
¾ cup matchstick-cut carrots
1 3-oz. pkg. ramen noodles (any flavor)
6 cups chopped napa cabbage
½ cup loosely packed Thai basil leaves, chopped
3 green onions, sliced
Crushed red pepper (optional)

1. For soft-cooked eggs: Place eggs in a 2-qt. saucepan; add cold water to cover by 1 inch. Bring to a rapid boil over medium-high heat. Remove from heat, cover, and let stand 7 to 8 minutes; drain. Run cold water over the eggs or place in an ice bath. Gently peel when cool enough to handle.
2. Meanwhile, for dressing: Whisk together white miso paste, sesame oil, rice vinegar, and olive oil. Drizzle 2 Tbsp. dressing over drained albacore tuna. Stir in sesame seeds.
2. Cook sugar snap peas and carrots in salted boiling water 1 minute; plunge into cold water. Coarsely crush ramen noodles (discard seasoning packet).
3. Combine noodles, cabbage, basil, green onions, and ½ cup dressing. Top with tuna, snap peas, carrots, and soft-cooked eggs. Pass remaining dressing and crushed red pepper. Makes 4 servings.
PER SERVING *516 cal, 32 g fat, 215 mg chol, 664 mg sodium, 26 g carb, 4 g fiber, 6 g sugars, 30 g pro.*

COME ON OVER

Long live the backyard BBQ—that on-the-fly shindig that starts on Saturday morning when you wake up and think, hey, we should have people over tonight. This is our cheat sheet to get it done and have fun.

FUSS-FREE APPETIZER

OPEN A JAR The easiest appetizer to serve is one you can pull out of the pantry and serve straight out of the jar. A small tray or metal cake pan will make a collection of jarred pickled veggies, tapenades, and spreads look intentional. And you can't go wrong with a chunk of sharp cheddar or goat cheese on the side.

GRILLED PORK AND PEACHES

When peaches hit the grill, they caramelize and create a sweet syrup that mingles with the spiced pork, making both of them taste even better. Toss on some fresh mint to finish.

HANDS-ON TIME 15 minutes
TOTAL TIME 50 minutes

¼	cup butter
2	tsp. ground cinnamon
1	tsp. ground cumin
1	tsp. ground turmeric
1	tsp. cayenne pepper
½	tsp. ground cardamom
¼	tsp. ground cloves
¼	tsp. ground nutmeg
1	tsp. salt
1	tsp. black pepper
2	Tbsp. packed brown sugar
2	1- to 1½-lb. pork tenderloins
4	to 6 fresh peaches and/or plums, halved or quartered
	Canola oil
	Fresh mint leaves

1. For spice paste: In a small saucepan stir together the first 10 ingredients (through black pepper) over medium heat until butter is melted. Remove from heat. Stir in sugar until nearly smooth; let stand until paste forms.

2. Trim fat from pork; pat dry. Rub pork evenly with spice paste. Grill on the rack of a covered grill, using indirect heat, 30 to 35 minutes or until done (145°F). Lightly brush peaches and/or plums with canola oil; grill cut sides down, directly over heat, 2 to 3 minutes or until lightly charred. Slice pork; serve with fruit and top with mint. Makes 8 to 12 servings.
PER SERVING *190 cal, 8 g fat, 89 mg chol, 385 mg sodium, 4 g carb, 1 g fiber, 3 g sugars, 24 g pro.*

BBQ Sliders Grill pork tenderloin as directed. Instead of serving with peaches, thinly slice grilled pork. In a small saucepan warm 1 cup barbecue sauce; toss with sliced pork. Split 16 slider buns or cocktail rolls; fill with pork and top each with creamy coleslaw. Makes 16 sliders.

Pork Tostadas Grill pork tenderloin as directed, except chop the pork. Top tostada shells with chopped pork and toppings, such as avocados, tomatoes, Pickled Red Onions,*sliced jalapeños (tip, page 17), Cotija cheese, cilantro, and lime wedges. Makes 16 tostadas.

*Pickled Red Onions Place 1 cup sliced red onion in a bowl. In a small saucepan heat ½ cup water, ½ cup cider vinegar, and 2 Tbsp. sugar over medium heat, stirring to dissolve sugar. Pour over onion slices. Let stand 30 to 60 minutes; drain before using. Store in refrigerator up to 3 days.

WE'RE CROWNING PORK TENDERLOIN THE KING OF THIS SUMMER'S GRILL-OUTS. THE INEXPENSIVE CUT OF MEAT CAN BE SCALED UP OR DOWN, TAKES LITTLE TIME, AND TASTES EQUALLY DELICIOUS AT ROOM TEMPERATURE.

GRILLED PORK AND PEACHES

GIVE OUR BACK-POCKET GRILLED PORK TENDERLOIN RECIPE THREE DIFFERENT PARTY PERSONALITIES. EVEN IF YOU HOST THE SAME CREW ALL SUMMER, THEY'LL NEVER KNOW IT'S A REPEAT.

BBQ SLIDERS

PORK TOSTADAS

SELF-SERVE BAR

CHILL A FEW CANS...OF WINE
This former novelty has hit the mainstream, and there are some seriously delicious options. The investment is relatively low and the packaging is a built-in conversation starter. Put out a mix of whites, rosés, and sparklers to taste and share. Add a few stir-ins and you'll have an easy DIY cocktail setup. Sippable low-alcohol spritzers are made for summer get-togethers. Start with 3 parts wine to 1 part club soda, then improvise with bitters, citrus, and herbs.

THE ANYTHING GREEN CHOPPED SALAD

Lime-jalapeño dressing zips up a mix of raw and blanched green veggies.

HANDS-ON TIME 20 minutes
TOTAL TIME 50 minutes

6   oz. green beans, trimmed and chopped
6   oz. sugar snap peas and/or snow peas, trimmed (2 cups)
½   bunch asparagus (8 oz.), trimmed and chopped
1   medium English cucumber, chopped
1   medium zucchini, chopped
⅓   cup olive oil
3   limes (1 tsp. zest; ⅓ cup juice)
¼   cup chopped fresh cilantro
1   small jalapeño, seeded and finely chopped (tip, page 17)
1   tsp. ground cumin
2   cloves garlic, minced
½   tsp. salt
¼   tsp. crushed red pepper
⅓   cup pepitas, toasted (tip, page 27)
    Crumbled feta cheese or queso fresco (optional)

1. For salad: Blanch green beans, snap peas, and asparagus by cooking in a large pot of salted boiling water 2 minutes. Transfer to ice bath; let stand 1 minute. Drain and pat dry. In a large bowl combine blanched vegetables, cucumber, and zucchini.
2. For dressing: In a screw-top jar combine oil, lime zest and juice, cilantro, jalapeño, cumin, garlic, salt, and crushed red pepper. Cover; shake well. Pour dressing over salad; toss. Let stand 30 minutes. Top with pepitas and, if desired, feta cheese. Makes 9 cups.
PER ½ CUP *74 cal, 6 g fat, 45 mg sodium, 4 g carb, 1 g fiber, 1 g sugars, 2 g pro.*
Make Ahead Refrigerate salad and dressing separately in airtight containers up to 24 hours. Add dressing, pepitas, and cheese just before serving.

BEAN, CORN, AND TOMATO SALAD

Edamame, chickpeas, and a big handful of herbs add to this twist on tomatoes and corn.

TOTAL TIME 20 minutes

4   ears fresh corn
2   pt. grape and/or cherry tomatoes, halved if desired
1   15-oz. can chickpeas, rinsed and drained
1½ cups frozen shelled edamame, thawed
½   cup finely chopped red onion
¼   cup olive oil
¼   cup cider vinegar
1   tsp. honey
½   tsp. salt
¼   tsp. black pepper
⅓   cup torn fresh mint leaves
⅓   cup torn fresh basil leaves

1. For salad: Remove husks from corn. Scrub with a stiff brush to remove silks; rinse. Cut kernels from cobs; place in a serving bowl. Add tomatoes, chickpeas, edamame, and red onion.
2. For dressing: In a screw-top jar combine oil, vinegar, honey, salt, and pepper. Cover; shake well. Pour dressing over salad; toss. Top with mint and basil. Makes 9 cups.
PER ½ CUP *86 cal, 4 g fat, 64 mg sodium, 10 g carb, 3 g fiber, 3 g sugars, 3 g pro.*
Make Ahead Refrigerate salad and dressing separately in airtight containers up to 24 hours. Add dressing and herbs just before serving.

BEAN, CORN, AND
TOMATO SALAD

THE ANYTHING
GREEN CHOPPED
SALAD

POTATO PICCATA
SALAD
Recipe on page 128

ROUND OUT THE
SPREAD WITH A
SALAD THAT IS
VEGGIE-FORWARD,
BARELY REQUIRES A
RECIPE, AND CAN BE
PREPPED AHEAD.

FINISH WITH SOMETHING SWEET: THE BEST PARTS OF FRUIT CRISP—SEASONAL FRUIT AND NUTTY BROWN SUGAR CRUMBLE—TAKE FROZEN FORM IN THESE ICE CREAM BARS. WE LOVE STRAWBERRY OR PEACH—YOU CAN CUSTOMIZE WITH WHATEVER FRUIT YOU PLEASE.

POTATO PICCATA SALAD

Photo on page 127.

Dress up the humble summer staple with briny olives and capers and a lemon-and-mustard dressing.

TOTAL TIME 20 minutes

3 lb. small red or yellow potatoes, halved and/or quartered
½ cup pitted green olives, halved
½ cup chopped fresh parsley
2 Tbsp. capers
⅓ cup olive oil
2 lemons (1 tsp. zest; ⅓ cup juice)
1 shallot, finely chopped
1 Tbsp. coarse ground mustard
½ tsp. salt
¼ tsp. freshly ground black pepper
Grated Parmesan cheese (optional)

1. For salad: In a large saucepan combine potatoes and enough salted water to cover. Bring to boiling; reduce heat. Simmer, covered, 15 minutes or just until potatoes are tender. Drain well; cool slightly. Transfer to a serving bowl. Add olives, parsley, and capers.
2. For dressing: In a screw-top jar combine oil, lemon zest and juice, shallot, mustard, salt, and pepper. Cover; shake well. Pour dressing over potato mixture; toss. If desired, top with Parmesan. Makes 9 cups.
PER ½ CUP *97 cal, 5 g fat, 143 mg sodium, 13 g carb, 2 g fiber, 1 g sugars, 2 g pro.*
Make Ahead Refrigerate the dressed salad up to 24 hours. Add Parmesan just before serving.

SUMMER FRUIT CRISP ICE CREAM BARS

These bars are so versatile—any fruit-based ice cream flavor could be sandwiched between the crumbly crust. Or omit the fruit and try butter pecan or caramel ice cream.

HANDS-ON TIME 15 minutes
TOTAL TIME 6 hours 30 minutes, includes freezing

2 cups all-purpose flour
½ cup quick-cooking rolled oats
½ cup packed brown sugar
⅛ tsp. salt
1 cup butter
1 cup chopped pecans
1 gal. strawberry or peach ice cream
2 cups chopped fresh strawberries or peaches

1. Chill a large bowl at least 15 minutes.
2. Preheat oven to 400°F. In a bowl combine flour, oats, brown sugar, and salt. Cut in butter until pieces resemble coarse crumbs. Stir in nuts. Pat lightly into a 13×9-inch pan. Bake 15 minutes or until golden. Stir to crumble; let cool.
3. Remove half the crumbs; set aside. Spread remaining half evenly across bottom of baking pan. Place ice cream in the chilled bowl; stir to soften. Stir in fruit. Spread evenly over crumbs in pan. Top with reserved crumbs. Cover; freeze 6 hours or until firm. Let stand at room temperature 5 to 10 minutes before cutting. Makes 24 bars.
PER BAR *334 cal, 19 g fat, 46 mg chol, 127 mg sodium, 39 g carb, 2 g fiber, 21 g sugars, 5 g pro.*

SUMMER FRUIT CRISP
ICE CREAM BARS

how to cook
SAUCES

Everyone's go-to meal plan needs an occasional reset. These (mostly) no-cook sauces upgrade ho-hum chicken breasts, pasta night, and almost anything you can throw on the grill.

YOGURT-FETA DIP

YOGURT-FETA DIP

One sauce three ways: Tweak a creamy, tangy Greek yogurt dip for a flavorful marinade or herbal dressing.

TOTAL TIME 15 minutes

1	clove garlic, peeled
⅛	tsp. salt
½	cup plain Greek yogurt
½	cup chopped fresh parsley
¼	cup crumbled feta
1	lemon (1 tsp. zest; 1 Tbsp. juice)
1	Tbsp. minced chives
1	Tbsp. chopped fresh tarragon
1	Tbsp. olive oil

1. Use the flat side of a knife to mash garlic with salt into a paste.
2. In a food processor combine garlic paste and the remaining ingredients. Process until well combined. Makes about ¾ cup.
PER 2 TBSP. SERVING *27 cal, 2 g fat, 4 mg chol, 130 mg sodium, 1 g carb, 1 g sugars, 2 g pro.*

Creamy Yogurt-Feta Dressing Prepare Yogurt-Feta Dip, then thin to desired consistency with 2 to 4 Tbsp. milk. Season with salt and pepper. Makes about 1 cup.
PER 2 TBSP. SERVING *29 cal, 2 g fat, 3 mg chol, 86 mg sodium, 1 g carb, 1 g sugars, 2 g pro.*

Creamy Yogurt-Feta Marinade Prepare Yogurt-Feta Dip, increasing olive oil to 3 Tbsp. Pour over chicken; turn to coat. Marinate in the refrigerator up to 3 hours. Drain chicken; discard marinade. Roast or grill chicken. Makes about 1¼ cups.
PER 2 TBSP. SERVING *49 cal, 2 g fat, 3 mg chol, 86 mg sodium, 1 g carb, 1 g sugars, 2 g pro.*

ROMESCO SAUCE

TOTAL TIME 20 minutes

4	medium roma tomatoes, peeled, seeded, and chopped
1	¾-inch slice country-style bread (2 oz.), toasted and torn into pieces
⅔	cup chopped bottled roasted red sweet peppers
½	cup blanched whole almonds, toasted (tip, page 27)
¼	cup sherry vinegar or red wine vinegar
1	Tbsp. snipped fresh parsley
4	cloves garlic, smashed
1	tsp. smoked paprika
½	tsp. ground ancho chile pepper
⅛	tsp. cayenne pepper
¼	to ⅓ cup olive oil
	Salt

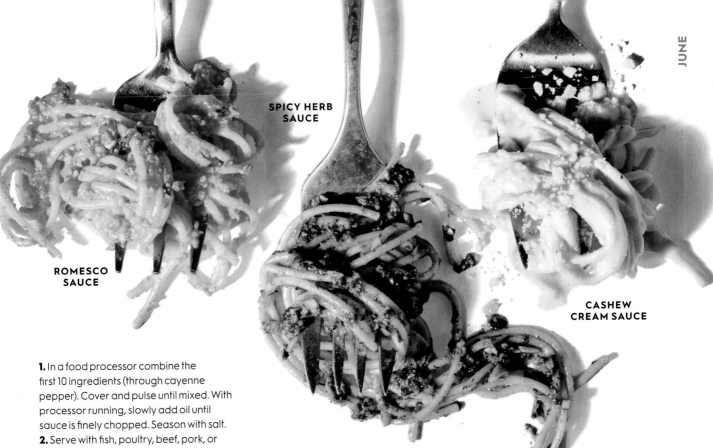

SPICY HERB SAUCE

ROMESCO SAUCE

CASHEW CREAM SAUCE

1. In a food processor combine the first 10 ingredients (through cayenne pepper). Cover and pulse until mixed. With processor running, slowly add oil until sauce is finely chopped. Season with salt.
2. Serve with fish, poultry, beef, pork, or vegetables. Makes 16 servings.
Storage Refrigerate sauce in an airtight container up to 1 week. Let stand at room temperature 30 minutes before serving.
PER SERVING *76 cal, 6 g fat, 61 mg sodium, 5 g carb, 1 g fiber, 1 g sugars, 2 g pro.*

SPICY HERB SAUCE

TOTAL TIME 20 minutes

2   cups lightly packed fresh cilantro leaves
1   cup lightly packed fresh Italian parsley leaves
1   to 2 jalapeños, stemmed, seeded, and halved (tip, page 17)
1   Tbsp. lemon juice
3   cloves garlic, peeled and halved
1   tsp. ground cumin
½   tsp. kosher salt
½   tsp. ground coriander
½   cup olive oil
¼   cup roasted, salted pumpkin seeds (pepitas)

1. In a food processor combine first 8 ingredients (through coriander). Process until finely chopped, stopping to scrape sides as necessary. With blender or processor running, slowly add oil in a steady stream until combined. Add 2 Tbsp. of the pumpkin seeds. Process until nearly smooth.

2. Transfer sauce to a serving bowl. Top with remaining pumpkin seeds. Makes 16 servings.
PER SERVING *84 cal, 9 g fat, 48 mg sodium, 1 g carb, 1 g pro.*

CASHEW CREAM SAUCE

HANDS-ON TIME 30 minutes
TOTAL TIME 2 hours 30 minutes, includes standing

1   cup raw cashews
1½ cups reduced-sodium chicken broth or vegetable broth
12 oz. dried pasta
1   Tbsp. olive oil
⅔   cup finely chopped shallot
2   cloves garlic, minced
1   Tbsp. chopped fresh thyme
⅓   cup dry white wine, reduced-sodium chicken broth, or vegetable broth
½   tsp. salt
½   tsp. black pepper
    Grated Parmesan cheese (optional)

1. In a bowl combine 1 cup raw cashews and 2 cups water. Let stand, covered, 2 hours; drain well.
2. In a food processor process cashews and 1 cup of the chicken broth until smooth and creamy. Add remaining ½ cup broth; cover and pulse until combined.
3. In a large pot cook pasta according to package directions. Drain, reserving 1 cup of the cooking water. Return pasta to pot; cover to keep warm.
4. Meanwhile, heat olive oil in a skillet over medium heat. Add shallot; cook and stir 3 minutes or until tender. Add garlic and thyme; cook 1 minute. Add white wine; stir to scrape up any browned bits. Stir in cashew mixture, salt, and pepper. Bring to boiling; reduce heat. Simmer 1 minute until thickened. Add reserved cooking liquid to reach desired consistency. If desired top with grated Parmesan cheese. Makes 6 servings.
PER SERVING *276 cal, 5 g fat, 336 mg sodium, 48 g carb, 3 g fiber, 4 g sugars, 9 g pro.*
Make Ahead Prepare sauce through Step 2. Refrigerate sauce in an airtight container up to 5 days. To serve, cook pasta as above. Heat sauce in a medium saucepan. Add to drained pasta and add reserved cooking water to reach desired consistency. If desired top with grated Parmesan cheese.

EVERY SUMMER HAS ITS HOT CONDIMENT TO TRY AT BACKYARD GRILL-OUTS AND TO KEEP IN YOUR FRIDGE TO RESCUE BORING VEGGIES.

FRESH HERB, TOMATO, AND CAPER SAUCE

START TO FINISH 10 minutes

- **2** cups snipped fresh Italian parsley
- **¼** cup sliced, toasted almonds (tip, page 27)
- **¼** cup snipped fresh oregano
- **2** Tbsp. lemon zest
- **2** Tbsp. capers, drained
- **⅔** cup olive oil
- **¼** cup lemon juice
- **½** tsp. salt
- **½** tsp. black pepper
- **4** oil-packed sun-dried tomatoes, finely chopped (¼ cup)

In a food processor combine parsley, almonds, oregano, and 2 Tbsp. lemon zest. Cover and pulse until finely chopped. Add capers; pulse to combine. Add olive oil, lemon juice, salt, and pepper; pulse until a saucy paste forms. Stir in sun-dried tomatoes. Makes 1½ cups.

PER SERVING *129 cal, 13 g fat, 143 mg sodium, 2 g carb, 1 g fiber, 10 g pro.*

Storage Store in an airtight container in the refrigerator up to 3 days or freeze in ¼-cup portions up to 1 month.

ROSE PARADE

One woman's passion for her favorite flower continues beyond the garden as she celebrates their beauty, fragrance, and flavor.

It all started with a $2 rose. Following a tradition that Danielle Dall'Armi and her husband, Bill Hahn, have when moving into a new house, the couple planted a rose bush in the yard of their Carpinteria, California home. That first rose didn't just thrive; it went absolutely crazy, growing 10 feet tall and just as wide. Danielle and Bill, who had grown roses as a hobby, thought maybe they were onto something bigger. They took a chance and planted 1,000 roses on half an acre, dubbed the place Rose Story Farm, and things snowballed from there. Over the past two decades, they've expanded—offering wholesale cut roses and mature plants along with design services—and blanketed 8 acres with more than 25,000 rose bushes in 120 fragrant varieties. "Fragrance is everything," Danielle says. "When you pick up a grocery store bouquet and put your nose right into the blooms, there's no fragrance. But a garden rose? The scent is unforgettable." Danielle knows the life span of a garden rose is short (typically three to four days) and hates to let so much as a single petal go to waste. Here's how she celebrates their beauty, fragrance, and flavor.

WHAT YOU NEED TO KNOW ABOUT EATING ROSES:

1. Only roses that have never been treated with chemicals should be eaten.

2. Because smell influences our sense of taste, the stronger a rose scent, the stronger it will taste.

3. The white inner tip of petals can be bitter. Snip them off if the flavor bothers you.

ROSE SPRING
ROLLS

ROSE SPRING ROLLS

Rose petals add both a decorative element and a light floral note against cucumber and peppery radishes in these spring rolls.

TOTAL TIME 45 minutes

- 6 oz. dried rice vermicelli noodles
- ½ cup fresh culinary rose petals (tip, page 139)
- 12 round rice papers
- 1¼ cups paper-thin radish and/or English cucumber slices
- ¼ cup fresh mint leaves
- ¼ cup fresh cilantro leaves
  Rose Dipping Sauce

1. In a large saucepan cook noodles in boiling, lightly salted water 2 to 3 minutes or just until tender; drain. Rinse under cold water; drain well. In a large bowl cut cooled noodles into short lengths. Toss with ¼ cup rose petals.
2. To assemble rolls: Pour warm water into a shallow bowl or pie plate. Working with one rice paper at a time, dip in water until pliable. Lay ¼ cup rice noodles about a third of the way up from the bottom, toward center of rice paper. Fold bottom edge up over filling; roll over once tightly. Place some of the vegetables, herbs, and remaining rose petals on paper above rolled portion. Tuck in sides. Continue rolling to seal rice paper to itself. Repeat with remaining rice papers. Serve with Rose Dipping Sauce. Makes 12 spring rolls.
Rose Dipping Sauce In a small bowl combine ¼ cup soy sauce and ¼ cup Rose Vinegar (recipe, page 139). Sprinkle with coarsely ground black pepper.
PER SPRING ROLL *104 cal, 310 mg sodium, 22 g carb, 1 g fiber, 1 g sugars, 2 g pro.*

ROSE, RASPBERRY, AND PISTACHIO SALAD

Photo on page 136.

TOTAL TIME 30 minutes

- 7 cups baby spinach and/or butterhead lettuce
- 2 cups fresh red raspberries
- 1 cup fresh culinary rose petals (tip, page 139)
- 1 cup thinly sliced red onion
- ½ cup roasted, salted shelled pistachios
- ⅓ cup chopped fresh tarragon and/or oregano
- ½ cup good-quality olive oil
- 3 Tbsp. Rose Vinegar (recipe, page 139) or champagne vinegar
- 1 tsp. Dijon-style mustard
- ½ tsp. freshly cracked black pepper
- ¼ tsp. sugar
- ⅛ tsp. bottled rose water (tip, page 134)
  Salt
  Shaved ricotta salata or Parmesan cheese

1. In an extra-large bowl combine spinach, raspberries, rose petals, red onion slices, pistachios, and herbs.
2. For dressing: In a screw-top jar combine oil, Rose vinegar, mustard, pepper, sugar, rose water, and a dash salt. Cover; shake well. Pour dressing over salad; toss gently to coat. Top with cheese. Makes 10 cups.
PER ½ CUP *84 cal, 7 g fat, 1 mg chol, 54 mg sodium, 4 g carb, 2 g fiber, 1 g sugars, 4 g pro.*

SPARKLING WINE AND ROSES COCKTAIL

Photo on page 137.

TOTAL TIME 10 minutes

- 1 750 ml. bottle sparkling rosé or Prosecco, chilled
- ½ cup ruby red grapefruit juice
  Rose Syrup (recipe, page 139), or purchased rose syrup
  Fresh culinary rose petals (tip, page 139)
  Grapefruit twists

In a pitcher stir together sparkling wine and juice. Add Rose Syrup 1 Tbsp. at a time to taste. Garnish with rose petals and grapefruit twists. Makes 6 servings.
PER 6-OZ. SERVING *118 cal, 7 mg sodium, 7 g carb, 0 g fiber, 5 g sugars, 0 g pro.*

ROSE-CANDIED ALMONDS

Photo on page 137.

Rose water and toasted cumin seeds flavor these sweet spiced nuts. Pair them with our Sparkling Wine and Roses Cocktail made with rose syrup and ruby red grapefruit juice.

HANDS-ON TIME 20 minutes
TOTAL TIME 1 hour

- ½ cup sugar
- 1½ tsp. bottled rose water (tip, page 139)
- 1 cup almonds (Marcona and/or regular), toasted (tip, page 27)
- ½ tsp. fine sea salt
- ½ tsp. cumin seeds, toasted*
- 2 Tbsp. julienned fresh culinary rose petals (about 16) (tip, page 139)

1. Line a shallow baking pan with foil; butter foil.
2. In a medium saucepan combine sugar, 2 Tbsp. water, and the rose water. Bring to boiling over medium-high heat, stirring to dissolve sugar. Stir in almonds. Reduce heat to medium; cook 4 to 5 minutes or until syrup thickens slightly, stirring often. Reduce heat to medium-low. Stir in salt and cumin seeds. Cook 7 to 8 minutes more or until sugar is caramelized and nuts are glazed, stirring frequently. (Caution: Mixture will be very hot.)
3. Spread nuts in a single layer in prepared pan. Sprinkle with rose petals; let cool. Break apart to serve. Store in an airtight container up to 1 week. Makes 1½ cups.
PER 3-TBSP. SERVING *156 cal, 9 g fat, 141 mg sodium, 17 g carb, 2 g fiber, 13 g sugars, 4 g pro.*

*Tip In a small skillet toast cumin seeds over medium heat 1 to 2 minutes or until aromatic and golden; cool.

ROSE, RASPBERRY,
AND PISTACHIO
SALAD
Recipe on page 135

**SPARKLING WINE
AND ROSES
COCKTAIL**
Recipe on page 135

**ROSE-CANDIED
ALMONDS**
Recipe on page 135

BAKED IN DONUT TRAYS, THESE PINK PEPPERCORN AND ROSE TEA CAKES HAVE ROSE WATER AND PETALS IN THE BATTER, A CREAM CHEESE GLAZE, AND A "CONFETTI" OF CRUSHED PINK PEPPERCORNS AND FRESH ROSE PETALS.

PINK PEPPERCORN AND ROSE TEA CAKES

HANDS-ON TIME 25 minutes
TOTAL TIME 50 minutes

Nonstick cooking spray
1½ cups cake flour or all-purpose flour
1 cup granulated sugar
½ tsp. baking soda
¼ tsp. baking powder
¼ tsp. salt
½ 8-oz. carton sour cream
⅓ cup vegetable oil
1 egg, beaten
¼ cup fresh culinary rose petals, chopped (or 2 Tbsp. dried rose petals), plus more fresh culinary petals for topping
1 tsp. bottled rose water
1 tsp. pink peppercorns, finely crushed, plus more for topping
1 recipe Cream Cheese Glaze

1. Preheat oven to 350°F. Coat a 3-inch donut pan or muffin pan with nonstick cooking spray.

2. In a large bowl whisk together flour, sugar, baking soda, baking powder, and salt. Add sour cream, oil, egg, ¼ cup water, the rose petals, rose water, and peppercorns, stirring until smooth after each addition. Spoon batter into prepared pan, filling each cup about half full. Cover; chill remaining batter.

3. Bake 12 to 15 minutes or until a toothpick comes out clean. Cool in pan 10 minutes. Remove from pan; cool completely. Repeat with reserved batter.

3. Dip tops of tea cakes in Cream Cheese Glaze. Immediately sprinkle with additional rose petals and peppercorns. Store glazed cakes in an airtight container up to 2 days or freeze unglazed cakes up to 1 month. Makes 15 tea cakes.

Cream Cheese Glaze In a medium mixing bowl beat 4 oz. softened cream cheese, ¾ cup powdered sugar, and 3 Tbsp. milk with a mixer on medium until smooth. Makes about 1½ cups.

PER TEA CAKE *191 cal, 8 g fat, 21 mg chol, 110 mg sodium, 28 g carb, 17 g sugars, 2 g pro.*

CULINARY PETALS For raw uses, you need fresh petals specified for culinary use. For cooking, use fresh and dried interchangeably; if fresh are called for, use half the amount of dried petals. Find fresh culinary petals and dried organic rose petals online. To keep petals fresh, wet a paper towel and place it in an airtight container. Place petals on the paper towel; cover and refrigerate up to 3 days.

ROSE WATER You'll need culinary rose water for the candied almonds and tea cakes, and to make Rose Syrup. Find rose water in large grocery stores or online.

ROSE SYRUP You can buy rose syrup, but if you already have a bottle of rose water, you can make the syrup. In a medium saucepan stir together 2 cups sugar and 1¼ cups water. Bring to boiling, stirring to dissolve sugar; reduce heat. Simmer, uncovered, 10 minutes, stirring occasionally. Stir in 2 Tbsp. bottled rose water (mixture will foam). Simmer, uncovered, 8 minutes more or until thickened, stirring occasionally. Remove from heat; cool. Pour into a clean dry bottle; seal tightly. Refrigerate up to 1 month. Makes about 2 cups.

ROSE VINEGAR Place ½ cup culinary rose petals or ¼ cup dried rose petals in a pint jar. In a small saucepan heat 1 cup apple cider vinegar over medium heat until warm. Pour over rose petals; stir gently. Cover jar with plastic wrap; seal with lid. Let stand up to 24 hours before using for best flavor. Strain and store in a cool, dry place up to 1 month. Makes 1 cup.

FAST *&* FRESH

Easy, healthful recipes for a better dinner tonight.

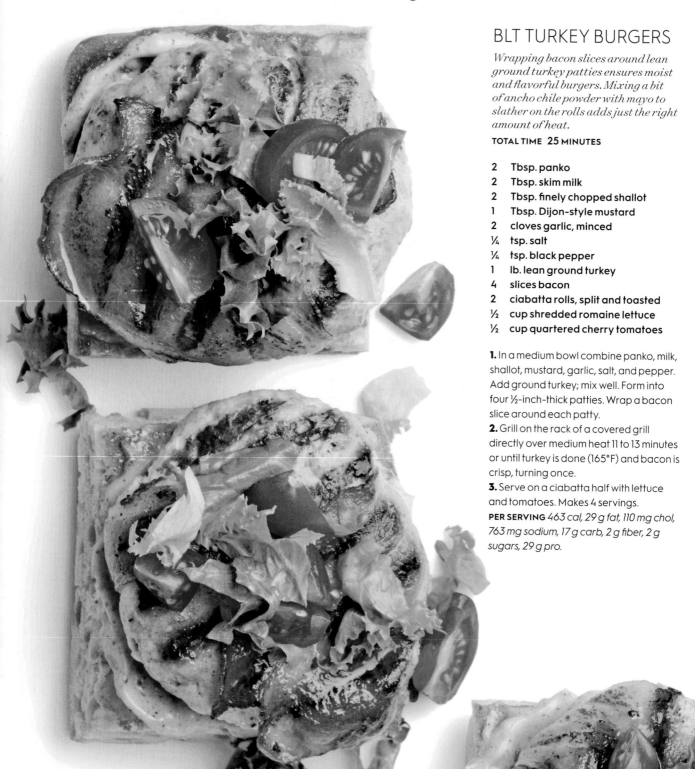

BLT TURKEY BURGERS

Wrapping bacon slices around lean ground turkey patties ensures moist and flavorful burgers. Mixing a bit of ancho chile powder with mayo to slather on the rolls adds just the right amount of heat.

TOTAL TIME 25 MINUTES

- 2   Tbsp. panko
- 2   Tbsp. skim milk
- 2   Tbsp. finely chopped shallot
- 1   Tbsp. Dijon-style mustard
- 2   cloves garlic, minced
- ¼   tsp. salt
- ¼   tsp. black pepper
- 1   lb. lean ground turkey
- 4   slices bacon
- 2   ciabatta rolls, split and toasted
- ½   cup shredded romaine lettuce
- ½   cup quartered cherry tomatoes

1. In a medium bowl combine panko, milk, shallot, mustard, garlic, salt, and pepper. Add ground turkey; mix well. Form into four ½-inch-thick patties. Wrap a bacon slice around each patty.
2. Grill on the rack of a covered grill directly over medium heat 11 to 13 minutes or until turkey is done (165°F) and bacon is crisp, turning once.
3. Serve on a ciabatta half with lettuce and tomatoes. Makes 4 servings.
PER SERVING *463 cal, 29 g fat, 110 mg chol, 763 mg sodium, 17 g carb, 2 g fiber, 2 g sugars, 29 g pro.*

GRILLED VEGGIE PASTA SALAD

Combine almost any vegetables on hand—mushrooms, cherry tomatoes, and eggplant are delicious additions.

TOTAL TIME 30 minutes

- 3 Tbsp. olive oil
- 1 medium red sweet pepper, quartered lengthwise
- 1 small zucchini, halved lengthwise
- ½ small red onion, cut into ½-inch slices
- 8 oz. asparagus spears, trimmed
- 4 cups cooked whole grain penne pasta
- 2 Tbsp. balsamic vinegar
- ½ tsp. salt
- ⅛ tsp. black pepper
- 2 Tbsp. fresh oregano leaves snipped

1. Lightly brush vegetables with 1 Tbsp. of the oil. Grill sweet pepper, zucchini, and onion on the rack of a covered grill directly over medium-high heat 10 minutes or until tender, turning once. Add asparagus the last 3 to 5 minutes, cooking until tender, turning once. Let cool slightly. Cut vegetables into ½-inch pieces.

2. In a large bowl combine vegetables and pasta. Add remaining 2 Tbsp. oil, the vinegar, salt, and pepper; toss to coat. Sprinkle with oregano. Makes 4 servings.

PER SERVING *348 cal, 15 g fat, 300 mg sodium, 49 g carb, 8 g fiber, 8 g sugars, 10 g pro.*

JERK CHICKEN AND PINEAPPLE SLAW

Sweet and tart join forces in this chunky pineapple and bok choy slaw. Jamaican jerk seasoning adds Caribbean heat to the chicken.

TOTAL TIME 25 minutes

- **3** heads baby bok choy, trimmed and thinly sliced
- **2** cups shredded red cabbage
- **½** pineapple peeled, cored, and chopped
- **2** Tbsp. cider vinegar
- **4** tsp. packed brown sugar
- **2** tsp. Jamaican jerk seasoning
- **4** halves skinless, boneless chicken breasts

1. For pineapple slaw: In an extra-large bowl combine bok choy, cabbage, and pineapple. In a small bowl stir together vinegar and 2 tsp. of the brown sugar. Drizzle over bok choy mixture; toss to coat.

2. In a small bowl combine remaining 2 tsp. brown sugar and the jerk seasoning. Rub on chicken.

3. Grill on the rack of a covered grill directly over medium heat 8 to 12 minutes or until chicken is done (165°F), turning once. Transfer to a cutting board and slice. Serve chicken with pineapple slaw. Makes 4 servings.

PER SERVING *316 cal, 8 g fat, 124 mg chol, 328 mg sodium, 20 g carb, 2 g fiber, 16 g sugars, 40 g pro.*

JERK CHICKEN
AND PINEAPPLE
SLAW

LAMB KABOBS WITH LEMON AND FETA

Raid the spice cabinet to make this bold, smoky rub. If you prefer, substitute beef sirloin steak for the lamb. Serve it with a quick mix of Greek yogurt and lemon juice or purchased tzatziki (a Greek sauce made with yogurt, cucumbers, lemon, and garlic). Serve with slices of pita bread toasted on the grill a minute or two.

TOTAL TIME 30 minutes

- 2   tsp. brown sugar
- 2   tsp. smoked paprika
- 2   tsp. turmeric
- ½   tsp. cinnamon
- ¼   tsp. cayenne pepper
- 1½ lb. lean boneless lamb
- 1   Tbsp. vegetable oil
- 2   lemons, halved
- ½   cup thinly sliced red onion
- ½   cup feta cheese
- ¼   cup fresh mint leaves
- ¼   cup pine nuts, toasted (tip, page 27) (optional)

1. If using wooden skewers, soak in water 30 minutes. In a small bowl combine brown sugar, paprika, turmeric, cinnamon, and cayenne.
2. Thinly slice meat diagonally across the grain into long strips. Thread meat accordion-style onto skewers, leaving ¼ inch between pieces. Lightly brush with oil; sprinkle with half the spice mixture.
3. Grill kabobs on the rack of a covered grill directly over medium heat 5 to 6 minutes or until meat is slightly pink in center, turning once. Add lemons, cut sides down, the last 2 to 3 minutes or until lightly charred.
4. Sprinkle meat with remaining spice mixture, onion, cheese, mint, and, if desired, pine nuts. Squeeze grilled lemons over meat. Makes 4 servings.

PER SERVING *421 cal, 16 g fat, 123 mg chol, 728 mg sodium, 24 g carb, 2 g fiber, 5 g sugars, 41 g pro.*

BERRY LEMONADE
Recipe on page 157

july

Summer gatherings mean juicy burgers with all the trimmings, tart in-season cherry pies, and make-ahead chilled desserts. These no-oven-required weeknight recipes will keep you cool.

157

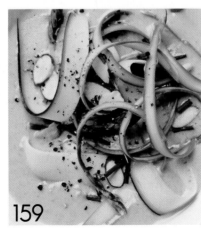

159

163

CHERRIES JUBILEE

Tart cherry season is too short to tolerate soggy crusts, runny fillings, and less-than-fresh toppings. These modern and classic cherry pie favorites have been perfected and tested, so all you have to do is get your hands on as much of this fleeting fruit as you can.

TANGY CREAM CHEESE AND CHERRY PIE

Throwback no-bake cherry cheesecake gets a lighter spin with Greek yogurt in the filling and an extra-crispy crust. The biggest update is swapping canned pie filling for fresh cherry topping.

HANDS-ON TIME 25 minutes
TOTAL TIME 5 hours 35 minutes, includes chilling

- 1 cup crushed graham crackers (about 20 squares)
- ½ cup panko
- 3 Tbsp. sugar
- ⅓ cup butter, melted
- ½ tsp. salt
- 1 8-oz. pkg. low-fat cream cheese, softened
- ¾ cup plain Greek yogurt
- ½ cup sugar
- 2 tsp. vanilla bean paste
- 1¼ cups heavy cream
- 2 cups fresh pitted tart red cherries or frozen unsweetened pitted tart red cherries, partially thawed
- 1 Tbsp. honey

1. Preheat oven to 350°F. In a large bowl combine graham crackers, panko, 3 Tbsp. sugar, the butter, and salt. Press into a 9-inch pie plate. Bake 10 minutes or until light brown; let cool.

2. In a large bowl beat cream cheese, Greek yogurt, ½ cup sugar, and the vanilla with a mixer on medium-high 2 minutes or until light and fluffy. In a second bowl beat cream on medium until soft peaks form (tips will curl). Fold into yogurt mixture. Spoon into piecrust; spread evenly. Cover; chill 4 hours.

3. In a saucepan heat cherries and honey 5 minutes or until heated through and juices release; cool. Spoon cherries over each serving. Makes 8 slices.

PER SLICE *498 cal, 33 g fat, 93 mg chol, 331 mg sodium, 45 g carb, 1 g fiber, 31 g sugars, 7 g pro.*

THE MODERN

Two updates to the classic no-bake cherry cheesecake make this cream cheese pie even more delicious.

THE CRUST Panko mixed with graham crackers gives this crust a crisp, pleasantly gritty bite.

THE CHERRIES Warming cherries with a spoonful of honey brings out their flavor.

TART CHERRIES—AKA SOUR CHERRIES—ARE THIN-SKINNED AND ARE AT PEAK SEASON FOR JUST TWO WEEKS IN LATE JULY. AT FARMERS MARKETS, LOOK FOR PLUMP BRIGHT RED FRUIT WITH STEMS INTACT.

MOST OF THE 34,000 ACRES OF TART CHERRIES GROWN IN THE U.S. ARE THE MONTMORENCY VARIETY. AND TWO-THIRDS OF THOSE ARE GROWN IN MICHIGAN. THANKFULLY, THESE RUBY-COLOR GEMS FREEZE WELL.

THE CLASSIC

The biggest disappointments with traditional cherry pie are undercooked pastry and a watery filling. Here's the solution to both.

THE CRUST No soggy bottom here. The key is to start at a high temp to set the pastry, then finish at a lower one.

THE CHERRIES Fresh and frozen cherries give different amounts of juice. Measure fruit and juice separately for a filling that's never soupy.

DOUBLE-CRUST CHERRY PIE

This pie checks all the "just right" boxes: flaky pastry, thickened cherry filling, and playful (not complicated) cutouts.

HANDS-ON TIME 55 minutes
TOTAL TIME 2 hours 10 minutes

6   cups fresh pitted tart red cherries or two 12-oz. pkg. frozen unsweetened pitted tart red cherries
1   cup sugar, plus more for sprinkling
3   Tbsp. cornstarch
     Pastry for Double-Crust Pie
     Milk

1. For fresh cherries, catch the juices as you pit them (it's fine if you get little or no juice from fresh cherries, but if they are extra-juicy, use up to ¼ cup). If using frozen cherries, thaw and reserve ¼ cup juice. In an extra-large bowl stir together sugar and cornstarch. Add cherries and reserved juice; toss.
2. Preheat oven to 450°F. Prepare pastry. On a lightly floured surface, roll one pastry ball from center to edges into a 12-inch circle. Ease pastry into pie plate without stretching it. Repeat rolling with second pastry ball.
3. Stir cherry mixture; transfer to pastry-lined pie plate. Trim bottom pastry even with edge of pie plate, reserving trimmings.

4. For pastry decorations: Using a 1-inch circle cookie cutter cut out circles on second pastry, reserving some circles for topping. Place pastry on filling; trim to ½ inch beyond edge of pie plate; reserve trimmings. Fold top pastry under bottom pastry; crimp edges as desired. Roll some of the reserved trimmings into slim lengths of rope, then cut into stems. Using a ½-inch leaf-shape cookie cutter or a paring knife, cut out leaves. Brush top pastry with milk. Arrange circles, leaves, and stems to form cherries on crust; brush with milk. Sprinkle with sugar. If you want to skip the decorations, cut three slits in top pastry to vent pie.
5. Place a foil-lined baking sheet on rack below pie in oven. Bake 15 minutes. Reduce oven to 375°F. Bake 1 hour more or until filling in center is bubbly. Cool on a wire rack. Makes 8 slices.
Pastry for Double-Crust Pie In a large bowl stir together 2½ cups all-purpose flour and 1 tsp. salt. Using a pastry blender cut in ½ cup shortening and ¼ cup cut up butter, until pieces are pea size. Sprinkle 1 Tbsp. cold water over part of the flour mixture; toss with a fork. Push moistened pastry to side of bowl. Repeat moistening flour mixture, using 1 Tbsp. cold water at a time (no more than ⅔ cup total), until all flour mixture is moistened. Gather dough into a ball, kneading gently until it holds together. Divide into two balls.
PER SLICE *473 cal, 19 g fat, 15 mg chol, 342 mg sodium, 72 g carb, 3 g fiber, 35 g sugars, 5 g pro.*

BURGER BASH

The juiciest hamburger in the country is in Charleston, South Carolina. The Secret? Marinade.

CHEVALO'S MARINATED BURGERS
Recipe on page 152

"There's only one thing separating an ordinary burger from an extraordinary one," Chevalo Wilsondebriano says. "It's got to be juicy to be unforgettable." Chevalo should know. He and his wife, Monique, built their booming food business, Charleston Gourmet Burger Co., around a simple technique they believe delivers the juiciest hamburgers: marinating the ground beef. After years of impressing friends and family with their signature burgers at cookouts, the couple bottled their secret: an all-natural meat marinade now sold in grocery stores around the country and on QVC (online shopping).

"Every single bite should be a wow, and there's only one way to make that happen," Monique says. "You can't brush a sauce on a patty and expect that to do it. You have to work the marinade into the meat with your bare hands and massage it into every morsel of the beef."

Then you need patience. The longer you let the mixture sit, the greater the reward. Chevalo recommends at least 30 minutes; marinating overnight produces the best results. That's what he does every Fourth of July when they host an annual burger bash.

The couple rounds out the menu with grilled corn on the cob topped with pimiento-cheese butter, a rice salad full of fresh fruit, and tangy buttermilk slaw that disappears almost as quickly as Chevalo's burgers. "Find me another food that is as universally loved as a hamburger," he says with a laugh. "I'm beginning to think a good, juicy burger is about as close as we're ever going to get to world peace."

"IF YOU TAKE A BITE AND YOU DON'T NEED A NAPKIN TO WIPE YOUR HANDS, I'VE GOT NEWS FOR YOU: YOUR MEAT ISN'T JUICY ENOUGH." CHEVALO WILSONDEBRIANO

CHEVALO'S BURGER CHECKLIST

1. THE MEAT Buy 80/20 ground beef. "It has the best fat content for moisture and flavor," Chevalo says.

2. THE MARINADE Gently work in the marinade with your hands just until distributed (until you don't see any of the marinade). Don't overwork the meat or the burger will be tough. Marinate at least 30 minutes.

3. THE SIZE Chevalo starts with a quarter pound of meat, shapes it into a ball, and flattens it to about ½ to ¾ inch thick and slightly bigger than the bun. The patties will cook more evenly and stay flat and not shrink if you press your thumb into the center to make a dimple.

4. THE TIMING Chevalo prefers the flavor from a charcoal grill, but a gas grill or cast-iron skillet on the stove also turns out delicious burgers. Cook 4 to 5 minutes on each side for medium doneness. If the meat is marinated, medium-well or even well-done burgers will still be juicy.

CHEVALO'S MARINATED BURGERS

Chevalo and Monique's marinade recipe is a closely guarded secret, but this version is pretty close. Chevalo serves his signature burgers from large boards loaded with toppings.

HANDS-ON TIME 25 minutes
TOTAL TIME 1 hour 5 minutes

¾	cup Worcestershire sauce
¼	cup ketchup
2	tsp. dried parsley
1½	tsp. onion powder
1½	tsp. garlic powder
½	tsp. salt
1	tsp. black pepper
2	lb. 80-percent lean ground beef
8	hamburger buns, split and toasted

1. In an extra-large bowl combine Worcestershire sauce, ketchup, dried parsley, onion powder, garlic powder, salt, and pepper. Add ground beef. Using your hands, mix thoroughly until just combined. (Overworking the meat will make it tough.) Divide evenly into eight ½- to ¾-inch-thick patties. Arrange in a baking pan. Cover; chill 30 minutes to 24 hours to marinate.

2. Press center of each patty to form a dimple, which keeps the patties from bulging in the center. Grill on rack of a covered grill directly over medium heat 8 to 10 minutes or until medium doneness (160°F), turning once. Serve in toasted buns. Makes 8 burgers.

PER BURGER *459 cal, 24 g fat, 108 mg chol, 779 mg sodium, 34 g carb, 2 g fiber, 10 g sugars, 25 g pro.*

PEACHY RICE SALAD
Recipe on page 157

GRILLED CORN WITH PIMIENTO-CHEESE BUTTER
Recipe on page 157

BUTTERMILK HERB SLAW
Recipe on page 157

BERRY
LEMONADE

EXTRA-TART BERRY LEMONADE IS THE COUPLE'S FAVORITE BEVERAGE. MONIQUE (CENTER) AND HER SISTERS, TORRI AND TONJA, ADD EASY SIDES THAT REFLECT THE FLAVORS OF CHARLESTON.

PEACHY RICE
SALAD

BUTTERMILK HERB SLAW

Photo on page 155.

Monique adds torn kale and pickled banana peppers to the traditional cabbage and carrot combo. The slaw is delicious on the burgers, too.

HANDS-ON TIME 30 minutes
TOTAL TIME 2 hours 30 minutes

3	cups shredded savoy or green cabbage
3	cups shredded red cabbage
3	cups torn curly kale
1	cup julienned carrots
½	cup drained banana pepper rings, plus 2 Tbsp. pickling liquid
½	cup sliced pickled okra (optional)
½	cup sliced green onions
¼	cup coarsely chopped fresh parsley
¼	cup chopped fresh chives
⅔	cup buttermilk
½	cup mayonnaise
3	Tbsp. red wine vinegar
2	tsp. Dijon-style mustard
1	tsp. sugar
1	clove garlic, minced
½	tsp. salt
¼	tsp. freshly ground black pepper

1. For salad: In a large bowl combine cabbages, kale, carrots, banana pepper rings, okra (if desired), green onions, parsley, and chives.
2. For dressing: In a medium bowl whisk together pickling liquid, buttermilk, mayonnaise, vinegar, mustard, sugar, garlic, salt, and black pepper. Toss salad with dressing. Chill, covered, 2 to 24 hours. Makes 12 cups.
PER 1 CUP *97 cal, 7 g fat, 5 mg chol, 236 mg sodium, 7 g carb, 2 g fiber, 3 g sugars, 2 g pro.*

PEACHY RICE SALAD

Carolina Gold rice is beloved in the South for its flavor, texture, and starch content. If you can't find it, substitute a long grain rice.

HANDS-ON TIME 20 minutes
TOTAL TIME 1 hour 40 minutes, includes chilling

1½	cups uncooked Carolina Gold rice
2	to 3 ripe peaches, halved, pitted, and sliced (2 cups)
1	cup fresh blueberries
1	cup cherry tomatoes, halved
½	cup torn fresh basil
½	cup thinly sliced red onion
1	to 2 Fresno or jalapeño chile peppers, stemmed, seeded, and sliced (tip, page 17) (optional)
⅓	cup cider vinegar
⅓	cup olive oil
2	Tbsp. red pepper jelly
2	Tbsp. minced fresh shallot
1	Tbsp. chopped fresh basil
1	tsp. Dijon-style mustard
¼	tsp. salt
¼	tsp. black pepper

1. Cook rice according to package directions. Fluff; spread in a shallow baking pan. Cover loosely; chill 1 hour.
2. For salad: In a large bowl combine cooled rice, peaches, blueberries, tomatoes, ½ cup torn basil, the red onion, and, if desired, chile pepper.
3. For vinaigrette: In a small bowl whisk together cider vinegar, olive oil, red pepper jelly, shallot, 1 Tbsp. chopped basil, the mustard, salt, and black pepper. Toss salad with dressing. Season with salt and black pepper to taste. Chill, covered, up to 8 hours. Stir before serving. Makes 9½ cups.
Make Ahead Refrigerate rice and vinaigrette in separate airtight containers up to 3 days.
PER ¾ CUP *171 cal, 6 g fat, 110 mg sodium, 26 g carb, 1 g fiber, 6 g sugars, 2 g pro.*

BERRY LEMONADE

HANDS-ON TIME 25 minutes
TOTAL TIME 4 hours 25 minutes

14	cups water
3	cups sugar
24	lemons
12	cups fresh raspberries
4	cups sliced fresh strawberries

1. For simple syrup: In a large saucepan heat 3 cups of the water and the sugar over medium heat, stirring until dissolved. Let cool.
2. Juice 20 lemons. (You should have 4 cups juice.) Slice remaining lemons.
3. For raspberry puree: In a food processor process 8 cups of the raspberries in batches until smooth. Strain through a fine-mesh sieve.
4. For lemonade concentrate: In a gallon container stir together simple syrup, lemon juice, and raspberry puree. Chill, covered, 4 to 24 hours.
5. In a 2-gallon jar stir together concentrate, remaining 11 cups water and 4 cups raspberries, and sliced strawberries. Serve over ice. Makes 22 cups.
PER 1 CUP *161 cal, 1 g fat, 6 mg sodium, 41 g carb, 5 g fiber, 33 g sugars, 1 g pro.*

GRILLED CORN WITH PIMIENTO-CHEESE BUTTER

Photo on page 155.

The rich pimiento-cheese combo stirred into softened butter melts over an ear of hot grilled corn. Is there anything else to say but "Yum"?

HANDS-ON TIME 15 minutes
TOTAL TIME 30 minutes

12	ears fresh corn on the cob
2	Tbsp. vegetable oil
½	tsp. salt
½	tsp. black pepper
1	4-oz. jar diced pimientos, drained
⅓	cup butter, softened
¼	cup mayonnaise
1	tsp. garlic powder
8	oz. sharp cheddar cheese, shredded (2 cups)
	Chopped fresh chives

1. Peel back husks from corn, leaving attached at base. Remove silks. Using 100-percent-cotton kitchen string, tie back husks, ears exposed. Rinse; pat dry. Brush with oil; sprinkle with salt and pepper. Grill on rack of a covered grill directly over medium heat 12 to 15 minutes or until crisp-tender, turning to brown evenly.
2. In a medium bowl stir together pimientos, butter, mayonnaise, garlic powder, and cheese. Top each grilled ear with butter mixture and chives. Makes 12 servings.
PER SERVING *253 cal, 18 g fat, 34 mg chol, 305 mg sodium, 18 g carb, 2 g fiber, 6 g sugars, 8 g pro.*
Make Ahead Refrigerate Pimiento-Cheese Butter in an airtight container up to 3 days. Let stand 30 minutes at room temperature to soften before using.

FAST & FRESH

Easy, healthful recipes for a better dinner tonight.

CHICKPEA-HERB FLATBREADS

CHICKPEA-HERB FLATBREADS

The base of this flatbread dish is a chunky spin on hummus, made with chickpeas, tahini (sesame seed paste), lemon, cumin, and lots of herbs.

TOTAL TIME 20 minutes

- ½   cup tahini
- 1   clove garlic , minced
- 2   Tbsp. lemon juice
- ⅛   tsp. salt
- 2   cups mixed herbs parsley, mint, and/or cilantro
- 2   15-oz. cans chickpeas, rinsed and drained
- ½   tsp. cumin
- ¾   tsp. salt
- 1   pt. cherry tomatoes, halved
- 1   medium cucumber, sliced
- 6   green onions, sliced
- 1   Tbsp. olive oil
- ⅛   tsp. black pepper
- 6   flatbread
      Lemon wedges

1. For sauce: In a small bowl whisk together tahini, ⅓ cup water, and the garlic until smooth. Set aside 2 Tbsp. Stir lemon juice and ⅛ tsp. salt into remaining sauce. Thin to drizzling consistency with water, if necessary.
2. For hummus, in a food processor combine 1½ cups herbs and reserved 2 Tbsp. sauce. Pulse until finely chopped. Add chickpeas, cumin, and ½ tsp. salt; pulse to form a coarse spread.
3. For salad: In a large bowl combine tomatoes, cucumber, green onions, and remaining ½ cup herbs. Add olive oil, remaining salt, and pepper; toss to combine. Spread hummus on each flatbread. Top with salad; drizzle with sauce. Serve with lemon wedges. Makes 6 servings.
PER SERVING *441 cal, 16 g fat, 847 mg sodium, 62 g carb, 9 g fiber, 7 g sugars, 16 g pro.*

CHILLED PEA SOUP WITH VEGETABLE NOODLES

CHILLED PEA SOUP WITH VEGETABLE NOODLES

A quick whirl in a blender transforms sweet peas, buttermilk, and lemon into a tangy, rich soup. To quickly thaw frozen peas, let them stand in hot water 2 minutes. Drain then rinse with cold water before using.

TOTAL TIME 20 minutes

- 2   cups frozen peas, thawed
- 2   cups buttermilk
- 1   tsp. lemon juice
- ½   tsp. salt
- 1   medium zucchini
- 8   oz. asparagus, trimmed
- ⅓   cup sliced almonds, toasted (tip, page 27)
- ¼   cup snipped chives
      Black pepper

1. In a blender combine peas, buttermilk, lemon juice, and salt. Cover; blend until smooth. Divide soup among four bowls.
2. Using a vegetable peeler, shave zucchini and asparagus into thin ribbons. Divide vegetables among bowls. Top each with toasted almonds and chives. Season to taste with additional salt and black pepper. Makes 4 servings.
PER SERVING *230 cal, 6 g fat, 8 mg chol, 699 mg sodium, 32 g carb, 6 g fiber, 13 g sugars, 14 g pro.*

CHICKEN AND STRAWBERRY PANZANELLA

Day-old bakery Italian bread works best for panzanella, an Italian bread salad. The drier the bread, the more it will soak up the dressing and juices from the strawberries. To quickly dry fresh bread, spread cubes on a baking sheet and bake in a 300°F oven 10 to 15 minutes, stirring once.

TOTAL TIME 25 minutes

- 2   to 2¼ lb. rotisserie chicken
- 1   shallot, finely chopped
- 2   Tbsp. sherry vinegar
- 2   tsp. Dijon-style mustard
- ¼   tsp. salt
- ¼   tsp. black pepper
- ⅓   cup olive oil
- 4   cups hearty Italian bread, cubed
- 1   5-oz. pkg. baby kale
- 1½ cups strawberries, sliced
- ¼   cup pine nuts, toasted (tip, page 27)

1. Remove meat from chicken, discarding skin and bones. Cut meat into bite-size pieces (about 3½ cups).
2. For dressing, in a small bowl combine shallot, vinegar, mustard, salt, and pepper. Whisk in oil in a steady stream until emulsified.
3. Arrange chicken, bread, kale, strawberries, and pine nuts on a platter. Drizzle with dressing. Season to taste with additional salt and pepper; toss. Makes 4 servings.
PER SERVING *552 cal, 33 g fat, 127 mg chol, 821 mg sodium, 28 g carb, 4 g fiber, 5 g sugars, 38 g pro.*

SESAME-SHRIMP NOODLE BOWL

Bean thread noodles (also called glass noodles, cellophane noodles, or Chinese vermicelli) can be found in the ethnic section of many grocery stores or at Asian markets. Cooked rice noodles work here, too.

TOTAL TIME 30 minutes

4	oz. bean thread noodles
⅓	cup rice vinegar
¼	cup soy sauce
¼	cup toasted sesame oil
1	lb. medium shrimp, cooked and peeled
12	oz. refrigerated firm tofu, drained, patted dry, and cubed
4	stalks celery, very thinly sliced
¼	head red cabbage, shredded (2¾ cups)
1	fresno chile pepper fresh, thinly sliced (tip, page 17)

1. Soak noodles in enough hot water to cover (about 1 qt.) 10 minutes or just until soft; drain. Rinse with cold water; drain. Meanwhile, in a large bowl whisk together vinegar, soy sauce, and sesame oil. Add noodles; stir to coat.

2. Add shrimp, tofu, celery, cabbage, and chile pepper to noodle mixture; toss gently. Season to taste with salt. Makes 4 servings.

PER SERVING *430 cal, 18 g fat, 183 mg chol, 748 mg sodium, 35 g carb, 3 g fiber, 6 g sugars, 33 g pro.*

the big CHILL

We love a good comeback story, especially when it's a no-bake dessert in time for peak summer heat. Give your oven the month off and make one of these updated spins on the retro icebox cake.

GINGER-LIME ICEBOX CAKE

This rendition pairs the best of Key lime pie and cheesecake: a big squeeze of lime juice and cream cheese in the filling. Gingersnap cookies spice it up.

HANDS-ON TIME 20 minutes
CHILL TIME 8 hours

2   8-oz. pkg. cream cheese, softened
¾   cup powdered sugar
6   to 8 limes (2 Tbsp. zest; ¾ cup juice)
1   tsp. vanilla
2   cups heavy cream
1   16-oz. pkg. gingersnaps

1. For filling: In a large bowl beat together cream cheese, sugar, 1 Tbsp. lime zest, the lime juice, and vanilla with a mixer on medium until smooth.

2. In a second large bowl beat heavy cream with mixer on medium until soft peaks form (tips curl). Fold into cream cheese mixture.

3. Spread ½ cup filling into a 9-inch springform pan. Top with a layer of gingersnaps (about 14). Repeat layers three times using 1½ cups filling total; spread remaining filling over top. (Reserve eight gingersnaps.) Chill, covered, 8 to 24 hours. Remove sides of pan. Crush reserved gingersnaps; press onto sides of cake. Top with remaining lime zest. Makes 12 slices.

PER SLICE *460 cal, 31 g fat, 83 mg chol, 319 mg sodium, 41 g carb, 1 g fiber, 18 g sugars, 6 g pro.*

AT THEIR MOST BASIC, ICEBOX CAKES ARE ALTERNATING LAYERS OF WHIPPED CREAM FILLING AND COOKIES THAT SOFTEN AS THEY CHILL.

S'MORES ICEBOX CAKE
Recipe on page 167

BERRY ICEBOX PIE
Recipe on page 167

TOASTED COCONUT
ICEBOX CAKE

THE LONGER YOU CHILL THESE, THE SOFTER THE LAYERS. CHILL TIMES RANGE FROM 6 TO 12 HOURS, AND THEY CAN BE MADE UP TO 24 HOURS AHEAD.

S'MORES ICEBOX CAKE

Photo on page 164.

An icon reimagined: graham crackers layered with a filling of marshmallow creme and mascarpone cheese. The broiler stands in for a campfire to give marshmallows that familiar torched flavor and to melt the chocolate.

HANDS-ON TIME 20 minutes
CHILL TIME 6 hours 15 minutes

1½ cups heavy cream
½ 7-oz. carton mascarpone cheese
 or 8-oz. pkg. cream cheese
½ cup powdered sugar
2 tsp. vanilla
1 7-oz. jar marshmallow creme
1¼ cups mini marshmallows
¾ cup mini semisweet chocolate chips
7 graham crackers, quartered

1. For filling: In a large bowl beat cream, mascarpone, sugar, and vanilla with a mixer on medium until soft peaks form (tips curl). Add marshmallow creme; beat until fluffy. Fold in 1 cup marshmallows and ½ cup chips.
2. Spread 1 cup filling into a 9×5-inch loaf pan. Spread a small spoonful of filling on one graham cracker quarter. Top with second cracker. Stand sandwiched crackers upright. Repeat with remaining crackers and filling to form rows. Chill, covered, 6 to 24 hours.
3. Preheat broiler. Top cake with remaining ¼ cup marshmallows and chips. Broil 3 to 4 inches from heat 1 minute or until golden. Cover loosely; chill 15 minutes before serving. Makes 12 slices.
PER SLICE *347 cal, 19 g fat, 46 mg chol, 66 mg sodium, 40 g carb, 29 g sugars, 3 g pro.*

BERRY ICEBOX PIE

Photo on page 165.

Blackberry preserves, sour cream, and orange zest flavor the barely sweet filling. Paired with vanilla wafers, it's reminiscent of berry shortcake. For crunchy contrast, save some cookies to layer on top before serving.

HANDS-ON TIME 20 minutes
CHILL TIME 8 hours

2 cups heavy cream
¾ cup sour cream
1¼ cups seedless blackberry preserves
2 tsp. orange zest
1 11-oz. pkg. vanilla wafers
1 cup fresh blackberries

1. For filling: In a large bowl beat cream with a mixer on high until stiff peaks form (tips stand straight). Fold in sour cream. Fold in ¾ cup preserves and the zest.
2. Spread 1⅓ cups filling into a 9-inch pie plate. Top with a layer of wafers, 1⅓ cups filling, and remaining ½ cup preserves. Repeat twice with filling and wafers, reserving some wafers for top. Chill, covered, 8 to 24 hours. Serve topped with reserved wafers and blackberries. Makes 12 slices.
PER SLICE *378 cal, 21 g fat, 53 mg chol, 130 mg sodium, 45 g carb, 1 g fiber, 27 g sugars, 3 g pro.*

TOASTED COCONUT ICEBOX CAKE

Toasted coconut flakes and whipped coconut cream surround buttery cookies in this cake inspired by a popular Girl Scout cookie. Finish with drizzles of fudge and caramel sauces.

HANDS-ON TIME 30 minutes
CHILL TIME 12 hours

1¼ cups shredded coconut
2 14-oz. cans unsweetened coconut milk, chilled at least 4 hours
1 cup heavy cream
½ cup powdered sugar
1 tsp. vanilla
1 6.75- to 7.5-oz. pkg. crisp caramel-flavor cookies (such as Pepperidge Farm Bordeaux) or shortbread cookies
 Hot fudge and caramel ice cream sauces

1. Preheat oven to 350°F. Spread coconut in a 15×10-inch baking pan. Bake 5 minutes or until toasted, shaking pan once; let cool.
2. For filling: Spoon solid coconut cream from top of cans of coconut milk into a large bowl (reserve liquid for another use). Beat with a mixer on medium until smooth. Add cream, sugar, and vanilla. Beat on high until stiff peaks form (tips stand straight).
3. Line an 8×4-inch loaf pan with plastic wrap, extending it over edges. Spread ¼ cup filling into prepared pan. Top with a layer of cookies, ¾ cup filling, and ¼ cup coconut. Repeat three times, reserving ¼ cup each filling and coconut. Cover; chill 8 to 24 hours.
4. To serve, unmold cake onto a platter. Top with reserved filling and coconut. Drizzle with warmed hot fudge and caramel sauces. Makes 8 slices.
PER SLICE *524 cal, 40 g fat, 34 mg chol, 202 mg sodium, 36 g carb, 2 g fiber, 22 g sugars, 4 g pro.*

MELON BAR

Sun-ripened melon gets even sweeter with a sprinkle of salt.

If you've never tried salt on watermelon, you might find the idea strange, but even the sweetest things taste more flavorful with a sprinkle. To turn this long-standing salty-sweet tradition into a party dessert station: Set out watermelon slices and wedges (cut up yellow, orange, and mini varieties, too) with a selection of purchased and homemade salt blends.

1. GRAY SEA SALT This French salt gets its color from the clay-lined salt ponds where it's harvested.

2. LEMON-BASIL SALT Stir together ½ cup sea salt flakes, ¼ cup sugar, zest of two lemons, 2 Tbsp. finely chopped fresh basil, and 1 tsp. cracked black pepper.

3. CHILE-LIME SEASONING A blend of chile pepper, salt, and dehydrated lime juice, this popular Mexican blend is a common sprinkle for mango, and can be found in most grocery stores.

4. LIME-MINT SALT Stir together ½ cup sea salt flakes, ¼ cup sugar, zest of two limes, and 2 Tbsp. finely chopped fresh mint.

GRAY SEA SALT

CHILE-LIME
SEASONING

LIME-MINT
SALT

LEMON-BASIL
SALT

HEIRLOOM TOMATO
AND GREEN
BEAN SALAD
Recipe on page 187

august

It's all things fresh with bountiful seasonal produce, and flavor is highlighted in uncomplicated recipes. For expert prep tips, learn how time spent on Sunday results in eating well during the week.

174

177

194

Garlic:

A LOVE STORY

Some folks—like this Iowa couple—find the fiery flavor of homegrown garlic downright irresistible. Plant some this fall and prepare to be wooed.

JORDAN CLASEN AND WHITNEY BREWER

How does a city boy who grew up thinking garlic was a type of salt become a garlic farmer? "I was obsessed the first time I tasted fresh garlic (roasted, with new potatoes) and wanted to grow it," says Jordan Clasen, owner of Grade A Gardens (gradeagardens.com), an organic farm in Johnston, Iowa. Armed with lessons learned from garlic mentors—local farmers and organic growers—Jordan planted his first garlic crop in 2010: 5,000 plants on half an acre. Since then he's grown more than 40 varieties and expanded to 60,000 plants on 12 acres. The long hours and hard work haven't paled Jordan's passion. He's going for his fourth blue ribbon in garlic braiding at the Iowa State Fair this summer. Now's the time to try for yourself. These recipes will convince you to fall for garlic, too.

GREEN GARLIC VS. SCAPES

Gardeners get two bonus ingredients when they grow their own garlic. Green garlic (aka spring garlic) is a young plant that's pulled before it has developed a bulb of cloves—the garlic equivalent of a green onion. Garlic scapes are curly, pencil-thick flower bud stems that hardneck varieties send up. Cutting off the scape directs energy into the bulb. Green garlic and scapes have subtle fresh garlic flavor.

GARLIC SCAPE AND
BASIL PESTO
Recipe on page 174

"WHAT'S THE BEST
WAY TO REMOVE
GARLIC SMELL? WHY
WOULD YOU?" ASKS
JORDAN CLASEN.

HONEY AND GREEN
GARLIC BUTTER
Recipe on page 174

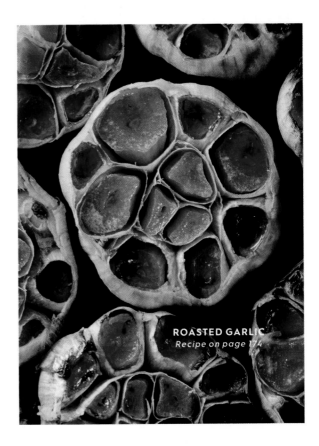

ROASTED GARLIC
Recipe on page 174

HONEY AND GREEN GARLIC BUTTER

Photo on page 173.

HANDS-ON TIME 5 minutes
TOTAL TIME 5 minutes

½   cup butter, softened
2   Tbsp. chopped green garlic or garlic scapes*
4   cloves garlic, minced
¼   tsp. salt
⅛   tsp. black pepper
1   tsp. honey

In a small bowl beat butter on medium 2 minutes or until light and fluffy. Add green garlic or garlic scapes, minced garlic, salt, black pepper, and honey; beat until combined. Serve on warm biscuits or corn bread or with hot cooked shrimp. Makes ½ cup.

*Tip Or use 2 Tbsp. chopped chives plus 1 clove garlic, minced.

EACH 1-TBSP. SERVING *106 cal, 12 g fat, 31 mg chol, 164 mg sodium, 1 g carb.*

QUICK GARLIC-ONION JAM

QUICK GARLIC-ONION JAM

HANDS-ON TIME 10 minutes
TOTAL TIME 30 minutes

3   Tbsp. butter
2   cups chopped sweet onions
2   to 3 recipes Roasted Garlic (recipe, right)
3   Tbsp. balsamic vinegar
2   Tbsp. packed brown sugar
2   Tbsp. water
½   tsp. salt
¼   tsp. crushed red pepper

In a large skillet heat butter over medium. Add sweet onions. Cook 15 minutes or until softened and starting to brown, stirring occasionally. Add Roasted Garlic, balsamic vinegar, packed brown sugar, water, salt, and crushed red pepper. Cook, uncovered, 5 minutes or until thickened. Let cool. Spread the jam over toasts and melted gruyère. Makes 1⅓ cups.

EACH 1-TBSP. SERVING *55 cal, 3 g fat, 4 mg chol, 72 mg sodium, 7 g carb, 2 g sugar, 1 g pro.*

ROASTED GARLIC

Photo on page 173.

HANDS-ON TIME 5 minutes
TOTAL TIME 1 hour 5 minutes

     Coarse kosher salt
1   large garlic bulb (2½ to 3 inches in diameter)
     Olive oil

Preheat oven to 350°F. Add a layer of kosher salt to bottom of roaster. Cut ½ inch from tip of bulb; place bulb cut side up in roaster. Drizzle with olive oil. Cover; roast 1 hour. Cool. Squeeze cloves from skin. Serve on toasted bread or toss with cooked pasta. Makes ¼ cup.

Tip A terra-cotta garlic roaster prevents overcooking. Soak it in water before using.

EACH SERVING *72 cal, 4 g fat, 5 mg sodium, 9 g carb, 1 g fiber, 2 g pro.*

GARLIC SCAPE AND BASIL PESTO

Photo on page 173.

TOTAL TIME 10 minutes

1¼ cups chopped garlic scapes or green garlic
¼   cup packed fresh basil leaves
¼   cup finely shredded Parmesan-Reggiano cheese
½   cup olive oil
     Salt and black pepper

In a food processor combine chopped scapes or green garlic, basil leaves and cheese until finely chopped. With the processor running, add olive oil in a steady stream until combined. Add additional olive oil to reach desired consistency. Season to taste with salt and pepper. Serve on crostini, pasta, or grilled chicken. Makes 1 cup.

EACH 1-TBSP. SERVING *67 cal, 7 g fat, 1 mg chol, 58 mg sodium, 1 g pro.*

new ways with
SPINACH

Fresh or frozen, the nutritious, tender dark leafy greens are endlessly versatile in the kitchen.

Its mildly grassy taste plays well with many other flavors, which makes it prime for sneaking in a few extra servings of veggies.

SPINACH
DUTCH BABY

SPINACH AND
RICE SOUP

SPINACH
SPAETZLE

OVERCOOKING CAN ZAP MANY NUTRIENTS. TO MAKE SURE YOU GET THE BIGGEST HEALTH BENEFIT FROM SPINACH, STEAM IT OR QUICKLY SAUTÉ IT.

SPINACH DUTCH BABY

HANDS-ON TIME 10 minutes
TOTAL TIME 40 minutes

- 3 Tbsp. olive oil
- ½ cup all-purpose flour
- ½ cup milk
- 3 eggs
- ½ tsp. salt
- ½ tsp. freshly ground black pepper
- 3 cups fresh spinach
- ½ cup shredded sharp white cheddar cheese (2 oz.)
- 2 cups cherry tomatoes
- 3 cloves garlic, minced
- 3 slices bacon, crisp-cooked and crumbled

1. Place 2 Tbsp. olive oil in a large skillet in a cold oven. Preheat oven to 425°F.
2. Meanwhile, in a medium bowl whisk together the flour, milk, eggs, salt, and black pepper until smooth. Chop enough of the spinach to equal ½ cup. Stir into batter. Pour batter into hot skillet. Bake 20 minutes. Sprinkle with cheese. Bake 5 minutes more or until puffed and golden. Remove and let stand 5 minutes.
3. While Dutch Baby stands, in a shallow baking pan combine tomatoes, garlic, and remaining 1 Tbsp. olive oil. Sprinkle with salt and pepper to taste. Bake 5 minutes. Remove from oven. Add remaining spinach; toss with tomatoes and garlic until wilted.
4. Top Dutch Baby with roasted tomatoes-wilted spinach, and crumbled bacon. Makes 4 servings.
EACH SERVING *325 cal, 21 g fat, 162 mg chol, 572 mg sodium, 19 g carb., 2 g fiber, 4 g sugar, 14 g pro.*

SPINACH AND RICE SOUP

TOTAL TIME 30 minutes

- 1 Tbsp. olive oil
- 1 small shallot, minced
- 1 cup uncooked jasmine rice
- 8 cups reduced-sodium chicken broth
- 1 bay leaf
- ¼ tsp. salt
- 3 eggs
- 1 lemon (1 tsp. zest; 3 Tbsp. juice)
- 3 cups chopped cooked chicken
- 1 10-oz. pkg. fresh spinach, coarsely chopped
- 1 Tbsp. chopped fresh dill weed
  Lemon wedges

1. In a large pot heat olive oil over medium. Add shallot; cook and stir 2 minutes. Add 1 cup uncooked jasmine rice; cook and stir 1 minute. Add chicken broth, bay leaf, and salt. Bring to boiling; reduce heat. Simmer, covered, 8 to 10 minutes or until rice is nearly tender.
2. In a bowl whisk together eggs and lemon juice. Slowly whisk in 1 cup hot broth. Whisk egg mixture into soup in pot. Cook and stir 2 minutes or until thickened. Remove bay leaf. Add 3 cups chopped cooked chicken, spinach, fresh dill, and lemon zest. Cook and stir until spinach is wilted. Serve with lemon wedges. Makes 8 servings.
EACH SERVING *250 cal, 7 g fat, 116 mg chol, 727 mg sodium, 21 g carb., 1 g fiber, 1 g sugar, 23 g pro.*

SPINACH SPAETZLE

TOTAL TIME 40 minutes

- 2 eggs
- ½ cup milk
- 4 fresh basil leaves
- ½ tsp. salt
- ¼ tsp. freshly ground black pepper
- ⅛ tsp. freshly ground nutmeg
- ½ 10-oz. pkg. frozen spinach, thawed and well drained
- 1½ cups all-purpose flour
- 2 Tbsp. butter
- 1 Tbsp. olive oil
- 1 12-oz. pkg. cooked Italian chicken sausage links, sliced
- ¼ cup finely shredded Asiago cheese

1. In a food processor combine eggs, milk, basil leaves, salt, black pepper, and nutmeg. Add spinach; pulse to combine. Add flour; process to combine. (Dough will be sticky.) Drop bits of dough into salted boiling water; cook until spaetzle rises to top. Remove to a colander; reserve ½ cup cooking liquid.
2. In a skillet heat butter and oil over medium-high. Add Italian chicken sausage; cook and stir until browned. Add spaetzle; cook and stir until browned (about 3 minutes). Stir in cooking liquid. Top with Asiago cheese. Makes 4 servings.
EACH SERVING *466 cal, 22 g fat, 183 mg chol, 953 mg sodium, 39 g carb., 2 g fiber, 2 g sugar, 26 g pro.*

FAST & FRESH

Easy, healthful recipes for a better dinner tonight.

EGGPLANT, GARLIC, AND HERB PASTA

EGGPLANT, GARLIC, AND HERB PASTA

Ricotta salata (an Italian sheep's milk cheese) is slightly drier than feta but with the same salty punch. We love it crumbled over pastas and salads or sliced on sandwiches.

TOTAL TIME 50 minutes

3   Tbsp. olive oil
    Salt
3   medium eggplant, quartered and sliced ¾ inch thick (3 lb. total)
6   cloves garlic, unpeeled
8   oz. dried whole wheat rotini pasta
3   Tbsp. fresh mint, chopped
2   Tbsp. fresh oregano, chopped
4   oz. ricotta salata or feta cheese, crumbled
1   small fresh red chile pepper, sliced

1. Preheat oven to 425°F. Coat two shallow baking pans with 2 Tbsp. olive oil. Sprinkle pans lightly with salt. Arrange eggplant slices and garlic in a single layer in pans. Drizzle with 1 Tbsp. olive oil. Sprinkle lightly with salt. Roast on separate oven racks 25 to 30 minutes or until eggplant is browned and softened.
2. Meanwhile, cook pasta according to package directions. Drain, reserving 1 cup cooking liquid. Return pasta to pot. Add eggplant. Squeeze garlic from cloves into pot. Add olive oil and ¾ cup reserved cooking liquid; toss to coat. Add herbs and, if desired, additional cooking liquid. Season to taste. Top with cheese and chile pepper. Makes 4 servings.
EACH SERVING *509 cal, 25 g fat, 25 mg chol, 730 mg sodium, 64 g carb, 17 g fiber, 14 g sugars, 16 g pro.*

CILANTRO-GINGER BULGUR WITH SHRIMP

CILANTRO-GINGER BULGUR WITH SHRIMP

Bulgur has a chewy texture and nutty taste. The longer the grain stands after cooking, the more liquid it soaks up, so dress any leftovers with additional lime juice and/or olive oil right before serving.

HANDS-ON TIME 20 minutes
TOTAL TIME 2 hours

1   cup uncooked bulgur
1   14.5-oz. can chicken broth
2   jalapeños, seeded and sliced (tip, page 17)
2   Tbsp. fresh ginger, grated
2   Tbsp. olive oil
½   tsp. salt
1   cucumber, seeded and sliced
2   green onions, thinly sliced
⅔   cup cilantro, chopped
2   Tbsp. lime zest, plus wedges
8   oz. fresh or frozen cooked shrimp, peeled and deveined

1. In a medium saucepan combine bulgur, broth, ¼ cup water, the jalapeños, ginger, oil, and salt. Bring to boiling; reduce heat. Simmer, covered, 12 to 15 minutes or until tender and most of the liquid is absorbed. Remove from heat. Let stand, covered, 10 minutes; fluff with a fork.
2. Transfer mixture to a large bowl. Stir in cucumber, green onions, cilantro, and lime zest. Fold in cooked shrimp. Drizzle with additional olive oil and season to taste with salt. Serve with lime wedges. Makes 6 servings.
EACH SERVING *171 cal, 5 g fat, 61 mg chol, 405 mg sodium, 21 g carb, 4 g fiber, 2 g sugars, 12 g pro.*

STRIPED BASS IN TOMATO BROTH

SPICE-RUBBED PORK CHOPS

Creativity in the spice department and quick pan-pickled shallots will make you feel like Top Chef on the Quickfire Challenge.

TOTAL TIME 30 minutes

2	tsp. fennel seeds
1	tsp. coriander seeds
½	tsp. kosher salt
4	½-inch thick (1½ to 2 lb. total) bone-in pork loin chops
1	Tbsp. olive oil
½	cup white balsamic vinegar
¼	cup shallot, thinly sliced
1	Tbsp. lemon juice
	Fresh parsley and mint leaves

1. In a 12-inch skillet heat fennel seeds and coriander seeds over medium heat 4 minutes or until toasted and fragrant, shaking skillet occasionally. Remove from pan. Cool slightly. Coarsely grind with a spice grinder or crush with a mortar and pestle. Combine with salt. Sprinkle on both sides of pork chops.
2. In the same skillet heat olive oil over medium-high heat. Add pork; cook 4 minutes. Turn; cook 3 minutes more or until done (145°F). Transfer to a plate; cover.
3. Add vinegar and shallot to skillet. Bring to boiling; reduce heat. Simmer, uncovered, 1 to 2 minutes or until syrupy, stirring to scrape up browned bits. Remove from heat. Stir in lemon juice. Spoon over pork. Top with fresh parsley and mint. Makes 4 servings.
EACH SERVING *337 cal, 18 g fat, 64 mg chol, 194 mg sodium, 17 g carb, 1 g fiber, 15 g sugars, 23 g pro.*

SERVE THE CHOPS WITH A FENNEL, BIBB LETTUCE, AND HERB CRUNCHY SALAD.

STRIPED BASS IN TOMATO BROTH

Striped bass, from the Atlantic Coast, has firm texture and mild, sweet taste. If you can't find it in your fish market, mahi-mahi or cod are nice substitutes.

TOTAL TIME 25 minutes

¾	cup dry white wine
3	Tbsp. extra-virgin olive oil
2	medium tomatoes, sliced
2	shallots, sliced ¼ inch thick
6	fresh thyme sprigs
½	tsp. salt
1	lb. skinless striped bass fillets, cut into 4 pieces

1. In a large skillet combine wine, olive oil, and ½ cup water. Add tomatoes, shallots, thyme sprigs, and salt. Bring to boiling; reduce heat. Simmer, uncovered, 3 to 5 minutes or until tomatoes begin to soften.
2. Place fish fillets in pan, spooning some of the broth over. Reduce heat to medium-low. Cook, covered, 5 to 7 minutes or until fish flakes when tested with a fork. Using a slotted spoon, transfer fish and tomatoes to shallow bowls. Discard thyme sprigs. Ladle broth and shallots into each bowl. Serve with toasted bread and top with additional fresh thyme. Makes 4 servings.
EACH SERVING *320 cal, 13 g fat, 90 mg chol, 376 mg sodium, 19 g carb, 1 g fiber, 3 g sugars, 23 g pro.*

SPICE-RUBBED
PORK CHOPS

CHILLED CORN SOUP
WITH CRISPY CORN
AND PANKO TOPPER

PRIME TIME

When corn, peaches, and tomatoes are at their seasonal best, we can't get enough. Because, let's face it, a winter tomato just doesn't come close. Here are a few new ways to enjoy all three at their peak.

CHILLED CORN SOUP WITH CRISPY CORN AND PANKO TOPPER

HANDS-ON TIME 30 minutes
TOTAL TIME 5 hours 20 minutes, includes chilling

- 1 Tbsp. unsalted butter
- 1 cup chopped white onion
- 1 clove garlic, minced
- 5 cups fresh corn kernels (cut from 10 ears), cobs halved and reserved
- 4 cups reduced-sodium chicken broth
- ½ tsp. salt
- 1 7-oz. carton plain whole milk Greek yogurt
- 1 Tbsp. olive oil
- ¼ cup panko
- ¼ cup crumbled feta cheese
- 1 Tbsp. chopped fresh dill weed
- 1 tsp. lemon zest

1. For soup: In a 4-qt. pot melt butter over medium heat. Add onion and garlic. Cook and stir 3 to 4 minutes or until softened. Add 4 cups corn kernels; cook 1 minute. Add reserved cobs and broth. Bring to boiling; reduce heat. Simmer, covered, 25 minutes. Remove from heat. Cool 20 minutes. Discard cobs.

2. Using an immersion blender, blend until smooth. Strain through a fine-mesh sieve into a bowl, pressing solids. Discard solids. Stir in salt. Chill, covered, at least 4 hours. Whisk yogurt into soup until smooth.

3. For topper: In a skillet heat olive oil over medium heat. Add remaining corn and the panko; cook 2 minutes or until browned. Sprinkle topper, feta, dill, and zest over soup. Makes 4 servings.

EACH SERVING *340 cal, 13 g fat, 23 mg chol, 991 mg sodium, 46 g carb, 5 g fiber, 17 g sugars, 16 g pro.*

PICKLED HARISSA CORN RELISH

HANDS-ON TIME 30 minutes
TOTAL TIME 24 hours

- ½ cup cider vinegar
- ½ cup water
- 1 Tbsp. harissa paste
- 2 to 3 tsp. sugar
- 1½ tsp. salt
- 1½ cups fresh sweet corn kernels (cut from 3 ears fresh sweet corn)
- ½ cup chopped sweet onion
- ½ cup chopped red sweet pepper
- ¼ cup sliced carrot
- ¼ cup thinly sliced radishes
- 1 Tbsp. chopped fresh cilantro

In a saucepan combine cider vinegar, water, harissa paste, sugar, and salt. Bring to boiling, stirring to dissolve sugar. Remove from heat; stir in corn kernels, onion, red sweet pepper, carrot, and radishes. Cool completely. Chill 24 hours. Stir in fresh cilantro before serving. Makes 8 servings.

EACH SERVING *43 cal, 465 mg sodium, 9 g carb., 1 g fiber, 4 g sugars, 1 g pro.*

Try it with Steak Serve over cumin-rubbed grilled ribeyes.

Try it with Pork Top shredded pork tenderloin and lettuce in a tortilla.

Try it with Burgers Use as a topper for beef or turkey burgers.

SWEET CORN

WHAT TO LOOK FOR Seek tight, bright green husks that have moist silks at the tops. Avoid yanking the husks all the way back to check kernels, which can quickly dry out ears.

HOW TO STORE For maximum sweetness, eat as soon as possible after corn is picked.

PICKLED HARISSA CORN RELISH

PEACHES

WHAT TO LOOK FOR Look for a golden hue beneath the blush. Green signifies the peach was picked too early.

HOW TO STORE Keep at room temperature, stem sides down, until ripe. (They should feel soft when squeezed.) To speed ripening, place in a paper bag for a day or two.

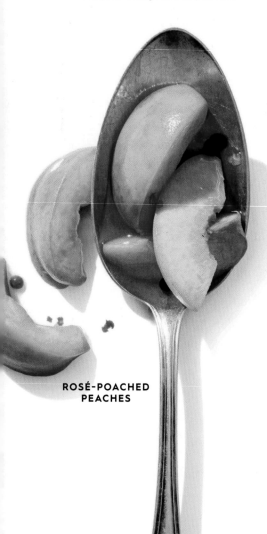

ROSÉ-POACHED PEACHES

PEACH-BERRY HOT HONEY CRISP

HANDS-ON TIME 25 minutes
TOTAL TIME 1 hour 25 minutes, includes cooling

- ½ cup all-purpose flour
- ½ cup regular rolled oats
- ½ cup packed light brown sugar
- ¼ tsp. ground cinnamon
- ¼ tsp. salt
- 5 Tbsp. unsalted butter, cut into small pieces
- 7 firm ripe peaches (2½ lb.), pitted and cut into ½-inch-thick wedges
- 1¼ cups fresh raspberries
- 1¼ cups fresh blueberries
- ½ cup granulated sugar
- 2 Tbsp. hot honey* (such as Mike's brand)
- ½ tsp. almond extract
- ¼ tsp. ground allspice
- 3 Tbsp. all-purpose flour

1. Lightly butter a 10-inch cast-iron skillet. For topping: In a medium bowl stir together ½ cup flour, the oats, brown sugar, cinnamon, and salt. Add butter; cut in until mixture forms clumps.
2. For filling: In a large bowl combine peaches, berries, granulated sugar, honey, almond extract, and allspice. Add 3 Tbsp. flour; toss well. Transfer to skillet. Sprinkle with topping.
3. Adjust grill** for indirect heat. Grill over medium heat 45 minutes or until filling is bubbly and topping is browned, rotating skillet occasionally. Remove; cool 20 minutes. Makes 8 servings.
*Tip Alternatively, stir in 2 Tbsp. honey and ½ tsp. crushed red pepper.
**Tip Alternatively, bake crisp in a 350°F oven 35 to 40 minutes.
EACH SERVING *317 cal, 8 g fat, 19 mg chol, 79 mg sodium, 61 g carb, 5 g fiber, 45 g sugars, 4 g pro.*

ROSÉ-POACHED PEACHES

HANDS-ON TIME 10 minutes
TOTAL TIME 20 minutes, plus chilling

- ½ cup rosé wine
- 1 Tbsp. sugar
- 1 tsp. whole black, pink, and/or green peppercorns, crushed
- 1 lb. fresh peaches, pitted and sliced

In a medium saucepan stir together the rosé, sugar, and crushed peppercorns. Bring to boiling; reduce heat. Simmer, uncovered, 5 minutes. Add peaches; stir gently. Return to boiling. Cook, uncovered, 1 minute more. Transfer mixture to a medium bowl. Chill, covered, up to 3 days. Makes 6 servings.
EACH SERVING *54 cal, 1 mg sodium, 10 g carb, 1 g fiber, 9 g sugars, 1 g pro.*
Try it with Ice Cream Spoon over vanilla.
Try it with Toast Serve over toasted bread smeared with goat cheese.
Try it with Shortcake Layer with whipped cream.

PEACH-BERRY HOT
HONEY CRISP

HEIRLOOM
TOMATO
AND GREEN
BEAN SALAD

HEIRLOOM TOMATO AND GREEN BEAN SALAD

HANDS-ON TIME 20 minutes
TOTAL TIME 30 minutes

- 8 oz. green beans, trimmed and chopped (2 cups)
- ¼ cup olive oil
- ½ cup Israeli couscous
- ½ tsp. salt
- 2 lb. assorted heirloom tomatoes, cut into wedges and/or sliced
- 2 cups assorted heirloom cherry tomatoes, halved
- 1½ cups matchstick-size strips jicama, daikon, or radish
- 3 Tbsp. lemon juice
- 3 Tbsp. drained capers
- 3 Tbsp. chopped fresh mint
- 2 Tbsp. chopped fresh parsley
- ¼ tsp. black pepper

1. In a medium saucepan cook green beans in boiling salted water 2 minutes. Drain and rinse under cold water; drain again.

2. Wipe out saucepan. Heat 1 Tbsp. oil over medium heat. Add couscous. Cook and stir 1 to 2 minutes or until lightly browned. Add ⅔ cup water and ¼ tsp. of the salt. Bring to boiling; reduce heat. Simmer, covered, 10 minutes or until tender and water is absorbed. Remove; let stand 5 minutes.

3. Arrange couscous, beans, tomatoes, and jicama on a platter. In a small bowl whisk together lemon juice, capers, mint, parsley, remaining salt, and pepper. Slowly whisk in remaining 3 Tbsp. oil. Pour over salad. Makes 8 servings.

EACH SERVING *148 cal, 7 g fat, 233 mg sodium, 19 g carb, 4 g fiber, 5 g sugars, 4 g pro.*

PLANK-SMOKED TOMATOES

HANDS-ON TIME 5 minutes
TOTAL TIME 1 hour 35 minutes, includes soaking plank

- 1 cedar grilling plank
- 1½ lb. whole ripe tomatoes, halved
- ½ tsp. kosher salt

Soak cedar grilling plank in water 1 to 2 hours; drain. Heat plank on rack of a covered grill directly over medium heat 3 to 5 minutes or until it begins to crackle and smoke. Sprinkle tomatoes with salt. Place on plank on grill rack. Grill, covered, 30 minutes or until softened and lightly browned. Remove; cool slightly. Makes 4 servings.

EACH SERVING *26 cal, 147 mg sodium, 6 g carb, 2 g fiber, 4 g sugars, 1 g pro.*

Try it with Pasta Toss with cooked pasta and shrimp. Drizzle with olive oil and top with fresh oregano.

Try it with Bread Serve on toasted bread spread with ricotta. Sprinkle with sea salt and fresh basil.

Try it with Chicken Serve alongside grilled chicken thighs.

TOMATOES

WHAT TO LOOK FOR A ripe tomato has deep color and gives a little when lightly squeezed.

HOW TO STORE Keep ripe tomatoes in a cool, dark place and use within a few days. Avoid refrigerating: Cold temperatures break down flavor compounds.

PLANK-SMOKED TOMATOES

PREP SCHOOL

Get a head start! Food blogger Tracy Benjamin's plan for a week of good eating and minimal cooking starts with a Sunday game plan.

For Tracy Benjamin, a disorganized fridge can throw the whole week off course. "If I don't corral all those bags of produce, I'll never want to cook," says Tracy, a photographer who chronicles her life in the kitchen on her food blog, Shutterbean. So most Sundays, once breakfast dishes have been cleared, coffee has been consumed, and her 9-year-old son and her husband have gone off to baseball practice or golf, Tracy sets aside a few hours in her San Francisco Bay Area kitchen to act, essentially, as her own sous chef. While she works with a few dinners in mind, her meal-prep strategy is more about preparing building blocks for the week than a precise menu. The goal is to have enough components to pull together any lunch or dinner in a few minutes, which pays off in less wasted food, more family time, and all-around smoother evenings. "I know my fridge can handle whatever the week throws at us," says Tracy.

"A VEGETABLE CHOPPING SESSION ON SUNDAY MEANS JUST ONE CLEANUP, WHICH SAVES A BIG CHUNK OF TIME DURING THE WEEK."

RESET-BUTTON
SALAD

CURRIED
ZUCCHINI
SOUP

RESET-BUTTON SALAD

Tracy Benjamin often puts together this salad on Monday nights to get the week off to a good start. "It helps reset my brain into remembering that healthy food can be so satisfying," she says.

TOTAL TIME 20 minutes

7   cups arugula
1½   cups cooked red quinoa
1   cup peeled and shredded beets
1   cup peeled and shredded carrots
¾   cup toasted walnuts (tip, page 27)
⅔   cup crumbled feta cheese
     Mom's Vinaigrette (recipe, below)

In a large bowl combine arugula, quinoa, beets, carrots, walnuts, and feta. Drizzle with Mom's Vinaigrette. Season to taste with salt and black pepper; toss. Makes 4 servings.

PER SERVING *490 cal, 39 g fat, 22 mg chol, 345 mg sodium, 26 g carb, 6 g fiber, 7 g sugars, 12 g pro.*

Make Ahead Refrigerate prepped ingredients in separate airtight containers: cooked quinoa up to 5 days, beet and carrots 3 days, walnuts 1 month.

MOM'S VINAIGRETTE

Tracy sometimes adds anchovies and Parmesan cheese to this vinaigrette for a simplified Caesar dressing.

TOTAL TIME 10 minutes

½   cup red wine vinegar
1   Tbsp. Dijon-style mustard
2   cloves garlic, minced
1   cup extra-virgin olive oil

In a small bowl whisk together vinegar, mustard, and garlic. Slowly add olive oil, whisking constantly until emulsified. Season to taste with salt and black pepper. Makes 1½ cups.

Make Ahead Refrigerate in an airtight container up to 1 month.

PER 1 TBSP. SERVING *81 cal, 9 g fat, 27 mg sodium.*

CURRIED ZUCCHINI SOUP

HANDS-ON TIME 20 minutes
TOTAL TIME 50 minutes

1   Tbsp. extra-virgin olive oil
1½   cups chopped onion
4   lb. zucchini, cut into 1-inch pieces
1   Tbsp. dried thyme, crushed
4   cups chicken stock
1   cup heavy cream
2   tsp. curry powder
¼   cup butter, melted
¼   cup all-purpose flour
     Homemade croutons

1. In a 6-qt. Dutch oven heat olive oil over medium. Add onion; cook 4 to 5 minutes or until tender. Add zucchini and thyme; cook, covered, 12 minutes or until zucchini is softened, stirring occasionally. Add stock, cream, and curry powder. Bring to boiling. In a small bowl combine melted butter and flour; stir into soup. Reduce heat; cook, uncovered, 15 minutes or until zucchini is tender, stirring occasionally. Let cool slightly.

2. Using an immersion blender, blend soup until creamy. (Or, working in batches, blend in a food processor or blender.) Season to taste with salt and black pepper. Top with croutons. Makes 8 servings.

Homemade Croutons Preheat oven to 350°F. Spread 2 cups cubed sourdough, Italian, or French bread in a single layer in a shallow baking pan. Drizzle with 2 Tbsp. olive oil and sprinkle with ¼ tsp. freshly ground black pepper and ⅛ tsp. kosher salt. Toss to coat. Bake 10 minutes. Stir; bake 8 to 10 minutes more or until crisp and brown, stirring once. Makes 2 cups.

Make Ahead In an airtight container, refrigerate up to 5 days or freeze up to 3 months.

PER SERVING *243 cal, 19 g fat, 49 mg chol, 604 mg sodium, 15 g carb, 3 g fiber, 8 g sugars, 6 g pro.*

A SUNDAY IN THE LIFE

Tracy shares how she gets a typical week's worth of food ready in 2 to 3 hours.

WARMING UP "I hard-boil eggs in my Instant Pot, setting out an ice bath for when they're done. I throw tomatoes in a 400°F oven to roast for 25 minutes. I also form meatballs and pop them in, to get the most mileage out of the hot oven."

CHOPPING "I get into a real rhythm as I chop vegetables. It's almost therapeutic. After prepping ingredients for a vegetable soup—often curried zucchini—and putting it on the stove, I chop vegetables for salads and bread for croutons."

TOASTING TIME "After pulling out the meatballs and tomatoes, I lower the oven to 325°F to toast walnuts for 8 to 10 minutes and croutons for 20."

BLITZING IT "The food processor comes out and pesto gets whirled. While I have a jar out, I'm reminded to make vinaigrette. After cleaning the food processor, I use it to make energy bars."

WRAPPING UP "I finish the soup with an immersion blender, make a quick tuna salad, and put everything away in clear dishes. I might finish by making banana bread or trail mix to treat myself for all the hard work. And now, the cleanup."

**PASTA WITH
ROASTED
TOMATOES AND
ARUGULA PESTO**
Recipe on page 194

GREEN BEAN SALAD
Recipe on page 197

PASTA WITH ROASTED TOMATOES AND ARUGULA PESTO

Photo on page 192.

TOTAL TIME 15 minutes

12   oz. dried spaghetti
1   cup Roasted Tomatoes
½   cup Arugula Pesto (recipe, below)
¼   cup grated Parmesan cheese
    Fresh basil leaves

Cook spaghetti according to package directions. In a large bowl toss together cooked pasta, Roasted Tomatoes, Arugula Pesto, and cheese. Top with basil. Makes 4 servings.

Roasted Tomatoes Place 6 roma tomatoes on a baking pan. Drizzle with 1 Tbsp. olive oil. Lightly season with salt and black pepper. Bake in a 400°F oven 25 minutes or until tomatoes are tender and beginning to char.

PER SERVING *517 cal, 21 g fat, 5 mg chol, 165 mg sodium, 68 g carb, 4 g fiber, 4 g sugars, 15 g pro.*

ARUGULA PESTO

Tracy says, "This pesto is delicious on everything—stirred into scrambled eggs and pasta or spread on sandwiches."

TOTAL TIME 15 minutes

2   cloves garlic, peeled
6   cups arugula
1   cup fresh basil leaves
1   cup toasted walnuts (tip, page 27)
½   cup extra-virgin olive oil
3   Tbsp. grated Parmesan cheese
2   Tbsp. lemon juice
½   tsp. salt
¼   tsp. black pepper

In a food processor chop garlic. Add arugula and basil; process until minced. Add walnuts, olive oil, cheese, lemon juice, salt, and pepper. Process until smooth and creamy. Makes 1⅔ cups.

PER 1 TBSP. *71 cal, 7 g fat, 33 mg sodium, 1 g carb, 1 g pro.*

CHICKEN-ZUCCHINI MEATBALLS

Double this recipe and freeze one batch for speedy 20-minute dinners like the meatball subs, right.

HANDS-ON TIME 20 minutes
TOTAL TIME 1 hour 5 minutes

1   cup finely shredded zucchini
¼   tsp. salt
1   lb. ground chicken
1   egg, lightly beaten
½   cup panko
½   cup grated Parmesan cheese
2   cloves garlic, minced
1   Tbsp. chopped fresh parsley
2   tsp. dried basil, crushed
¼   tsp. crushed red pepper

1. Preheat oven to 350°F. Line a 15×10-inch baking pan with foil; coat with nonstick cooking spray.
2. Line a colander with paper towels; add zucchini. Sprinkle ⅛ tsp. salt over zucchini. Let stand 20 minutes, pressing occasionally to remove moisture.
3. In a large bowl combine zucchini, chicken, egg, panko, cheese, garlic, parsley, basil, crushed red pepper, and remaining ⅛ tsp. salt. Shape rounded tablespoons of mixture into 20 meatballs; place in prepared pan. Bake 25 minutes or until cooked through (165°F). Makes 20 meatballs.

PER MEATBALL *103 cal, 5 g fat, 61 mg chol, 175 mg sodium, 3 g carb, 10 g pro.*

Make Ahead Refrigerate in an airtight container up to 5 days or freeze up to 3 months.

CHICKEN-ZUCCHINI MEATBALL SUBS

"Having meatballs on hand gives us all kinds of options," Tracy says. She works her chicken-zucchini version into pasta, salads, her son's lunch box, or—along with purchased marinara and crusty rolls—weeknight subs.

TOTAL TIME 20 minutes

4   hoagie rolls, split
1   cup shredded mozzarella cheese, (4 oz.)
12   Chicken-Zucchini Meatballs (recipe, left)
12   cups purchased marinara sauce
¼   cup shredded fresh basil

1. Preheat oven to 425°F. Place rolls on a baking sheet. Sprinkle insides with 2 Tbsp. cheese each. Bake 5 to 8 minutes or until lightly toasted.
2. Meanwhile, place meatballs and sauce in a medium saucepan. Bring to boiling; reduce heat. Simmer, uncovered, 3 to 5 minutes (10 minutes if frozen) or until meatballs are heated through, stirring occasionally.
3. Spoon meatballs and sauce onto toasted rolls. Top with remaining cheese. Bake 3 minutes more or until cheese is melted. Top with basil. Makes 4 subs.

PER SUB *574 cal, 17 g fat, 108 mg chol, 1,528 mg sodium, 74 g carb, 5 g fiber, 10 g sugars, 33 g pro.*

CHICKEN-ZUCCHINI
MEATBALL SUBS

HIPPIE
BANANA BREAD

WHEN TRACY HAS RIPE BANANAS, THEY GO INTO THIS BREAD, DENSE WITH NUTRIENTS FROM WALNUTS, PEPITAS, SUNFLOWER SEEDS, AND DRIED CHERRIES. SHE SAYS, "MY FAMILY IS REALLY HAPPY WHEN THERE'S BANANA BREAD ON THE COUNTER. WHO AM I TO DENY THEM?"

GREEN BEAN SALAD

Photo on page 193.

Tracy uses Mom's Vinaigrette recipe (page 191) to dress all her salads.

TOTAL TIME 15 minutes

- 12 oz. green beans, trimmed
- ¼ cup sliced almonds, toasted (tip, page 27)
- 2 Tbsp. chopped fresh mint
- 3 Tbsp. Mom's Vinaigrette (recipe, page 185)

Place a steamer basket in a large saucepan or skillet; add water to just below basket. Add green beans. Cover and bring to boiling. Steam 7 minutes or until crisp-tender. Top with almonds and mint. Drizzle with Mom's Vinaigrette. Makes 4 servings.

PER SERVING *122 cal, 10 g fat, 26 mg sodium, 7 g carb, 3 g fiber, 3 g sugars, 3 pro.*

LEMON-PARSLEY TUNA SALAD

TOTAL TIME 15 minutes

- 2 5-oz. cans solid white tuna (water pack), drained
- ⅓ cup plain Greek yogurt
- ¼ cup toasted walnuts, chopped (tip, page 27)
- ¼ cup minced red onion
- ¼ cup sweet pickle relish
- 1 Tbsp. Dijon-style mustard
- 1 Tbsp. chopped fresh parsley
- 1 tsp. lemon zest
  Salt and black pepper

In a medium bowl stir together all ingredients. Season to taste with salt and pepper. Makes 2 cups.

PER ½ CUP *177 cal, 7 g fat, 31 mg chol, 554 mg sodium, 8 g carb, 1 g fiber, 6 g sugars, 20 g pro.*

HEALTHY ENERGY BARS

HANDS-ON TIME 20 minutes
TOTAL TIME 4 hours 20 minutes, includes freezing

- 1½ cups cashews
- ¼ cup regular rolled oats
- 6 Medjool dates, pitted and chopped
- 2 Tbsp. maple syrup
- 1 Tbsp. instant espresso powder
- ¼ tsp. sea salt
- ½ cup chopped toasted walnuts (tip, page 27)
- ⅓ cup chopped bittersweet chocolate

1. In a food processor process cashews and oats 30 seconds or until chopped. Add dates, maple syrup, espresso powder, and salt; process 30 seconds or until mixture resembles cookie dough. Add walnuts and chocolate; process 20 seconds or until combined.
2. Line an 8-inch square baking pan with parchment, extending parchment over two sides of pan. Place oat mixture in pan; top with another piece of parchment. Press evenly into pan. Remove parchment from top of bars. Cover with plastic; freeze 4 hours. Using parchment, lift out of pan. Cut into 2-inch bars. Makes 16 bars.

PER BAR *138 cal, 9 g fat, 37 mg sodium, 15 g carb, 2 g fiber, 10 g sugars, 3 g pro.*

Make Ahead Refrigerate in an airtight container up to 5 days or freeze up to 2 months.

HIPPIE BANANA BREAD

Tracy's husband jokingly coined this bread "hippie" because of the abundance of good-for-you ingredients.

HANDS-ON TIME 20 minutes
TOTAL TIME 1 hour 30 minutes

- 1 cup all-purpose flour
- ½ cup almond flour
- 1 tsp. baking soda
- 1 tsp. salt
- ¼ tsp. ground cinnamon
- ½ cup olive oil
- ½ cup packed brown sugar
- ¼ cup maple syrup
- 1½ tsp. vanilla
- 2 eggs
- 3 ripe bananas, mashed (about 1 cup)
- ½ cup chopped toasted walnuts (tip, page 27)
- ½ cup dried cherries
- ¼ cup raw sunflower kernels
- ¼ cup pepitas

1. Preheat oven to 350°F. Butter an 8×4-inch loaf pan. Line with parchment paper, extending parchment over two sides of pan. Lightly butter parchment.
2. In a bowl combine flours, baking soda, salt, and cinnamon.
3. In a large bowl stir together olive oil and brown sugar, breaking up any lumps. Add maple syrup and vanilla; stir until smooth. Add eggs, one at a time, stirring well after each addition. Stir in bananas. Add flour mixture, stirring just until combined. Stir in walnuts, cherries, sunflower kernels, and pepitas. Spoon batter into pan.
4. Bake 1 hour or until a toothpick inserted in the center comes out clean. Cool in pan on wire rack 10 minutes. Using parchment, lift bread out of pan. Remove parchment; cool completely. Makes 12 slices.

PER SLICE *334 cal, 19 g fat, 31 mg chol, 318 mg sodium, 37 g carb, 3 g fiber, 21 g sugars, 6 g pro.*

CREAM PUFFS WITH CHOCOLATE SAUCE
Recipe on page 206

september

This month we're talking flavor—and lots of it. Memorable weeknight meals and French chocolate desserts. Learn how uncomplicated truly good food can be with lessons from the pros.

202

205

211

FAST & FRESH

Easy, healthful recipes for a better dinner tonight.

MEET ANNA KOVEL With 25-plus years as a cook in restaurants and test kitchens, Anna shares how to think on your feet, cook in season, and use what's on hand to keep meals interesting.

TUNA MELTS WITH OLIVES AND LEMON

The Strategy: Stock the pantry with protein. Cans of oil-packed tuna (or salmon, sardines, or chickpeas) provide the makings of a spontaneous dinner. "Tuna packed in oil has a firmer, silkier texture than water-packed. You'll notice there's no mayo. Instead, use the oil the tuna comes in to give this salad rich flavor, plus a lot of lemon to brighten it."

TOTAL TIME 25 minutes

- 8   thick slices artisanal Italian bread
- 3   5-oz. cans tuna packed in olive oil
- ¼   cup each pitted green olives, chopped
- ¼   cup cornichons, chopped
- 1   large lemon (2 tsp. zest; 1 Tbsp. juice)
- 2   tsp. Dijon-style mustard
- ¼   tsp. black pepper
- ¼   lb. havarti cheese, thinly sliced
       Watercress (optional)

1. Preheat broiler. Arrange bread slices on a baking sheet. Broil 4 inches from heat 2 minutes or until lightly toasted, turning once. In a medium bowl combine undrained tuna, olives, cornichons, lemon zest and juice, mustard, and pepper. Stir to combine and to break up tuna.
2. Divide tuna mixture among bread slices; top with cheese. Broil 1½ to 2 minutes or until cheese is melted. If desired, top with watercress. Makes 4 servings.
PER SERVING *644 cal, 24 g fat, 75 mg chol, 1,397 mg sodium, 58 g carb, 4 g fiber, 4 g sugars, 44 g pro.*

CHICKEN AND VEGETABLE GREEN CURRY

The Strategy: Clean out the fridge. A one-pot curry calls for small amounts of leftovers. "Vary the ingredients to use what you have," Anna says. "Spinach could be added in place of mustard greens, and tofu or shrimp instead of chicken."

HANDS-ON TIME 20 minutes
TOTAL TIME 45 minutes

1 Tbsp. vegetable oil
3 Tbsp. Thai green curry paste
¼ cup thinly sliced red onion
4 cups 1½-inch pieces eggplant and/or zucchini
1 14-oz. can unsweetened coconut milk
4 oz. green beans, trimmed and chopped
1 cup corn kernels
3 cups chopped mustard greens
2 cups shredded cooked chicken
1 tsp. salt
1 lemon, half juiced, half cut into wedges

1. In a 5- to 6-qt. pot heat oil over medium-high. Add curry paste; cook and stir 1 minute or until fragrant. Add onion and a pinch of salt. Cook 2 minutes. Add eggplant and/or zucchini; cook 6 to 7 minutes or until golden brown, stirring occasionally.

2. Stir in coconut milk and 2½ cups water. Bring to boiling over high heat. Add green beans and corn. Reduce heat to medium-low. Simmer, uncovered, 5 minutes or until vegetables are tender. Stir in greens, chicken, and salt. Heat through. Stir in lemon juice. Serve with lemon wedges. Makes 4 servings.

PER SERVING *509 cal, 25 g fat, 25 mg chol, 730 mg sodium, 64 g carb, 17 g fiber, 14 g sugars, 16 g pro.*

THE STRATEGY: MAKE A BIG BATCH. COOK A POT OF SEASONED BLACK BEANS AND KEEP IN 2-CUP PORTIONS AS THE BASE FOR QUICK MEALS.

STEAK AND BLACK BEAN BURRITO

Anna makes her own quick salsa for these burritos. She combines half a chopped white onion, one 4-oz. can fire-roasted diced green chiles, a squeeze of lime juice, and salt.

HANDS-ON TIME 30 minutes
TOTAL TIME 1 hour

1   tsp. ground cumin
1   tsp. dried oregano
1   tsp. ground chili
1   tsp. coarse salt
8   oz. sirloin steak
4   tsp. vegetable oil
¾   cup sliced white onion
1   tsp. cumin seeds, crushed
1   clove garlic, minced
2   cups Big-Batch Black Beans (recipe, right)
4   large flour tortillas, warmed
    Toppings, such as chopped cherry tomatoes, sour cream, shredded cheese, and/or salsa (optional)

1. For the spice mix, in a small bowl stir together the first four ingredients (through salt). Pat steak dry; rub with spice mix. Let stand 30 minutes. In a skillet heat 2 tsp. oil over medium-high heat. Add steak. Cook 5 minutes or until browned. Turn; cook 3 to 5 minutes more or until steak is medium rare (145°F). Remove; let rest. Add onion and a pinch salt to hot skillet. Reduce heat to medium; cook and stir 7 minutes or until golden brown and softened.
2. Meanwhile, heat a small saucepan over medium-high. Add cumin seeds; cook and stir 1 minute or until fragrant. Add 2 tsp. oil and garlic. Reduce heat to medium; cook 1 minute. Stir in beans and ½ cup of their cooking liquid; heat through. Fill tortillas with sliced steak, onion, beans, and desired toppings. Makes 4 servings.
PER SERVING *503 cal, 13 g fat, 29 mg chol, 1,071 mg sodium, 69 g carb, 11 g fiber, 4 g sugars, 29 g pro.*

BIG-BATCH BLACK BEANS

You can always turn to canned black beans, but Anna makes them and seasons them as she likes.

HANDS-ON TIME 20 minutes
TOTAL TIME 1 hour 10 minutes, plus overnight soaking

2   lb. dried black beans, rinsed
    Fresh herb sprigs, such as oregano, thyme, and/or cilantro
1   medium white onion, halved
2   garlic cloves, peeled
1   bay leaf
½   cinnamon stick
1   dried ancho chile
1   Tbsp. coarse salt

1. Add beans to an 8-qt. pot; add cold water to cover by 4 inches. Refrigerate overnight. (To quick-soak: Boil water rapidly 1 minute. Remove from heat. Let stand, covered, 1 hour.)
2. Tie herb stems together with kitchen string. Add onion, garlic, bay leaf, cinnamon stick, ancho chile, and herbs to the beans. Add additional cold water to cover by 4 inches. Bring to boiling; reduce heat to medium-low. Simmer, uncovered, 45 minutes or just until tender, stirring occasionally. Add 1 Tbsp. coarse salt. Cook 20 to 30 minutes more or until beans are soft but not falling apart. Let cool in cooking liquid. Discard bay leaf, cinnamon, chile, and herbs. Makes 10 cups.
PER ½-CUP *627 cal, 3 g fat, 682 mg sodium, 115 g carb, 28 g fiber, 5 g sugars, 39 g pro.*

RECIPE IDEAS: USE THEM UP

Divide beans and the cooking liquid into small portions. Refrigerate up to 5 days or freeze up to 6 months. Here are Anna's favorite ways to turn them into full meals.

RICE BOWL Add cooked sweet peppers, onions, or poblano peppers to the mix. "I love the mild heat and bitterness of poblanos. I char the peppers a bit to soften them."

QUESADILLAS "For a vegetarian option, I might add a little sweet potato with the beans." She tosses 1-inch sweet potato rounds with oil, salt, pepper, and a little chili powder, then roasts them until tender. Chop into small pieces before adding to quesadillas.

HEARTY SOUP "If you have enough liquid, you don't even need broth." Using an immersion blender, she whirls the beans in their cooking liquid until smooth, then salts to taste. Top with a dollop of sour cream, diced red onion, and hot sauce.

**BIG-BATCH
BLACK BEANS**

**STEAK AND BLACK
BEAN BURRITO**

AU CHOCOLAT

We asked cookbook author, former pastry chef, and Paris transplant David Lebovitz to help us interpret chocolate with a French accent.

In the world of chocolate desserts, the classic French recipes hold a kind of iconic status. Mousse that's somehow both cloudlike and almost too intense to bear. Impossibly fudgy flourless chocolate cake. All that decadence (and names like gâteau victoire) sometimes comes with a side of intimidation. But mastering these treats is easier than it sounds.

If you need a few French chocolate lessons, David Lebovitz is your guy. "Chocolate occupies my thoughts nearly every day," he says. After close to two decades as a pastry chef, David moved to Paris to devote himself to writing full time. (He has published six cookbooks, including *The Great Book of Chocolate*.) He has spent the past 15 years exploring Paris and its food—tasting, testing, and sharing discoveries on his blog at davidlebovitz.com. We like to think of him as a modern-day Julia Child, translating French cooking and baking for another generation of American home cooks.

FLOURLESS CHOCOLATE CAKE (GÂTEAU VICTOIRE)

"Because this cake has only six ingredients, the chocolate shines. Use your favorite bittersweet chocolate or experiment with different cacao percentages," David says. Typically, the higher the percentage, the stronger the chocolate flavor. (For baking, David recommends staying between 55 and 70 percent cacao.)

HANDS-ON TIME 25 minutes
TOTAL TIME 3 hours 30 minutes, includes cooling

    Natural unsweetened or Dutch-process cocoa powder for dusting pan and topping cake
12 oz. bittersweet or semisweet chocolate (55 to 70 percent cacao), chopped
¾ cup heavy cream
3 Tbsp. coffee-flavor liqueur (such as Kahlúa), strong coffee, or 1 tsp. instant espresso powder
6 large eggs, at room temperature
6 Tbsp. sugar

1. Preheat oven to 350°F. Butter a 9-inch springform pan. Line bottom with parchment paper; butter paper. Dust pan with cocoa powder. Wrap bottom and sides of pan with an 18-inch-wide sheet of heavy foil. (This ensures no water gets into pan during baking.)

2. Set a large heatproof mixing bowl over a medium saucepan of simmering water, being careful that water doesn't touch bottom of bowl. Add chopped chocolate, heavy cream, and liqueur to bowl. Heat 8 minutes or until melted, smooth, and glossy, stirring occasionally. Remove bowl from heat; let cool 30 minutes.

3. In a large mixing bowl beat eggs and sugar with a mixer on high 5 minutes or until thick and light in color. (To test: Lift mixture from bowl; a ribbon will form as it falls back into bowl.) Working in three batches, gently fold egg mixture into chocolate mixture. Transfer to prepared pan.

4. Place springform pan in a roasting pan on oven rack. Add enough hot water to reach halfway up sides of springform pan. Bake 40 minutes or until top is evenly set across surface. Remove roasting pan; let stand 2 minutes. Transfer springform pan to a wire rack. Remove foil; let cool completely at room temperature (2 to 3 hours).

5. Transfer cake from pan to a serving platter. Dust top with additional cocoa powder. To ease slicing, wet and wipe knife clean between cuts. Makes 12 slices.

Make Ahead Cover loosely with plastic and refrigerate up to 3 days. Let stand at room temperature 1 hour before serving.
PER SLICE *277 cal, 20 g fat, 113 mg chol, 48 mg sodium, 24 g carb, 2 g fiber, 19 g sugars, 5 g pro.*

"CHOCOLATE IS THE MOST UNIVERSALLY PROVOKING AND ADDICTIVE FLAVOR," SAYS DAVID.

"SAUCES ARE FORGIVING, SO YOU CAN EXPERIMENT WITH HIGHER CACAO PERCENTAGES. YOU'LL BE SURPRISED HOW THEY IMPACT FLAVOR AND TEXTURE."

DAVID'S SECRETS

Two standout ingredients—corn syrup and cocoa powder—contribute to the characteristic syruplike consistency and intense color of this sauce.

WINNING TEXTURE Corn syrup is unconventional in French cooking but David adds it to give this sauce bright sheen and luxurious body. You can substitute agave syrup.

RICH COLOR "Pastry chefs often use unsweetened cocoa powder in combo with other chocolates to add dimension and achieve a deeper, darker final color," David says.

CREAM PUFFS WITH CHOCOLATE SAUCE (PÂTE À CHOUX AVEC SAUCE CHOCOLAT)

"Of all the sauces I've made, this is the most versatile—rich in taste, super glossy, and not loaded with butter or cream. I love how it goes with anything—cream puffs, chocolate cake, ice cream—or alone by the spoonful."

HANDS-ON TIME 30 minutes
TOTAL TIME 1 hour 10 minutes

½   cup unsalted butter, room
    temperature, cut up
¼   tsp. salt
1   cup all-purpose flour
4   large eggs
2   oz. bittersweet or semisweet
    chocolate (55 to 70 percent cacao),
    chopped
¾   cup natural unsweetened or
    Dutch-process cocoa powder
½   cup sugar
¼   cup light-color corn syrup or agave
    nectar
3   cups vanilla ice cream
¼   cup sliced almonds, toasted (tip,
    page 27)

1. Preheat oven to 425°F. Line a baking sheet with parchment paper.
2. For cream puffs: In a medium saucepan combine 1 cup water, the butter, and salt. Cook and stir over high heat until butter is melted.
3. Add flour all at once. Stir vigorously until dough forms a smooth ball that doesn't separate or stick to sides of pan. Remove from heat. Transfer dough to bowl of a stand mixer fitted with paddle attachment; let rest 2 minutes. Add eggs, one at a time, beating until well combined after each addition.
4. Drop dough by heaping tablespoons 1 inch apart onto prepared baking sheet to make 12 puffs. Bake 5 minutes. Reduce oven to 375°F. Bake 30 minutes more or until golden brown; rotate baking sheet once during the last 7 minutes of baking. Transfer to a wire rack; let cool.
5. For chocolate sauce: Place chopped chocolate in a small bowl. In a medium saucepan combine ¾ cup water, the cocoa powder, sugar, and corn syrup. Bring to boiling over high heat, whisking until smooth. Pour over chopped chocolate. Let stand 5 minutes. Whisk until smooth. Cover with plastic until ready to use. Store any remaining sauce in refrigerator up to 10 days.
6. Split cream puffs; fill with ice cream. Top with chocolate sauce and almonds. Makes 12 cream puffs.
PER CREAM PUFF *363 cal, 22 g fat, 132 mg chol, 113 mg sodium, 40 g carb, 3 g fiber, 27 g sugars, 7 g pro.*

"A PERFECT MOUSSE STICKS TO YOUR TASTE BUDS THEN HITS YOU WITH A WALLOP OF PURE CHOCOLATE FLAVOR. IT NEITHER NEEDS NOR WANTS ADORNMENT," DAVID SAYS.

CHOCOLATE MOUSSE (MOUSSE AU CHOCOLAT)

The base of this mousse is a custard known as crème anglaise.

HANDS-ON TIME 15 minutes
TOTAL TIME 2 hours 45 minutes , includes chilling

- ¾ cup whole milk
- 2 Tbsp. sugar
- 4 egg yolks
- 10 oz. bittersweet or semisweet chocolate (55 to 70 percent cacao), finely chopped
- 2 tsp. rum or Cognac
- ½ cup heavy cream

1. To make crème anglaise: In a medium saucepan heat milk and sugar over medium 1 to 2 minutes or until 130°F, stirring occasionally. In a large bowl whisk egg yolks until smooth. Slowly pour warm milk into yolks, whisking constantly. Pour mixture back into saucepan; cook over medium heat 5 minutes or until crème anglaise thickens and coats the back of a spoon (169°F to 173°F), stirring constantly. Do not allow crème anglaise to boil.

2. Place chopped chocolate in a large bowl. Strain crème anglaise through a fine-mesh sieve over chocolate. Let stand 1 minute. Stir until chocolate has melted and mixture is smooth. Stir in rum. Let cool 30 minutes.

3. In a large bowl beat cream with a mixer on medium up to 2 minutes or until soft, droopy peaks form. Do not overbeat. Cream should move loosely in bowl.

4. Fold one-third of chocolate mixture into whipped cream. Fold whipped cream mixture into chocolate mixture just until there are no visible streaks. Chill, covered, at least 2 hours before serving. Makes 8 servings.

PER SERVING *296 cal, 23 g fat, 111 mg chol, 18 mg sodium, 24 g carb, 2 g fiber, 19 g sugars, 5 g pro.*

DAVID'S SECRETS

"Classic French mousse recipes call for melting the chocolate over a double boiler, which can lead to overheating or graininess."

EASY MELTING Skip the double boiler. Instead, David prepares a hot custard and strains it onto chopped chocolate; its heat does the melting.

THE RIGHT SIZE Finely chop the chocolate (smaller than ½ inch). "Avoid using chips; many are designed to keep their shape and not melt."

FEELING YOUR OATS

Make the morning hustle easy and nutritious. Bake a pan of delicious break-apart oat crisps on Sunday to crunch or throughout the week.

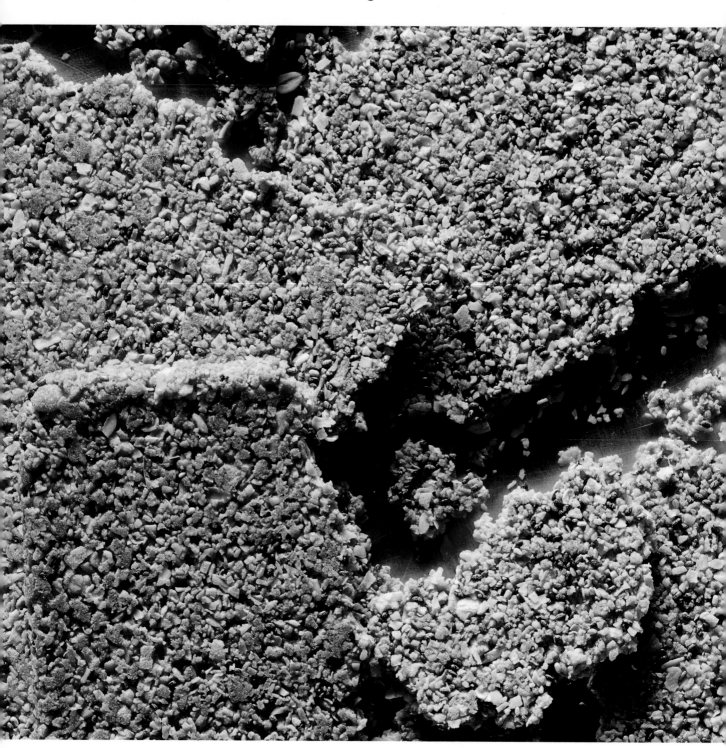

1. CEREAL Crumble and serve with milk and fresh berries.

COCONUT-CHIA OAT CRISPS

Chia seeds are rich in omega-3 fatty acids, fiber, and protein. Or opt for flaxseed meal (ground flaxseed), which gives the crisps a nutty flavor and crumbly texture.

HANDS-ON TIME 20 minutes
TOTAL TIME 1 hour 40 minutes

Nonstick cooking spray
1 cup regular rolled oats
½ cup oat bran
½ cup flaked or shredded coconut
⅓ cup packed brown sugar
¼ cup whole wheat flour
3 Tbsp. almond or peanut butter
1 Tbsp. honey
⅛ tsp. baking soda
⅛ tsp. salt
2 Tbsp. chia seeds or flaxseed meal

1. Preheat oven to 325°F. Coat a 15×10-inch baking pan with nonstick cooking spray. In a food processor combine oats, oat bran, coconut, brown sugar, and flour. Process until finely ground. Add nut butter, 2 Tbsp. water, the honey, baking soda, and salt. Process until combined. Transfer mixture to a large bowl. Stir in chia seeds. (Mixture will be crumbly.)
2. Press oat mixture firmly into prepared pan. Bake 18 to 20 minutes or until golden. Cool in pan on a wire rack. (Mixture crisps as it cools.)
3. Release oat crisp from pan. Break into pieces. Store in an airtight container at room temperature up to 1 week. Makes 8 servings.
PER SERVING *169 cal, 7 g fat, 73 mg sodium, 25 g carb, 5 g fiber, 9 g sugars, 5 g pro.*

2. PARFAIT Top a cup of yogurt and fresh fruit with pieces.

3. TOAST Smear large chunks with nut butter and top with banana slices.

how Ayesha Curry scores
BIG WITH FLAVOR

By day she runs a growing food empire. By night she's committed to putting nutritious, high-flavor meals on the table for her family. The wife of NBA star Stephen Curry is a master of the balancing act.

For Ayesha Curry, a memorable meal is home-cooked and full of flavor. Author of The New York Times best-selling cookbook *The Seasoned Life* and host and executive producer of ABC's upcoming Family Food Fight, Ayesha has become known for her ability to reinvent menu staples with high-impact seasonings and unique ingredient combinations. "Steph and I look at our calendars every weekend and carve out a few nights each week when we can cook together and reconnect as a family over a meal," says Ayesha.

HARISSA-SPICED CHICKEN

"Smoky flavors have become a part of my palette, and smoked paprika is a nice way to introduce that essence," says Ayesha, who pairs the spice with harissa (a spicy Middle Eastern blend of chiles, cumin, and garlic) and chili powder to add kick to chicken thighs.

HANDS-ON TIME 15 minutes
TOTAL TIME 1 hour 25 minutes

¼ cup olive oil
2 Tbsp. harissa seasoning or paste
1 large lemon (1 Tbsp. zest; 2 Tbsp. juice)
1 Tbsp. honey
1 tsp. ground cumin
1 tsp. smoked paprika
1 tsp. chili powder
4 cloves garlic, minced
6 bone-in, skin-on chicken thighs (2½ to 3 lb.)
2 garlic bulbs, halved horizontally
½ tsp. salt
½ tsp. black pepper
¼ cup chopped fresh Italian parsley

1. Preheat oven to 400°F. Line a 15×10-inch baking pan with foil.

2. In a bowl stir together olive oil, harissa, lemon juice, honey, cumin, smoked paprika, chili powder, and half the minced garlic.
3. Place chicken, skin sides up, and garlic bulbs in prepared pan; spoon harissa mixture over all. Sprinkle with salt and pepper. Chill, covered, 30 minutes.
4. Bake 35 minutes or until done (175°F). Squeeze roasted garlic bulbs to release cloves into a bowl. Turn oven to broil; broil chicken 5 inches from heat 1 to 2 minutes or until skin browns. Top chicken with lemon zest, remaining minced garlic, and the parsley. Serve with roasted garlic cloves. Makes 6 servings.
PER SERVING *513 cal, 39 g fat, 184 mg chol, 346 mg sodium, 6 g carb, 1 g fiber, 3 g sugars, 32 g pro.*

ROASTED RED PEPPER RICE

HANDS-ON TIME 30 minutes
TOTAL TIME 1 hour

2 red sweet peppers
1 Tbsp. butter
1 Tbsp. olive oil
1 to 2 cloves garlic, minced
1½ cups uncooked jasmine rice
2 to 3 tsp. smoked paprika
2 cups chicken broth
1 large lemon (1 Tbsp. zest; 2 Tbsp. juice)
1 1-inch piece fresh ginger, peeled
¼ tsp salt
¼ tsp. black pepper

1. Preheat broiler. Line a baking sheet with foil. Cut peppers in half; remove stems and seeds. Place, cut sides down, on prepared baking sheet. Broil 4 inches from heat 5 to 10 minutes or until charred. Wrap in foil; let stand 20 minutes. Remove skins; finely chop peppers.

2. In a large saucepan heat butter and olive oil over medium-high. Add garlic; cook 1 to 2 minutes or until fragrant and soft. Add rice and paprika. Cook 1 to 2 minutes more, stirring occasionally. Add chopped peppers, broth, 1 cup water, the lemon zest and juice, ginger, salt, and black pepper.
3. Bring to boiling; reduce heat. Simmer, covered, 20 to 25 minutes or until rice is tender and liquid has been absorbed. Remove from heat; discard ginger. Season to taste with additional salt and black pepper. Makes 6 servings.
PER SERVING *215 cal, 4 g fat, 5 mg chol, 563 mg sodium, 39 g carb, 1 g fiber, 1 g sugars, 3 g pro.*

KALE, HALLOUMI, AND PEACH SALAD

Prosciutto and Halloumi cheese, plus peaches and pecans, inspire the girls to eat this salad. Working olive oil into kale by hand tenderizes the leaves.

HANDS-ON TIME 25 minutes
TOTAL TIME 40 minutes

3 oz. very thinly sliced prosciutto (about 8 slices) or bacon
½ cup olive oil, plus 1 Tbsp.
1 lemon (2 tsp. zest; 1 Tbsp. juice)
1 Tbsp. lime juice
1 Tbsp. orange juice
1 Tbsp. balsamic vinegar
1 small shallot, finely chopped
1 Tbsp. honey
1 tsp. Dijon-style mustard
1 clove garlic, minced
½ tsp. black pepper
6 cups stemmed and coarsely chopped fresh kale
2 peaches, pitted and sliced
½ cup crumbled Halloumi cheese or feta cheese
¼ cup toasted pecans, coarsely chopped (tip, page 27)
Salt

1. Preheat oven to 350°F. Place prosciutto slices on a nonstick baking sheet without overlapping. Bake 15 minutes or until crisp; let cool. Break into pieces.

2. For citrus vinaigrette: In a screw-top jar combine the ½ cup olive oil, lemon zest, citrus juices, vinegar, shallot, honey, mustard, garlic, and pepper. Cover; shake.

3. Place kale and 1 Tbsp. oil in a bowl. Massage kale until softened. Top with half the peaches, cheese, and pecans. Toss with vinaigrette. Season with salt. Top with remaining peaches, cheese, and pecans, and prosciutto. Makes 8 servings.

PER SERVING *260 cal, 21 g fat, 9 mg chol, 397 mg sodium, 12 g carb, 3 g fiber, 7 g sugars, 8 g pro.*

BRAISED CABBAGE AND CARROTS

"My family loves the combo of cabbage and carrots in this dish. And seasonings like cumin make the vegetables exciting," Ayesha says.

HANDS-ON TIME 15 minutes
TOTAL TIME 35 minutes

2   Tbsp. olive oil
½   cup chopped onion
1   to 2 cloves garlic, minced
1   medium head green cabbage, cored and coarsely sliced (10 cups)
½   medium head purple cabbage, cored and coarsely sliced (5 cups)
8   oz. baby carrots with tops, trimmed and quartered lengthwise
2   cups vegetable stock or chicken stock
1   tsp. dried thyme, crushed
1   tsp. smoked paprika
1   tsp. ground cumin
    Salt and black pepper

In an 8-qt. Dutch oven heat olive oil over medium-high. Add onion and garlic; cook 1 minute or until fragrant and soft. Add cabbages, carrots, stock, thyme, paprika, and cumin. Bring to boiling; reduce heat to medium-low. Cook, covered, 20 to 25 minutes or until cabbage is tender. Season with salt and pepper. Makes 8 servings.

PER SERVING *87 cal, 4 g fat, 287 mg sodium, 12 g carb, 4 g fiber, 7 g sugars, 2 g pro.*

OLIVE OIL AND ROSEMARY LOAF

HANDS-ON TIME 15 minutes
TOTAL TIME 1 hour, plus cooling

Nonstick cooking spray
2¼   cups all-purpose flour
2   tsp. baking powder
1   Tbsp. finely chopped fresh rosemary
1   Tbsp. sugar
1½   tsp. salt
1   cup milk
2   eggs
¼   cup olive oil
2   cloves garlic, minced
    Fresh rosemary sprigs
    Sea salt flakes

1. Preheat oven to 350°F. Coat a 9×5-inch loaf pan with nonstick cooking spray.

2. In a bowl combine flour, baking powder, rosemary, sugar, and salt.

3. In a bowl whisk together milk, eggs, olive oil, and garlic. Add flour mixture to egg mixture. Stir to combine. (Dough will be wet.) Using a spatula dusted with flour, transfer dough to prepared pan. Press rosemary sprigs on top; sprinkle with sea salt flakes. Bake 40 to 45 minutes or until golden and a toothpick inserted near center comes out clean. Let cool 10 minutes. Remove from pan; cool. Makes 16 slices.

PER SLICE *114 cal, 4 g fat, 24 mg chol, 296 mg sodium, 15 g carb, 1 g fiber, 2 g sugars, 3 g pro.*

CINNAMON DROP BISCUITS

HANDS-ON TIME 20 minutes
TOTAL TIME 35 minutes

2   cups all-purpose flour
1   Tbsp. baking powder
1   tsp. granulated sugar
1   tsp. salt
10   Tbsp. cold unsalted butter, cut up
1¼   cups buttermilk
1   tsp. vanilla
2   Tbsp. melted butter
2   Tbsp. packed brown sugar
1   tsp. ground cinnamon

1. Preheat oven to 400°F. Line a baking sheet with parchment paper.

2. In a large bowl combine flour, baking powder, granulated sugar, and salt. Using a pastry blender, cut in cold butter until mixture resembles coarse crumbs. Make a well. Stir in buttermilk and vanilla just until combined.

3. Drop dough into ¼-cup mounds onto prepared baking sheet to form 12 biscuits. Brush with melted butter. In a small bowl combine brown sugar and cinnamon; sprinkle over tops. Bake 15 to 17 minutes or until golden brown and a toothpick comes out clean. Let cool. Makes 12 biscuits.

PER BISCUIT *200 cal, 12 g fat, 32 mg chol, 281 mg sodium, 20 g carb, 1 g fiber, 4 g sugars, 3 g pro.*

Make Ahead Freeze biscuits in an airtight container up to 3 weeks. To thaw, bake 10 minutes at 350°F.

PEAR-HONEY SORBET

HANDS-ON TIME 15 minutes
TOTAL TIME 1 hour 30 minutes, plus overnight freezing

1   lb. pears, such as Bartlett, peeled, cored, and sliced (about 2½ cups)
½   cup sugar
¼   cup honey
1   to 2 Tbsp. chopped candied ginger
1   Tbsp. lemon juice

1. In a saucepan combine pears, 1 cup water, the sugar, honey, candied ginger, and lemon juice. Bring to boiling; reduce heat. Simmer, uncovered, 10 to 15 minutes or until pears are soft and begin to break apart. Remove from heat; let cool. (You will have about 2¼ cups pears and liquid.)

2. Transfer to a blender; blend until smooth. Freeze in an airtight container overnight or until firm. Makes 4 servings.

PER SERVING *237 cal, 5 mg sodium, 61 g carb, 3 g fiber, 52 g sugars.*

CANDY CORN
CUPCAKES
Recipe on page 228

october

Treat yourself to cooking lessons: easy-to-prep delicata squash, Spanish-style fare, and fun to make (and eat) Halloween sweets. See what's new with the *New Cook Book.*

220

238

240

say hello to
DELICATA SQUASH

In the world of winter squash, having thin skin is good.

KALE, FENNEL,
AND ROASTED
DELICATA SALAD

KALE, FENNEL, AND ROASTED DELICATA SALAD

HANDS-ON TIME 15 minutes
TOTAL TIME 40 minutes

- 1 lb. delicata squash, washed, halved lengthwise, seeded (reserve seeds), and cut into 1-inch slices
- ¼ cup olive oil plus 4 tsp.
- ¼ cup golden raisins
- 1 Tbsp. sherry vinegar
- 2 Tbsp. lemon juice
- 1 Tbsp. white miso paste
- 1 small clove garlic, minced
- 6 cups curly kale, stemmed and leaves torn
- 1 small fennel bulb, trimmed, quartered, cored, and thinly sliced (¾ cup)

1. Preheat oven to 450°F. Place squash in a shallow baking pan. Drizzle with 1 Tbsp. of the olive oil; sprinkle with ½ tsp. salt and ¼ tsp. black pepper. Roast 10 minutes; turn over. Roast 10 minutes more or until brown and tender. Remove squash; set aside pan. Reduce oven to 400°F.

2. Meanwhile, wash seeds in cold water to remove all pulp; pat dry. In same baking pan toss together seeds, 1 tsp. olive oil, ⅛ tsp. salt, and ⅛ tsp. black pepper. Bake 5 minutes or until toasted.

3. For pickled raisins: In a small microwave-safe bowl combine raisins, vinegar, and 1 Tbsp. water. Microwave on high 1 minute or until bubbly. Let cool.

4. For miso-lemon vinaigrette: In a bowl whisk together lemon juice, miso paste, and garlic until smooth. Whisking constantly, gradually add remaining ¼ cup olive oil until emulsified.

5. In a large bowl toss kale, squash, and fennel with miso-lemon vinaigrette. Place on platter. Spoon pickled raisins over; top with toasted seeds. Makes 4 servings.

PER SERVING *285 cal, 19 g fat, 538 mg sodium, 26 g carb, 6 g fiber, 15 g sugars, 7 g pro.*

CROSTINI WITH DELICATA SQUASH BUTTER

CROSTINI WITH DELICATA SQUASH BUTTER

HANDS-ON TIME 30 minutes
TOTAL TIME 1 hour

- 1¾ to 2 lb. delicata squash, washed, trimmed, halved lengthwise, and seeded
- 5 Tbsp. olive oil plus 1 tsp.
- 1 bulb garlic, plus 1 clove, halved
- ½ cup fresh sage leaves
- 1 cup thinly sliced shallots
- 30 ½-inch slices baguette
- 2 lemons (1 Tbsp. zest; 2 tsp. juice)
- ½ 15-oz. container whole-milk ricotta cheese

1. Preheat oven to 425°F. Place squash halves cut sides up in a shallow baking pan; brush with 1 Tbsp. olive oil. Sprinkle with ¼ tsp. salt and ⅛ tsp. black pepper. Cut ½ inch off tip of garlic bulb to expose cloves. Remove loose outer layers. Add to baking pan. Drizzle with 1 tsp. olive oil. Bake 30 to 40 minutes or until squash is very tender; let cool.

2. Meanwhile, in a small saucepan heat remaining 4 Tbsp. olive oil over medium. In two batches, cook sage 30 seconds or until crisp. Use a slotted spoon to transfer to a plate lined with paper towels. In two batches, cook shallots 3 to 5 minutes or until crisp. Transfer to plate with sage. Sprinkle all with ⅛ tsp. salt. Pour shallot-sage oil into a bowl.

3. Preheat broiler. Brush both sides of bread slices with shallot-sage oil; set aside remaining oil. Place bread on a baking sheet; broil 3 to 4 inches from heat 1 to 2 minutes or until golden brown, turning once. Rub toasts with halved garlic clove; sprinkle with ⅛ tsp. salt.

4. For Delicata Butter: Squeeze roasted garlic cloves from bulb into a food processor. Spoon squash pulp into the food processor. Pulse until smooth. Add lemon juice, ⅛ tsp. salt, and ⅛ tsp. black pepper. Pulse until combined.

5. In a bowl stir together reserved shallot-sage oil, lemon zest, cheese, ¼ tsp. salt, and ¼ tsp. black pepper.

6. Spread Delicata Butter on toasts. Top with cheese spread, fried sage, and fried shallots. Makes 30 crostini.

PER CROSTINI *142 cal, 7 g fat, 7 mg chol, 275 mg sodium, 16 g carb, 1 g fiber, 2 g sugars, 5 g pro.*

CRISPY DELICATA
RINGS WITH HERBED
BUTTERMILK DIP
Recipe on page 220

**PORK, GINGER,
AND DELICATA
STIR-FRY**
Recipe on page 220

DELICATA SQUASH, KNOWN FOR ITS DELICATE EDIBLE RIND, HAS A SWEET, NUTTY TASTE REMINISCENT OF A SWEET POTATO.

CRISPY DELICATA RINGS WITH HERBED BUTTERMILK DIP

Photo on page 218.

HANDS-ON TIME 30 minutes
TOTAL TIME 55 minutes

   Nonstick cooking spray
¼   cup all-purpose flour
½   cup mayonnaise
⅓   cup buttermilk
1   Tbsp. Dijon-style mustard
1½ cups panko
2   Tbsp. chopped fresh Italian parsley
½   tsp. salt
½   tsp. black pepper
1½ lb. delicata squash, washed, trimmed, seeded,* and cut into ½-inch rings
   Herbed Buttermilk Dip

1. Preheat oven to 400°F. Line two large baking sheets with foil; coat with nonstick cooking spray.
2. Place flour in a shallow dish. In a second dish combine mayonnaise, buttermilk, and mustard. In a third dish combine panko, parsley, salt, and pepper.
3. One ring at a time, dip in flour; shake off excess. Dip in mayo mixture; let excess drip back into dish. Coat with panko mixture. Place on prepared baking sheet.
4. Bake 15 minutes or until bottoms begin to brown. Turn rings; rotate pans. Bake 8 to 10 minutes more or until brown and tender; cool 5 minutes. Serve warm with Herbed Buttermilk Dip. Makes 8 to 10 servings.
*Tip Use a melon baller or spoon to scoop seeds from ends of squash.
Herbed Buttermilk Dip In a small bowl combine ½ cup plain Greek yogurt and ¼ cup buttermilk. Stir in 1 Tbsp. chopped fresh chives; 1 Tbsp. chopped fresh Italian parsley; 2 tsp. chopped fresh dill weed; 2 cloves garlic, minced; ½ tsp. onion powder; ⅛ tsp. salt; and ¼ tsp. black pepper. Makes ¾ cup.
PER SERVING *124 cal, 7 g fat, 5 mg chol, 275 mg sodium, 12 g carb, 1 g fiber, 4 g sugars, 4 g pro.*

PORK, GINGER, AND DELICATA STIR-FRY

Photo on page 219.

TOTAL TIME 45 minutes

¾   cup reduced-sodium chicken broth
¼   cup reduced-sodium soy sauce
2   Tbsp. rice vinegar
1   Tbsp. balsamic vinegar
1   Tbsp. red curry paste
3   Tbsp. vegetable oil
1   tsp. crushed red pepper
½   lb. pork tenderloin, cut into 1-inch cubes
3   cloves garlic, minced
1   Tbsp. grated fresh ginger
1   lb. delicata squash, washed, trimmed, quartered lengthwise, seeded, and cut into 1-inch pieces
6   oz. green beans, trimmed and cut into 1-inch pieces
6   green onions, trimmed and cut into 1-inch pieces
   Hot cooked rice

1. For sauce: In a small bowl combine broth, soy sauce, vinegars, and curry paste.
2. In an extra-large skillet heat 1 Tbsp. oil over medium-high. Add crushed red pepper; cook and stir 30 seconds. Add pork cubes; cook and stir 2 to 3 minutes or just until edges are brown but centers are still pink. Add garlic and ginger; cook and stir 1 minute. Transfer to a plate.
3. In the same skillet heat 1 Tbsp. oil over medium-high. Add squash; cook and stir 7 minutes or until browned and tender. Transfer to plate with pork.
4. In the same skillet heat remaining 1 Tbsp. oil over medium-high. Add green beans. Cook and stir 3 minutes. Add green onions; cook 2 to 3 minutes or until browned and blistered. Reduce heat to medium; add sauce, squash, and pork. Bring to boiling; reduce heat. Simmer, uncovered, 3 to 4 minutes or until pork is cooked through and sauce begins to thicken. Serve over rice. Makes 4 servings.
PER SERVING *329 cal, 12 g fat, 37 mg chol, 789 mg sodium, 35 g carb, 4 g fiber, 8 g sugars, 19 g pro.*

BAKED DELICATA EGG CUPS WITH CRISPY HERBED CRUMBS

HANDS-ON TIME 25 minutes
TOTAL TIME 1 hour

3   Tbsp. olive oil
1   large clove garlic, gently smashed and peeled
½   cup coarse fresh bread crumbs*
¾   tsp. salt
¼   tsp. black pepper
¼   cup finely shredded Parmesan cheese
1   Tbsp. chopped fresh Italian parsley
1   lb. delicata squash, washed and trimmed
4   eggs
   Hot sauce (optional)

1. Preheat oven to 425°F. In an 8- or 9-inch cast-iron or oven-safe skillet heat 2 Tbsp. olive oil over medium heat. Add garlic; cook 3 to 4 minutes or until golden brown, turning occasionally. Remove garlic; finely chop. Add bread crumbs to skillet; cook 4 minutes or until golden. Transfer to a small bowl; stir in chopped garlic, ¼ tsp. salt, and ⅛ tsp. black pepper; let cool. Stir in cheese and parsley.
2. Cut squash into four 1¾- to 2-inch rings. Using a spoon or melon baller, scoop out seeds and flesh to shape a 1½- to 2-inch-diameter cup.
3. Wipe skillet. Add remaining 1 Tbsp. olive oil, then add squash, turning to coat with oil. Sprinkle with ¼ tsp. salt. Bake 15 minutes; turn squash. One at a time, crack an egg into a small cup or bowl; slide into a squash ring. Repeat with remaining eggs. Sprinkle eggs with remaining ¼ tsp. salt and ⅛ tsp. black pepper. Bake 10 to 12 minutes or until whites are set. Top with crumb mixture. If desired, serve with hot sauce. Makes 4 servings.
*Tip For fresh bread crumbs, pulse 1 slice bread in a food processor.
EACH SERVING *218 cal, 17 g fat, 190 mg chol, 629 mg sodium, 7 g carb, 1 g fiber, 3 g sugars, 10 g pro.*

BAKED DELICATA
EGG CUPS WITH
CRISPY HERBED
CRUMBS

SWEET & SPOOKY

Have no fear—the tricks to these playful Halloween treats are fun, creative, and worthy of cheers.

HAUNTED HOUSE

A 10-inch chocolate sugar cookie cutout is the base for this hair-raising home. Decorate with chocolate graham shutters, stick candy pillars, plus candy corn and pumpkin landscaping. For dramatic effect, prop it up by affixing stands.

START TO FINISH 4 hours

	Pattern pieces, page 224
1	cup butter, softened
1	cup sugar
1	egg
½	tsp. vanilla
2	cups all-purpose flour
¾	cup unsweetened cocoa powder
	Pinch of salt
	Desired-color hard rectangular candies
	Chocolate-flavor candy coating, melted
	Cocoa-Cream Cheese Frosting (recipe, page 225) or canned chocolate frosting
	Assorted candy corn, candy pumpkins, and/or stick candy
	Black, chocolate, and orange decorating icing

1. Copy and cut out pattern pieces; cover with contact paper or plastic wrap.

2. In a large bowl beat butter and sugar with a mixer on medium until combined. Beat in egg and vanilla. In a small bowl whisk together the flour, cocoa powder, and salt. Gradually add flour mixture to butter mixture, beating until a soft dough forms. Shape dough into a ball. Chill 30 minutes.

3. Preheat oven to 350°F. Line a cookie sheet with parchment paper. Roll dough between two pieces of parchment paper to ¼-inch thickness.

4. Remove parchment paper from rolled dough. Arrange House and Chimney pattern pieces on dough, leaving at least 1 inch between each. With a sharp paring knife, cut dough around pattern pieces and place on prepared baking sheet. Remove scraps; reroll as needed. If desired, cut additional rectangles to make door panels and shutters. To stand the house, cut two 3×2-inch rectangles.

5. Bake 12 minutes or until firm. Cool on parchment paper.

6. For windows, line a baking sheet with foil. Crush colored hard candies. Bake candies on prepared sheet 5 minutes or until melted; let cool. Break into pieces large enough to fill windows. Drizzle with melted chocolate-flavor candy coating to resemble broken glass; let cool until chocolate is set. Attach windows to back of cookie with melted candy coating. Pipe panes on windows using chocolate decorating icing.

7. Spread Cocoa-Cream Cheese Frosting or purchased chocolate frosting to resemble roof shingles. Using frosting, attach baked pieces or chocolate graham crackers for front door, shutters, and chimney.

8. Attach candy corn, candy pumpkin, and stick candy for pillars and landscaping using additional melted chocolate candy coating. Pipe on details using black, chocolate, and orange decorating icing. Let stand until icing is set.

9. To stand house, attach each rectangle to the back of the house at a 90° angle with a generous amount of melted candy coating. Be sure the stands are perfectly parallel so the house does not fall over. To keep the house upright until chocolate sets, support the house between heavy objects, such as canned food.

MADE OF MELTED HARD CARAMEL CANDIES, THESE WINDOWS EERILY GLOW.

HAUNTED HOUSE PATTERNS

Photo on page 222.

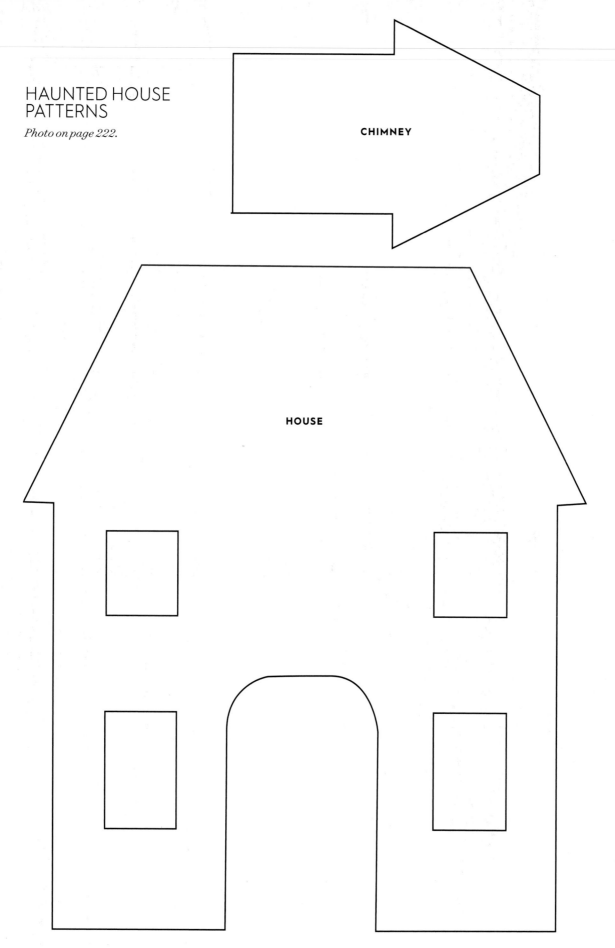

CHIMNEY

HOUSE

SPIRITED COOKIES

Make easy ghostly embellishments. Swipe an offset spatula through large dots of frosting, pipe chocolate frosting with a small round tip for eyes and mouth.

HANDS-ON TIME 50 minutes
TOTAL TIME 1 hour 10 minutes

- 1   cup butter, softened
- 1   cup sugar
- 1   egg
- ½   tsp. vanilla
- 2   cups all-purpose flour
- ¾   cup unsweetened cocoa powder
      Pinch salt
      Creamy White Frosting or canned white frosting
      Cocoa-Cream Cheese Frosting or canned chocolate frosting

1. In a large bowl beat butter and sugar with a mixer on medium until combined. Beat in egg and vanilla. In a small bowl whisk together flour, cocoa powder, and salt. Gradually beat flour mixture into butter mixture until a soft dough forms. Working on a lightly floured surface, shape dough into a ball. Chill 30 minutes.

2. Roll dough between two pieces of parchment to ¼-inch thickness. Preheat oven to 350°F. Line cookie sheets with parchment paper.

3. Remove top sheet of parchment from dough. Use a 2½-inch round cutter to cut dough. Place 2 inches apart on prepared sheets. Bake 10 to 12 minutes or until firm and slightly crisp. Let cool.

4. Using a pastry bag fitted with a large round tip or a plastic bag with a corner snipped off, pipe three large dollops of Creamy White Frosting. Using an offset spatula pull from center of dollop toward edge of cookie to shape ghosts. Pipe on dots of Cocoa-Cream Cheese Frosting for ghost-eyes and mouth. Cover and refrigerate leftover frostings for another use. Makes 48 servings.

PER SERVING *155 cal, 8 g fat, 19 mg chol, 51 mg sodium, 21 g carb, 1 g fiber, 15 g sugar, 1 g pro.*

Creamy White Frosting In a large bowl beat 1 cup shortening, 1½ tsp. vanilla, and ½ tsp. almond extract with a mixer on medium 30 seconds. Gradually add 2 cups powdered sugar, beating well. Add 2 Tbsp. milk. Gradually beat in 2 cups additional powdered sugar and 1 to 2 Tbsp. additional milk to reach spreading consistency. Makes 3 cups.

Cocoa-Cream Cheese Frosting In a large mixing bowl beat one 8-oz. pkg. cream cheese, softened; ½ cup butter, softened; and 2 tsp. vanilla with a mixer on medium until light and fluffy. Gradually beat in 5 cups powdered sugar and ½ cup unsweetened cocoa powder to reach spreading consistency. Makes 3½ cups.

CREEPY
COBWEB
BARK

CREEPY COBWEB BARK

Form silky strands for the chocolate web by pulling a toothpick through concentric circles of melted white chocolate on a base of melted milk chocolate. Halved black raspberry gummy candies and black licorice bear an eerie resemblance to the real deal.

HANDS-ON TIME 20 minutes
TOTAL TIME 50 minutes, including chilling

- 6 oz. chocolate candy coating, chopped (1 cup)
- 6 oz. milk chocolate, chopped (1 cup)
- 1 Tbsp. shortening
- 4 oz. white baking chocolate, chopped
  Black raspberry gummy candies, halved
  Black licorice, cut into 1- to 2-inch pieces

1. Line a large baking sheet with heavy foil; grease foil.
2. In a large microwave-safe bowl combine chocolate candy coating, milk chocolate, and shortening. Microwave, uncovered, 1½ to 2 minutes or until melted, stirring every 30 seconds.
3. Pour melted chocolate onto prepared baking sheet. Spread to a circle about ¼ inch thick.
4. In a separate microwave-safe bowl, microwave white baking chocolate 30 to 60 seconds or until melted, stirring every 15 seconds. Transfer melted white chocolate to a piping bag fitted with a small open tip or a plastic bag; snip off a small corner. Pipe concentric circles on chocolate. Pull a toothpick or a bamboo skewer from center to outer edges, wiping toothpick between each pull. To resemble spiders, top chocolate with gummy candy and licorice.
5. Chill until firm, about 30 minutes. Use foil to lift from baking sheet. Serve intact, letting your guests serve themselves or break into pieces to serve. Refrigerate leftover candy between layers of waxed paper in an airtight container up to 2 weeks. Makes 36 servings.

EACH SERVING *77 cal, 4 g fat, 2 mg chol, 26 mg sodium, 10 g carb, 8 g sugar, 1 g pro.*

MONSTER MASH CUPCAKES

MONSTER MASH CUPCAKES

Dip pretzel sticks into candy melts, attach candy eyes, then tuck among spikes of creamy frosting.

HANDS-ON TIME 40 minutes
TOTAL TIME 1 hour 45 minutes, including cooling

- 2 cups all-purpose flour
- ¾ cup unsweetened cocoa powder
- 1 tsp. baking soda
- ¾ tsp. baking powder
- ½ tsp. salt
- ¾ cup butter, softened
- 2 cups sugar
- 3 eggs
- 2 tsp. vanilla
- 1½ cups milk
  Creamy White Frosting (recipe, page 225) or canned white frosting
  Green food coloring
- 48 to 60 pretzel sticks
  White candy coating, melted
- 48 to 60 candy eyeballs

1. Preheat oven to 350°F. Line twenty-four to thirty 2½-inch muffin cups with paper bake cups.
2. In a medium bowl stir together flour, cocoa powder, baking soda, baking powder, and salt. In a large bowl beat butter with a mixer on medium 30 seconds. Gradually beat in sugar, ¼ cup at a time, until combined. Scrape sides of bowl; beat 2 minutes more. Add eggs, one at a time, beating well after each addition. Beat in vanilla. Alternately add flour mixture and milk to butter mixture, beating on low after each just until combined.
3. Spoon batter into prepared muffin cups, filling each about two-thirds full.
4. Bake 18 to 22 minutes or until a toothpick inserted near centers comes out clean. Cool cupcakes in pan 5 minutes. Remove from pans. Cool on wire racks.
5. To decorate, tint frosting green. Using a pastry bag fitted with a large round tip or plastic bag with one corner snipped, pipe long spikes on cupcakes. Dip pretzel sticks in melted coating and attach candy eyeballs while still moist. Insert two pretzels into each cupcake. Let stand until set. Makes 24 servings.

EACH SERVING *352 cal, 16 g fat, 40 mg chol, 201 mg sodium, 50 g carb, 1 g fiber, 39 g sugar, 13 g pro.*

CANDY CORN CUPCAKES

Pipe frosting in colorful layers to mimic iconic candy corn, then crown it with the real thing.

HANDS-ON TIME 40 minutes
TOTAL TIME 1 hour 45 minutes, including cooling

- 2½ cups all-purpose flour
- 2½ tsp. baking powder
- ½ tsp. salt
- ¾ cup butter, softened
- 1¾ cups sugar
- 3 eggs, room temperature
- 1½ tsp. vanilla
- 1¼ cups milk
  Creamy White Frosting (recipe, page 225) or canned white frosting
  Orange and yellow food coloring
  Candy corn (optional)

1. Preheat oven to 350°F. Line twenty-four to thirty 2½-inch muffin cups with paper bake cups.
2. In a medium bowl stir together flour, baking powder, and salt. In a large bowl beat butter with a mixer on medium 30 seconds. Gradually beat in sugar, ¼ cup at a time, until combined. Scrape sides of bowl; beat 2 minutes more. Add eggs, one at a time, beating well after each addition. Beat in vanilla. Alternately add flour mixture and milk to butter mixture, beating on low after each just until combined.
3. Spoon batter into prepared muffin cups, filling each about two-thirds full.
4. Bake 18 to 22 minutes or until a toothpick inserted near center comes out clean. Cool in pans 5 minutes. Remove from pans; cool on wire racks.
5. To decorate, divide frosting into three portions. Tint one portion orange, one portion yellow, and leave remaining portion white. Using separate pastry bags fitted with a large round tip or plastic bags with one corner snipped, pipe frosting onto each cupcake, stacking colors like candy corn. If desired, top with a candy corn. Makes 24 servings.

EACH SERVING *327 cal, 15 g fat, 40 mg chol, 162 mg sodium, 46 g carb, 1 g fiber, 385 g sugar, 3 g pro.*

CHOCOLATE SPIDEY CUPCAKES

These lovable spiders have Mallomar® bodies and licorice laces for legs (chocolate frosting holds them in place). Make eyes from halved tiny marshmallows and dragées affixed with frosting.

HAND-ON TIME 40 minutes
TOTAL TIME 1 hour 55 minutes, including cooling and standing

- 2½ cups all-purpose flour
- 2½ tsp. baking powder
- ½ tsp. salt
- ¾ cup butter, softened
- 1¾ cups sugar
- 3 eggs
- 1½ tsp. vanilla
- 1¼ cups milk
  Cocoa-Cream Frosting (recipe, page 225) or canned chocolate frosting
  Black shoestring licorice
- 48 chocolate-covered marshmallow cookies (such as Mallomars)
  Tiny marshmallows
  Black sugar pearl dragées

1. Preheat oven to 350°F. Line forty-eight 1¾-inch muffin cups with paper bake cups.
2. In a medium bowl stir together flour, baking powder, and salt. In a large bowl beat butter with a mixer on medium 30 seconds. Gradually beat in sugar, about ¼ cup at a time, until combined. Scrape sides of bowl; beat 2 minutes more. Add eggs, one at a time, beating well after each addition. Beat in vanilla. Alternately add flour mixture and milk to butter mixture, beating on low after each just until combined.
3. Spoon batter into prepared muffin cups, filling each about two-thirds full.
4. Bake 10 to 12 minutes or until a toothpick inserted near center comes out clean. Cool in pans 5 minutes. Remove from pans; let cool on wire racks.
5. To decorate, frost cupcakes with frosting. For legs, press short pieces of licorice into frosting on each side. Top each with cookies. For eyes, cut marshmallows in half; attach a dragée to each with frosting. Attach eyes to cookies with frosting. Makes 48 servings.

EACH SERVING *248 cal, 9 g fat, 30 mg chol, 162 mg sodium, 40 g carb, 1 g fiber, 29 g sugar, 2 g pro.*

NINE-EYED CREATURE CUPCAKES

Decorate a beastly mane with a profusion of googly eyes—the more the spookier!

HANDS-ONE TIME 40 minutes
TOTAL TIME 1 hour 45 minutes, including cooling

- 2 cups all-purpose flour
- ¾ cup unsweetened cocoa powder
- 1 tsp. baking soda
- ¾ tsp. baking powder
- ½ tsp. salt
- ¾ cup butter, softened
- 2 cups sugar
- 3 eggs
- 2 tsp. vanilla
- 1½ cups milk
  Creamy White Frosting (recipe, page 225) or canned white frosting
  Blue food coloring
  Assorted sizes candy eyeballs

1. Preheat oven to 350°F. Line twenty-four to thirty 2½-inch muffin cups with paper bake cups.
2. In a medium bowl stir together flour, cocoa powder, baking soda, baking powder, and salt. In a large bowl beat butter with a mixer on medium 30 seconds. Gradually beat in sugar, ¼ cup at a time, until combined. Scrape sides of bowl; beat 2 minutes more. Add eggs, one at a time, beating well after each. Beat in vanilla. Alternately add flour mixture and milk to butter mixture, beating on low after each just until combined.
3. Spoon batter into prepared muffin cups, filling each about two-thirds full.
4. Bake 18 to 22 minutes or until a toothpick inserted near center comes out clean. Cool cupcakes in pan 5 minutes. Remove from pans; let cool on wire racks.
5. To decorate, tint frosting blue. Using a pastry bag fitted with a medium star tip, pipe short spikes on cupcakes. Attach candy eyeballs while frosting is still moist. Makes 24 servings.

EACH SERVING *335 cal, 16 g fat, 40 mg chol, 180 mg sodium, 48 g carb, 1 g fiber, 38 g sugar, 3 g pro.*

CANDY CORN CUPCAKES

CHOCOLATE SPIDEY CUPCAKES

NINE-EYED CREATURE CUPCAKES

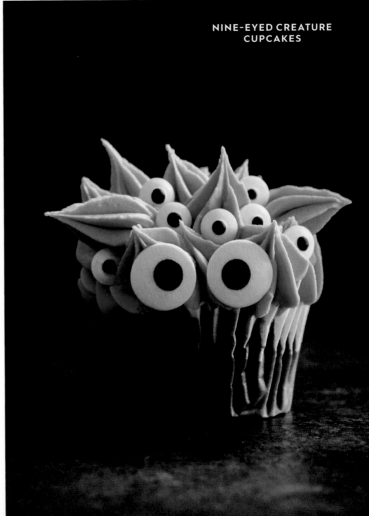

MIMIC CANDY CORN'S YELLOW, ORANGE, AND WHITE BY PIPING LAYERS OF FROSTING WITH A LARGE ROUND TIP. NOT CREEPY, JUST SWEET, THIS THRILLER GETS ITS MANE FROM A STAR PIPING TIP. THE MORE CANDY EYES, THE MORE BEASTLY.

SPANISH LESSONS

As temperatures turn cool in Upstate New York, this creative couple shows how to celebrate—with a Spanish-style paella party.

"Paella is a party waiting to happen," says Mario Pollan of the dish that's a frequent centerpiece of dinners that he and his partner, Daniel Buenos, host at their home in Westerlo, New York. "It's one of those versatile, colorful, anything-goes comfort foods that has minimal prep and no last-minute fussing. The pan goes from stove to table, and everyone helps themselves, so we feel like guests rather than hosts." Actually, hosting comes naturally to these two event planners. They regularly coordinate weddings and private parties at M&D Farm, 58 acres of fields and gardens around their 1800s farmhouse and wisteria-covered barn.

Paella, too, comes naturally to Daniel, who grew up in Andalusia (a region of southern Spain), where he says there are as many paellas as there are cooks, and most recipes are handed down. His came from his grandmother, and he has tweaked it along the way. His current version is by no means classic. For example, rather than traditional short grain bomba rice, he prefers parboiled rice because it retains its shape as it soaks up wine and spice flavors. For an extra-smoky dimension, he usually adds a roasted vegetable—in this case it's Brussels sprouts. Depending on the season, it could be zucchini or asparagus.

When fall sets in and friends gather around a table in the couple's open-sided barn, Daniel's paella is the highlight of a relaxed evening that stretches over several courses. Daniel and Mario set out a bounty of Spanish-style appetizers on a big round table to encourage mingling. Bowls of pumpkin soup signal time to make way to the dining table. Then Daniel brings out the paella, a crisp radicchio and roasted butternut squash salad, and a fennel salad. Guests top off their glasses and the conversation flows. "In my family, we savored our food while we savored each other's company," Daniel says. "We enjoy continuing that custom."

PORK AND CHICKEN PAELLA WITH BRUSSELS SPROUTS

"IN MY FAMILY, WE SAVORED OUR FOOD WHILE WE SAVORED EACH OTHER'S COMPANY," DANIEL SAYS. "WE ENJOY CONTINUING THAT CUSTOM."

PORK AND CHICKEN PAELLA WITH BRUSSELS SPROUTS

Converted, or parboiled, rice has been soaked, steamed, and dried in the husk to stay firmer and less sticky when cooked—which is ideal for paella.

HANDS-ON TIME 20 minutes
TOTAL TIME 40 minutes

Roasted Brussels Sprouts
6   Tbsp. olive oil
1   lb. pork loin (center cut), cut into 1-inch pieces
1   lb. skinless, boneless chicken breasts, cut into 1-inch pieces
1   large red, green, and/or yellow sweet pepper, cut into 1-inch pieces
3   Tbsp. minced garlic
1   Tbsp. fresh thyme leaves
1   bay leaf
1   Tbsp. sweet paprika
1   tsp. black pepper
¼   cup dry white wine
1   8-oz. can tomato sauce
2½   cups uncooked converted rice
1   cup chicken broth
½   tsp. salt

1. Prepare Roasted Brussels Sprouts. Meanwhile, in a 15-inch paella pan,* heat olive oil over medium. Add pork and chicken. Cook and stir 2 to 3 minutes or until browned. Transfer to a bowl; set aside. Add sweet pepper to pan; cook and stir 2 minutes or until softened. Add garlic, thyme, bay leaf, paprika, and pepper; cook and stir 1 minute. Add wine; cook 30 seconds. Add tomato sauce and ¼ cup water; cook and stir 1 minute. Stir in rice.
2. Return pork and chicken to pan. Add 4 cups water, the chicken broth, and salt. Bring to boiling. Cook, uncovered, over high 18 minutes or until most of the liquid is evaporated. Add Roasted Brussels Sprouts. Reduce heat to medium; cook 2 minutes more. Turn off heat. Cover; let stand 5 minutes. Discard bay leaf. To make a crust, aka socarrat,** reheat on high, without stirring, 1 to 2 minutes or until edges look dry. Makes 8 servings.
Roasted Brussels Sprouts Preheat oven to 425°F. Place 1 lb. halved Brussels sprouts in a shallow baking pan. Add 2 Tbsp. olive oil, ½ tsp. salt, and ½ tsp. black pepper; toss to coat. Roast 20 minutes or until tender and brown, stirring once.
PER SERVING *491 cal, 14 g fat, 73 mg chol, 473 mg sodium, 56 g carb, 3 g fiber, 3 g sugars, 34 g pro.*

*Tip A paella pan is wide and flat to ensure rice cooks evenly. If you don't have one, use a heavy 12- to 14-inch skillet with 2- to 2½-inch depth.
**Socarrat is the crusty bottom of a paella, a result of brief high heat to slightly caramelize rice in the bottom of the dish. Some cooks find socarrat highly desirable.

RADICCHIO AND ROASTED BUTTERNUT SQUASH SALAD

HANDS-ON TIME 20 minutes
TOTAL TIME 45 minutes

¼   cup extra virgin olive oil
¼   cup sherry vinegar or apple cider vinegar
1   small shallot, finely chopped
2   tsp. chopped fresh oregano plus more for topping
1   tsp. fennel seeds, crushed
1   tsp. honey
½   tsp. salt
½   tsp. black pepper
½   medium butternut squash, peeled and sliced into 2-inch wedges (or 2 cups cubed)
1   to 2 heads radicchio (12 to 14 oz. total)
1   medium fennel bulb, cored and thinly sliced (1 cup)
3   Tbsp. roasted, salted pepitas or almonds

1. Preheat oven to 400°F. For vinaigrette: In a small bowl whisk together olive oil, vinegar, shallot, oregano, fennel seeds, honey, salt, and black pepper.
2. In a 15×10-inch baking pan toss squash in 2 Tbsp. vinaigrette. Bake, uncovered, 25 to 30 minutes, stirring once, or until tender and starting to brown; let cool.
3. Coarsely chop radicchio; place in a large mixing bowl. Add squash and fennel slices. Toss with remaining vinaigrette. Top with pepitas and additional oregano. Makes 6 to 8 servings.
PER SERVING *148 cal, 11 g fat, 137 mg sodium, 12 g carb, 2 g fiber, 3 g sugars, 3 g pro.*

PORK AND CHICKEN
PAELLA WITH
BRUSSELS SPROUTS

RADICCHIO
AND ROASTED
BUTTERNUT
SQUASH SALAD

SHRIMP IN
GARLIC-PEPPER
SAUCE

TORTILLA
ESPAÑOLA

DANIEL SERVES HOMEMADE SPECIALTIES—
GARLICKY SHRIMP AND TORTILLA ESPAÑOLA
COMPLEMENTED BY READY-TO-SERVE NIBBLES:
BREADSTICKS, POTATO CHIPS, ANCHOVIES AND
OLIVES, LOCAL CHEESES, AND PAPER-THIN SLICES
OF PROSCIUTTO.

SHRIMP IN GARLIC-PEPPER SAUCE

In Spain, this dish is traditionally cooked in a shallow clay casserole known as a cazuela. The glazed interior of this dish is appreciated for retaining heat.

TOTAL TIME 25 minutes

1   lb. large fresh or frozen shrimp in shells (12 count)
½   cup olive oil
1   bulb garlic, halved crosswise
¼   tsp. black peppercorns
1   Fresno or jalapeño chile peppers, stemmed and thinly sliced (tip, page 17)
⅛   tsp. salt
⅛   tsp. paprika
1   Tbsp. chopped fresh Italian parsley
    Crusty bread for dipping

1. Thaw shrimp, if frozen. Peel and devein shrimp, leaving tails intact. Pat dry with paper towels.
2. In a 10-inch skillet or clay pot (follow manufacturer's instructions) add olive oil, garlic, shrimp (in an even layer), peppercorns, chile pepper, salt, paprika, and parsley. Heat over medium until oil begins to bubble. Cook 2 minutes or until garlic is golden brown and shrimp is opaque, stirring occasionally. Remove from heat. Serve with crusty bread. Makes 6 servings.
PER SERVING *298 cal, 20 g fat, 122 mg chol, 287 mg sodium, 14 g carb, 1 g fiber, 1 g sugars, 18 g pro.*

TORTILLA ESPAÑOLA

This potato omelet is a classic Spanish tapa.

HANDS-ON TIME 25 minutes
TOTAL TIME 1 hour

2   cups vegetable oil
¼   cup olive oil
1½ lb. russet potatoes, peeled and cut into ½-inch pieces
1½ cups chopped onion
½   tsp. salt
5   thin slices Serrano ham or prosciutto, halved crosswise
1   fresh mild chile pepper, such as Cubanelle or Anaheim, stemmed, seeded, and cut into ½-inch strips (tip, page 17)
8   large eggs

1. In a 10-inch skillet heat oils over medium 10 to 15 minutes or until oil reaches 350°F. Meanwhile, in a large bowl toss together potatoes, onion, and ¼ tsp. of the salt.
2. Working in two batches, cook ham in hot oil 1 minute or until browned, carefully turning once (oil may splatter). Transfer to a plate lined with paper towels. Add pepper strips to skillet. Cook 2 minutes or until lightly browned and softened. Transfer to plate with ham.

3. Increase heat to medium-high. Carefully add potato-onion mixture. Cook 15 minutes or until tender and golden brown, stirring occasionally. (If necessary, reduce heat to medium to prevent overbrowning.) Using a slotted spoon, transfer potato-onion mixture to a bowl. Drain all but 3 Tbsp. oil from skillet. Reheat oil in skillet over medium.
4. In a large bowl whisk together eggs and remaining ¼ tsp. salt. Stir in potato-onion mixture. Transfer to hot skillet. Cook 10 minutes, running a spatula around edge of skillet and lifting egg mixture so uncooked portion flows underneath. When bottom is browned and top is still slightly moist in center, invert onto a 12-inch plate. Using a wide spatula, slide back into skillet. Cook 5 minutes more or until browned. Invert onto a clean plate. Top with ham and peppers. Makes 8 servings.
PER SERVING *359 cal, 26 g fat, 189 mg chol, 326 mg sodium, 23 g carb, 2 g fiber, 3 g sugars, 10 g pro.*

THE ROASTED WHOLE PUMPKIN SERVING "BOWL" HAS SEASONAL APPEAL WHILE INTENSIFYING THE FLAVOR OF THE CREAMY SAVORY SOUP.

PUMPKIN SOUP WITH MANCHEGO CROUTONS

HANDS-ON TIME 30 minutes
TOTAL TIME 3 hours 10 minutes

1 2½-lb. fresh pie pumpkin or one 15-oz. can pumpkin
½ lb. rustic bread, cut into 1-inch cubes
1 oz. Manchego cheese, finely shredded (¼ cup)
3 Tbsp. olive oil
1½ cups chopped onion
4 cloves garlic, minced
3 cups reduced-sodium chicken broth
1 medium russet potato, peeled and chopped
4 oz. Gruyère cheese, shredded (1 cup)
¼ cup heavy cream
1 tsp. salt
½ tsp. black pepper

1. Preheat oven to 375°F. Line a 15×10-inch baking pan with foil.
2. Halve pumpkin; remove seeds* and strings. Place cut sides down on prepared pan. Bake 1 hour or until tender; remove. Turn upright; let cool. Scoop out pulp; discard skin. Working in batches, place pumpkin in a blender or food processor; blend or process until smooth. Transfer to a fine-mesh sieve lined with a double thickness of 100-percent-cotton cheesecloth. Let stand 1 hour, then press lightly to remove liquid. Discard liquid. (You should have 1¾ cups pumpkin.)

3. For croutons: Increase oven to 400°F. Line a 15×10-inch baking pan with foil. Spread bread cubes in pan. Toss with 2 Tbsp. olive oil to coat. Sprinkle with Manchego. Bake 18 to 20 minutes or until golden brown, stirring once.
4. Meanwhile, in a 4- to 5-qt. pot heat 1 Tbsp. olive oil over medium-high. Add onion and garlic. Cook and stir 4 minutes or until tender. Add broth, 1 cup water, and the potato. Bring to boiling; reduce heat. Simmer, covered, 15 minutes or until potato is tender. Stir in pumpkin. Using an immersion blender, blend until smooth. (Or, working in batches, process in a blender.) Simmer over medium. Slowly add Gruyère, stirring until melted. Stir in cream, salt, and black pepper; heat through. Top soup with croutons. Makes 8 servings.
To Serve in a Pumpkin Bowl Preheat oven to 400°F. Cut off top portion of a 6-lb. pumpkin; remove seeds and strings. Place right side up on a baking sheet lined with foil; brush inside and out with vegetable oil. Roast 40 minutes or just until golden brown and tender; let cool. Fill with soup.
***To Toast Seeds** Rinse seeds to remove strings; pat dry. Spread in a shallow baking pan; sprinkle with ⅛ tsp. salt and ⅛ tsp. black pepper. Roast in a 400°F oven 5 to 8 minutes, stirring once. Sprinkle toasted seeds on soup, mix with dried fruit and nuts, or use for snacking.
PER SERVING 308 cal, 14 g fat, 28 mg chol, 672 mg sodium, 34 g carb, 3 g fiber, 4 g sugars, 12 g pro.

THE WINE LIST

Spanish wines and spirits are often on menus and store shelves. These are a few of Mario and Daniel's favorites. "We love to experiment and show our guests how these beverages enhance the flavors of the foods we serve," Mario says.

VERMOUTH You may be familiar with vermouth (a fortified wine flavored with botanicals) in cocktails. In Spain, however, vermouth is often sipped as an aperitif. Daniel prefers sweet red vermouth served over ice with soda water and a wedge of lemon as a refreshing drink any time of day. Spanish red vermouths are light, smooth, and slightly sweet.

CAVA These bubbles are Spain's equal to French Champagne and Italian Prosecco. Look for brut, the driest form, which has an uncomplicated flavor. "It's a chameleon," Daniel says, "because it goes as well with savory dishes as it does dessert."

TEMPRANILLO This Spanish red is Mario and Daniel's house wine. Its strong fruit flavors and aromas complement hearty comfort foods like Daniel's paella. They say it takes the bite out of cool weather too.

SHERRY A fortified wine, sherry (Jerez in Spanish) is made from white grapes grown near the city of Jerez de la Frontera in Andalusia. Its nutty flavors pair well with desserts. "Sip it slowly to appreciate all its subtleties," Daniel says.

DANIEL'S PAELLA IS THE HIGHLIGHT OF A RELAXED EVENING THAT STRETCHES OVER SEVERAL COURSES.

CINNAMON-RAISIN BREAD PUDDING

Daniel remembers while he was growing up that his mother and grandmother ended meals with pieces of ripe fruit. He prefers something richer for gatherings—this raisin bread pudding.

HANDS-ON TIME 25 minutes
TOTAL TIME 1 hour 30 minutes

- 24 slices cinnamon-raisin bread (two 12- to 16-oz. pkg.)
- ¼ cup unsalted butter, softened
- 1 17- to 18-oz. jar Seville orange marmalade or orange marmalade
- ¼ cup raisins
- ¼ cup packed brown sugar
- ½ tsp. ground cinnamon
- 2 cups heavy cream
- 1 14-oz. can sweetened condensed milk
- 2 eggs
  Blood orange and mandarin orange slices, and fresh rosemary sprigs (optional)

1. Preheat oven to 350°F. Butter two 8-inch round cake pans. Line with parchment paper. Butter paper.
2. Spread 12 slices bread slices with 1 tsp. softened butter; spread remaining 12 with 2 tsp. marmalade each. Sandwich slices with butter and marmalade together. Trim off crusts. Diagonally cut each sandwich into quarters; arrange in prepared pans, stacking and overlapping to fit snugly. In a small bowl stir together raisins, brown sugar, and cinnamon; sprinkle over top.
3. In a large bowl whisk together cream, condensed milk, and eggs. Pour over bread. Press bread down to absorb cream mixture. Bake 45 minutes or until a knife inserted in center comes out clean. Let cool 20 minutes in pans on a wire rack.
4. Meanwhile, in a small saucepan warm remaining marmalade over low heat.
5. Loosen sides of bread from pans. Invert one pan onto a platter; shake gently to loosen bottom. Remove parchment. Spread with half the warm marmalade. Invert second pan onto a baking sheet or wire rack, then invert again onto a rimless baking sheet, top up; gently slide onto first layer. Top with remaining marmalade. Serve within 2 hours. If desired, top with slices of blood orange, mandarin orange, and fresh rosemary sprigs. Makes 16 slices.
PER SLICE *443 cal, 19 g fat, 77 mg chol, 243 mg sodium, 65 g carb, 2 g fiber, 46 g sugars, 7 g pro.*

gold
RUSH

Ground cherries may be the tastiest, easiest-to-grow fruit you've never heard of, producing a profusion of sweet yellow orbs through fall.

Pop a ground cherry into your mouth and you might struggle to describe the flavor. It tastes a little like pineapple. Or is it peach? And is that a hint of corn? In any case, this little-known member of the tomato family (husks hint at the relationship to tomatillo) offers a taste of summer all the way through fall.

To grow ground cherries—also known as husk cherries—sow seeds in a warm, sunny spot indoors six to eight weeks before the last frost. Transplant seedlings to a sunny part of the garden that has average garden soil. (Or sow seeds outside after the chance of frost has passed.) Mulch with straw and water weekly when there's no rain. Fruits ripen on the bushy plants from around August through October.

You'll know they're ready to eat when they drop to the ground. Peel off the inedible husks, then snack on them fresh or cook them into a quick compote. Look for ground cherries at farmers markets or buy seeds at seedsavers.com.

SPICED GROUND CHERRY COMPOTE

HANDS-ON TIME 15 minutes
TOTAL TIME 45 minutes

4   cups fresh ground cherries, husked and washed
1   cup sugar
    Zest of half a lemon
    Juice of 1 lemon
⅛   tsp. ground nutmeg
1   vanilla bean

1. In a medium-size heavy saucepan combine the first five ingredients (through nutmeg). With a small knife split the vanilla bean lengthwise and scrape seeds from pod. Add seeds to cherry mixture; discard pod.
2. Bring cherry mixture to boiling over medium-high heat, stirring frequently. Reduce heat and simmer, uncovered, 30 minutes, stirring occasionally. Refrigerate in an airtight container up to 1 week. Makes 12 servings.
EACH SERVING *91 cal, 22 g carb, 17 g sugar, 1 g pro.*

IT TASTES A LITTLE LIKE PINEAPPLE. OR IS IT PEACH? AND IS THAT A HINT OF CORN?

A NEW PLAID

Chances are you have a version of the iconic *Better Homes & Gardens New Cook Book* on your kitchen shelf. Slide that old edition aside to make room, because this cookbook just got a makeover. The 17th edition looks and cooks differently than its predecessors: More recipes with global flavors and fresh ingredients, a photo with every recipe to inspire and teach, and answers to common cooking questions.

CARAMEL MERINGUE PIE

Dulce de leche caramel sauce is generally near sweetened condensed milk in grocery aisles.

HANDS-ON TIME 50 minutes
TOTAL TIME 5 hours 40 minutes, including chilling

Baked Pastry Shell (recipe, right)
Meringue for Pie (recipe, right)
½ cup sugar
¼ cup cornstarch
2¼ cups half-and-half or milk
⅓ cup dulce de leche
4 egg yolks (left over from the Meringue for Pie recipe)
1 Tbsp. butter
1½ tsp. vanilla or vanilla bean paste

1. Prepare Baked Pastry Shell. Preheat oven to 325°F. Prepare Meringue for Pie.
3. For filling: In a medium saucepan stir together sugar and cornstarch. Gradually stir in half-and-half then dulce de leche. Cook and stir over medium-high 5 minutes or until thick and bubbly; reduce heat. Cook and stir 2 minutes more. Remove from heat.
4. Gradually stir 1 cup hot half-and-half mixture into egg yolks. Combine all in saucepan. Bring to a boil, stirring constantly; reduce heat. Cook and stir 2 minutes more. Remove from heat. Stir in butter and vanilla.
5. Beat meringue briefly with a mixer to refresh. Pour hot filling into baked pastry shell. Immediately spread meringue over filling, sealing to edge of pastry. Using the back of a spoon, swirl meringue to make peaks. Bake 20 to 25 minutes or until meringue is golden and a thermometer registers 160°F. Let cool on a wire rack 1½ hours. Chill 3 to 6 hours before serving. Makes 8 slices.
PER SLICE *407 cal, 18 g fat, 117 mg chol, 260 mg sodium, 55 g carb, 1 g fiber, 32 g sugars, 7 g pro.*

BAKED PASTRY SHELL

TOTAL TIME 30 minutes

1½ cups all-purpose flour
½ tsp. salt
¼ cup shortening
¼ cup cold butter, cut into pieces
¼ to ⅓ cup cold water

1. In a bowl stir together flour and salt. Using a pastry blender, cut in shortening and butter until pea size. Sprinkle 1 Tbsp. water over part of the flour mixture; toss with a fork. Push moistened pastry to side of bowl. Repeat 1 Tbsp. at a time until mixture begins to come together. Gather pastry into a ball, kneading gently until it holds together.
2. On a lightly floured surface, slightly flatten pastry. Roll pastry to form a 12-inch-diameter circle.
3. Fold pastry circle into fourths; transfer to a 9-inch pie plate. Unfold; ease pastry into plate without stretching it.
4. Trim to ½ inch beyond edge of plate. Fold under extra pastry even with pie plate's edge; crimp as desired.
5. Preheat oven to 450°F. Prick bottom and sides of pastry. Line with a double thickness of foil. Bake 8 minutes. Remove foil. Bake 6 to 8 minutes more or until golden. Let cool on a wire rack.
Make Ahead Fit the pastry dough in a freezer-to-oven pie pan, slide the unbaked pastry shell and pan into a resealable freezer bag, and freeze up to 3 months. Bake as directed.

MERINGUE FOR PIE

HANDS-ON TIME 15 minutes
TOTAL TIME 30 minutes

4 eggs*
½ cup water
2 tsp. cornstarch**
1 tsp. vanilla
½ tsp. cream of tartar***
½ cup sugar

1. Separate eggs; set aside yolks for pie filling. Place egg whites in a clean glass or copper bowl; let stand until room temperature.
2. In a 1-cup liquid measure whisk to combine the water and cornstarch. Microwave 45 to 60 seconds or until boiling, stirring once. Set aside.
3. Add vanilla and cream of tartar to egg whites. Beat with a mixer on medium 1 minute or until soft peaks form (tips curl). Add sugar 1 Tbsp. at a time, beating on high. Gradually beat in the warm cornstarch mixture until stiff glossy peaks form (tips stand straight).
***Tip** Cold eggs separate more cleanly because yolks are firm and less likely to break. Room-temp whites are less viscous and beat into a foam more quickly. Separate first, then let stand to reach room temp.
****Tip** Cornstarch stabilizes the meringue, helps prevent shrinking, lowers the chance of beading—those golden liquid droplets on the surface—and makes for smoother cut edges.
*****Tip** Cream of tartar is an acid that helps egg whites expand and hold the foam structure.

BEATING EGG WHITES TO THE RIGHT STAGE IS KEY TO A TALL, FLUFFY MERINGUE.

SCONES

LEARN IT, CHANGE IT. THE SECRET TO PERSONALIZING RECIPES IS HAVING KITCHEN CONFIDENCE. START BY MASTERING THE TECHNIQUES TO THIS BAKERY-STYLE SCONE, THEN ADD YOUR FAVORITE STIR-INS, SUCH AS ½ CUP CHOPPED FRUIT OR TOASTED NUTS.

SCONES

HANDS-ON TIME 25 minutes
TOTAL TIME 35 minutes

2½ cups all-purpose flour
¼ cup granulated sugar
1 Tbsp. baking powder
¼ tsp. salt
½ cup cold butter,* cut up
1 egg, lightly beaten
⅓ cup heavy cream
⅓ cup sour cream
  Coarse sugar

1. Preheat oven to 400°F. Line a baking sheet with parchment paper. In a large bowl stir together flour, sugar, baking powder, and salt. Using a pastry blender, cut in cold butter until mixture resembles coarse crumbs. Make a well in center of flour mixture.
2. In a bowl combine egg, heavy cream, and sour cream. Add egg mixture all at once to flour mixture. Using a fork, stir just until moistened.
3. Turn dough out onto a lightly floured surface. Knead 10 to 12 strokes or until nearly smooth.** Divide in half. Pat or lightly roll each dough half into a 6-inch circle. Cut circles into six wedges.
4. Place wedges 2 inches apart on prepared baking sheet. Brush with additional heavy cream and sprinkle with coarse sugar. Bake 12 to 14 minutes or until bottoms are golden. Let cool on a wire rack. Makes 12 scones.

*Tip For flaky layers, keep the butter cold so it begins to melt in the oven, not before.
**Tip Overworking causes dense, tough scones. Stop while dry flour still shows in the dough.

PER SCONE *223 cal, 12 g fat, 49 mg chol, 243 mg sodium, 25 g carb, 1 g fiber, 5 g sugars, 4 g pro.*

GLUTEN-FREE PEANUT BUTTER COOKIES

GLUTEN-FREE PEANUT BUTTER COOKIES

If gluten-free treats aren't on your radar, we'd like to call attention to this little discovery. It takes only three ingredients (that are probably on your shelves) to make these delicious gluten-free cookies.

HANDS-ON TIME 20 minutes
TOTAL TIME 40 minutes

1 cup sugar
1 cup peanut butter
1 egg

1. Preheat oven to 375°F. Grease cookie sheets or line with parchment. In a bowl stir together sugar, peanut butter, and egg. Drop by rounded teaspoons onto prepared cookie sheets. (If desired, roll in sugar before dropping.) Flatten with a fork. Bake 10 to 13 minutes or until set in centers. Cool on wire racks. Makes 32 cookies.

PER COOKIE *78 cal, 4 g fat, 6 mg chol, 36 mg sodium, 9 g carb, 8 g sugar, 2 g pro.*

APPLE-MAPLE
SPICE CAKE
Recipe on page 250

november

Aromatics wafting from the kitchen are unmistakable—warm spices partner with both sweet and savory dishes. Let the holiday season begin.

254

262

264

Baking
FALL FLAVORS

These recipes give us all the flavors we crave with a few twists—it's the season for change, after all.

CRANBERRY-WALNUT TART

Underneath gorgeous cranberries you'll find sweet vanilla cream filling over a walnut-studded shortbread crust. Most seasonal recipes have cranberries cooked in a lot of sugar to tame their pucker; here we embrace it. Coarsely chopped with oranges and sprinkled with just enough sugar to bring out their juices, the berries in this tart topper will delight your taste buds.

HANDS-ON TIME 30 minutes
TOTAL TIME 1 hour

1¼ cups all-purpose flour
¾ cup sugar plus 1 Tbsp.
4 tsp. orange zest
⅓ cup cold butter, cut up
1¼ cups coarsely chopped walnuts
½ cup heavy cream
1 tsp. vanilla
2¼ cups fresh or frozen cranberries, thawed, if frozen
2 oranges, peeled and sectioned

1. Preheat oven to 400°F. Line a 14×5-inch rectangular (or 9-inch round) tart pan and a baking sheet with foil.
2. In a large bowl combine flour, 1 Tbsp. sugar, and 2 tsp. of the orange zest. Cut in butter until pieces resemble fine crumbs. Stir in 3 Tbsp. ice cold water just until dough is moistened. Gather dough in a ball, kneading until it holds together.
3. Press dough into bottom and up sides of prepared pan. Place pan on lined baking sheet. Bake 7 to 8 minutes or until set and golden. Transfer to a wire rack. Top with walnuts.
4. In a medium saucepan combine ½ cup sugar and the cream. Bring to boiling, stirring to dissolve sugar. Cook and stir 1 minute. Remove from heat. Stir in vanilla. Pour over walnuts. Bake 20 minutes or until top is brown. Cool on a rack.
5. Meanwhile, in a food processor pulse until coarsely chopped the remaining ¼ cup sugar, 2 cups of the cranberries, 2 tsp. zest, and orange sections. Transfer to a bowl; stir in remaining cranberries. Let stand at least 30 minutes, stirring occasionally. Spoon over tart. Makes 10 servings.

Sectioning Citrus Cut a thin slice off the top and bottom, then cut off the peel and white pith. Working over a bowl to catch juices, slice between the flesh and membrane on each side of segments to free slices.
Make Ahead Knead and shape dough into a disc, wrap tightly in plastic, and freeze up to 1 month. Thaw at room temperature 1 hour or until pliable. When ready to bake, proceed with Step 3.
PER SLICE *282 cal, 14 g fat, 15 mg chol, 8 mg sodium, 36 g carb, 3 g fiber, 20 g sugars, 4 g pro.*

AS WARM AND COZY INSTINCTS REV UP AT THE FIRST SIGN OF AUTUMN, PULL OUT COMFY SWEATERS AND REVISIT QUINTESSENTIAL FLAVORS OF APPLES, PUMPKIN, AND WARM SPICES.

CARAMEL APPLE FANS, THIS ONE'S FOR YOU. FINISH THIS APPLE BUNDT CAKE WITH A LUSCIOUS MAPLE-CARAMEL SAUCE.

TYPES OF CINNAMON

Most cinnamon on grocery store shelves is cassia. It is harvested from the inner bark of cassia trees, which originated in southern China. Cassia is sometimes referred to as Chinese cinnamon. Ceylon cinnamon, grown in Sri Lanka, is considered the authentic cinnamon. It's worth trying for its delicate, complex citrus flavor. Because Ceylon is often used in Mexican cooking, look for it at Latin markets or specialty spice shops.

APPLE-MAPLE SPICE CAKE

Chopped apples and apple butter in the batter result in moist, tender texture. Go for firm, sweet-tart apples, such as Gala and/or Granny Smith. Both soften when baked or cooked while retaining their shape without juicing excessively. If freshly grating a whole nutmeg, use half the amount called for.

HANDS-ON TIME 35 minutes

TOTAL TIME 3 hours 20 minutes, including cooling

1½	cups all-purpose flour
½	cup whole wheat flour
2	tsp. baking powder
1½	tsp. ground cinnamon
½	tsp. baking soda
½	tsp. salt
½	tsp. ground nutmeg
⅛	tsp. ground cloves
4	medium Gala and/or Granny Smith apples
1	cup butter, softened
1	cup granulated sugar
2	eggs
1	cup apple butter
¼	cup maple syrup plus 2 Tbsp.
⅔	cup packed brown sugar
⅓	cup heavy cream

1. Preheat oven to 350°F. Butter and flour a 10-inch fluted tube pan.

2. In a medium bowl whisk together the flours, baking powder, cinnamon, baking soda, salt, nutmeg, and cloves.

3. Core and finely chop apples.

4. In a large bowl beat ⅔ cup butter with a mixer on medium-high 30 seconds. Add granulated sugar; beat 2 minutes. Add eggs, one at a time, beating well after each addition. Beat in apple butter and ¼ cup maple syrup. (Batter may appear curdled.) Gradually beat in flour mixture on low until combined. Fold in half the apples. Spread batter evenly into prepared tube pan.

5. Bake 45 minutes or until toothpick inserted near center comes out clean. Cool in pan on wire rack 10 minutes. Remove cake from pan; let cool slightly on wire rack.

6. Meanwhile, for apple topping: In a large skillet melt remaining ⅓ cup butter over medium. Add remaining apples; cook and stir 1 to 2 minutes or until softened. Stir in brown sugar and cream. Bring to boiling, stirring to dissolve sugar. Boil gently, uncovered, 2 to 3 minutes. Remove from heat. Stir in remaining 2 Tbsp. maple syrup; cool slightly. Spoon over warm cake; pass remaining. Makes 12 slices.

PER SLICE *540 cal, 19 g fat, 79 mg chol, 383 mg sodium, 90 g carb, 4 g fiber, 66 g sugars, 4 g pro.*

EXTEND SHORTCAKE SEASON BEYOND SUMMER BERRIES. PAIR THE RICH BISCUIT-LIKE LAYER WITH SPICED, HONEY-STEEPED PEARS, THEN TOP WITH POMEGRANATE SEEDS.

SHEET-PAN SHORTCAKE WITH MASCARPONE CREAM AND PEARS

Enhance the richness and stability of the whipped topping by beating in mascarpone, the soft Italian cheese with delicate flavor that blends well with cream.

HANDS-ON TIME 25 minutes
TOTAL TIME 2 hours

¼	cup honey plus 3 Tbsp.
2	Tbsp. lemon juice
½	tsp. ground cardamom
2	ripe firm red and/or green pears (such as Anjou or Bosc), cored, halved, and thinly sliced
2¾	cups all-purpose flour
⅓	cup sugar
2	tsp. baking powder
¼	tsp. baking soda
¼	tsp. salt
1¼	cups cold butter, cut up
¾	cup buttermilk
1	egg
1½	cups heavy cream
¼	cup mascarpone cheese
½	cup pomegranate seeds (see How-To, right)

1. In a large bowl combine ¼ cup honey, lemon juice, and cardamom. Add pears; toss. Cover; let stand 1 to 2 hours, stirring occasionally.

2. Preheat oven to 350°F. In an extra-large bowl combine flour, sugar, baking powder, baking soda, and salt. Cut in butter until mixture resembles coarse crumbs. Make a well in center of flour mixture. In a small bowl whisk together buttermilk and egg. Add egg mixture to flour mixture, stirring with a fork just until moistened. (Dough will be crumbly.)

3. Using floured hands, press dough evenly in a 15×10-inch baking pan. Brush with additional buttermilk; sprinkle with additional sugar. Bake 25 minutes or until light brown. Let cool in pan on wire rack.

4. In a large bowl beat heavy cream, mascarpone cheese, and remaining 3 Tbsp. honey with a mixer on medium-high 3 minutes or until stiff peaks form. Top shortcake with whipped cream, pears with spiced sauce, and pomegranate seeds. Makes 16 slices.

Make Ahead Store without topping at room temperature up to 24 hours.

PER SLICE *367 cal, 25 g fat, 81 mg chol, 266 mg sodium, 33 g carb, 1 g fiber, 15 g sugars, 4 g pro.*

HOW TO DESEED A POMEGRANATE

SCORE THE TOP Trim top and bottom to expose the seeds. Make two 1-inch-deep cuts across the top to loosen the fruit.

SUBMERGE IN WATER Working in a bowl of water, split the fruit in half. Separate seeds from the peel and white membranes.

DISCARD MEMBRANES The white membranes are too bitter to eat. Use a slotted spoon to remove and discard them.

THIS HOLIDAY DESSERT—LAYERS OF SPICED PUMPKIN BREAD, BOURBON-SCENTED CREAM, AND CANDIED PECANS—DESERVES CENTERPIECE STATUS.

PUMPKIN BREAD TRIFLE

The beauty of the trifle is that after you prepare each segment, it takes only 15 minutes to assemble. Let it chill while you eat turkey dinner—or up to 8 hours if you really like to plan ahead.

HANDS-ON TIME 1 hour
TOTAL TIME 2 hours

3¾ cups granulated sugar
1   15-oz. can pumpkin
1   cup vegetable oil
4   eggs
3⅓ cups all-purpose flour
2   tsp. baking soda
2   tsp. pumpkin pie spice
1   tsp. salt
1½ cups chopped pecans
2½ cups heavy cream
1   8-oz. carton sour cream
1   cup powdered sugar
2   Tbsp. bourbon or milk
     Pomegranate seeds (optional)
     Caramel ice cream topping
     (optional)

1. Preheat oven to 350°F. Grease bottoms and 2 inches up sides of two 9×5-inch loaf pans.
2. In a large bowl stir together 3 cups granulated sugar, pumpkin, oil, ⅔ cup water, and eggs until combined. In a medium bowl whisk together flour, baking soda, pumpkin pie spice, and salt. Stir into pumpkin mixture. Spoon into prepared pans. Bake 1 hour or until a toothpick inserted near centers comes out clean. Cool in pans on a wire rack 10 minutes. Remove from pans; cool completely.
3. Grease a baking sheet. Place pecans close together in a single layer on prepared pan. In a small saucepan bring 3 Tbsp. water and remaining ¾ cup granulated sugar to boiling, without stirring, over medium. Cook, without stirring, 6 minutes or until golden, brushing pan sides with water to prevent crystals from forming. Pour over pecans. Let cool; break into pieces.
4. In a bowl beat heavy cream, sour cream, powdered sugar, and bourbon with mixer on high until stiff peaks form.
5. Cut one loaf into 1-inch cubes. (Freeze second loaf up to 1 month.) In a large trifle dish make three layers each of bread cubes, pecans, cream, and, if desired, pomegranate seeds and caramel ice cream topping. Serve immediately or chill up to 8 hours. Makes 16 servings.
PER SERVING *685 cal, 39 g fat, 97 mg chol, 338 mg sodium, 80 g carb, 2 g fiber, 57 g sugars, 7 g pro.*

CIDER SIPPER

Invite apple cider to your next happy hour, letting it make a grand entrance dressed in pomegranate red and chock-full of fruit and spice.

ICED MULLED POMEGRANATE CIDER

HANDS-ON TIME 25 minutes
TOTAL TIME 3 hours, includes chilling

6   cups apple cider
2   cups pomegranate juice
½   cup pomegranate molasses or honey*
2   3-inch pieces stick cinnamon
2   whole star anise
1   orange, thinly sliced
1   apple, cored and cut into thin wedges
½   to 1 cup brandy

1. In a large nonreactive pot heat apple cider, pomegranate juice, and pomegranate molasses over medium until steaming, stirring occasionally. Add cinnamon sticks and star anise; remove from heat. Stir in orange slices and apple wedges. Let cool to room temperature. Transfer to a large pitcher or storage container.
2. Cover and refrigerate until chilled (2 to 4 hours) or up to 1 day. Stir in brandy before serving. Makes 12 servings.
*Tip Pomegranate molasses adds a deep tangy note that balances the sweetness of cider. Look for it at large grocery stores.
PER SERVING *174 cal, 16 mg sodium, 43 g carb, 1 g fiber, 27 g sugars.*

IN ADDITION TO LOOKING EXOTIC, STAR ANISE DELIVERS A SWEET, MILD LICORICE NOTE.

HOW SWEET THEY ARE

It's time to give thanks for the sweet potato—the versatile veggie for all seasons that can be prepared in all sorts of savory, citrusy, and sweet ways.

Hmm, you might be thinking, another story about sweet potatoes in November. But hold on a sec. You won't find recipes for marshmallow-topped casseroles here. Not because we don't love them, but because you probably already have that handled. Instead, we focus on the adaptability of these nutritious tubers: How they can be sliced, diced, spiralized, or roasted whole. How they take to familiar pairings (garlic and butter or broccoli) as well as less-expected ones (pineapple, pomegranate, or coconut) to yield inspiring new dishes. We offer even more reasons to love this deliciously sweet and virtuous staple.

THE NUMBER OF SWEET POTATO TYPES AVAILABLE KEEPS INCREASING. LOOK FOR SOME OF THESE IN GROCERY STORES AND FARMERS MARKETS. OR PLANT AND GROW A FEW.

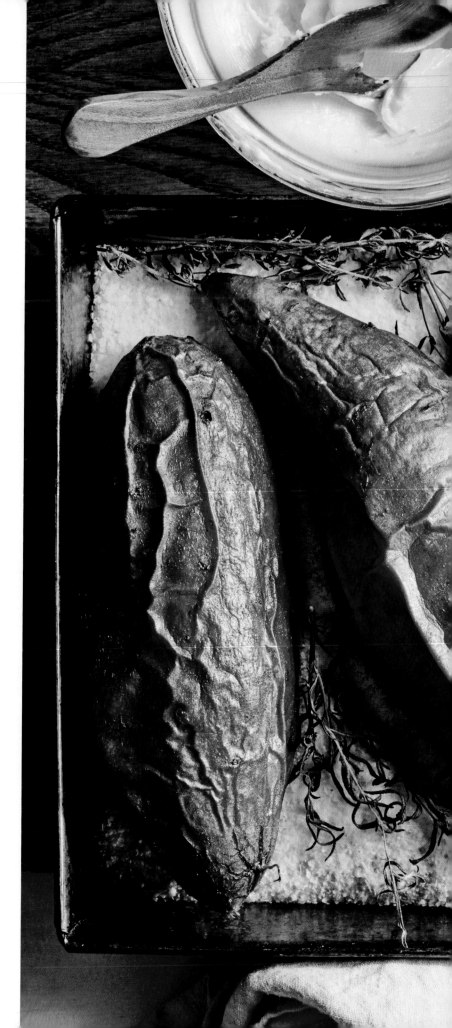

SALT-ROASTED SWEETS

Once you taste the magic alchemy of salt roasting, you'll reconsider regular baking. The bed of salt absorbs moisture from the sweet potatoes and herbs, then the sweet potatoes reabsorb the trapped moisture. The result: sweet, salty perfection. Roast a head of garlic alongside; then stir the cloves into softened butter to spread on top.

HANDS-ON TIME 10 minutes
TOTAL TIME 1 hour 25 minutes

1½ cups kosher salt
4 medium sweet potatoes, scrubbed and dried (about 2 lb.)
1 bulb garlic
8 fresh rosemary and/or thyme sprigs
2 Tbsp. olive oil
¼ cup butter, softened

1. Preheat oven to 450°F. Spread salt evenly in a 2-qt. rectangular baking pan. Press potatoes lightly into salt (just enough to stay in place). Cut ½ inch from tip of garlic bulb to expose cloves. Leaving bulb intact, remove loose, papery outer layers. Place garlic (cut side up) and herbs around potatoes. Drizzle garlic with 1 Tbsp. oil. Cover baking pan with foil.
2. Bake 1 hour. Remove garlic; let cool. Discard herbs. Brush potatoes with remaining oil. Bake, uncovered, 15 minutes more or until tender.
3. Squeeze garlic cloves into a small bowl. Add softened butter; stir to combine. Remove potatoes from salt and halve lengthwise. Serve with garlic butter. Makes 8 servings.
PER SERVING *236 cal, 15 g fat, 31 mg chol, 155 mg sodium, 24 g carb, 3 g fiber, 5 g sugars, 2 g pro.*

SWEET POTATO AND PINEAPPLE GRATIN
Recipe on page 262

POMEGRANATE-GLAZED
SWEET POTATOES
Recipe on page 262

THE OLD FARMER'S ALMANAC ONCE CALLED SWEET POTATOES "THE HEALTHIEST VEGETABLE OF THEM ALL."

SWEET POTATO AND PINEAPPLE GRATIN

Photo on page 260.

Pineapple adds a touch of sweetness to balance the mild heat of the chile peppers. Cotija—an aged Mexican cheese made with cow's milk—provides salty, creamy deliciousness.

HANDS-ON TIME 20 minutes
TOTAL TIME 1 hour 50 minutes

1 medium pineapple, peeled and cored
1 tsp. cumin seeds, lightly crushed
1 cup heavy cream
1 medium poblano pepper, stemmed, seeded, and finely chopped (tip, page 17)
2 cloves garlic, minced
1 tsp. salt
¼ tsp. black pepper
1½ lb. sweet potatoes, very thinly sliced
½ cup sliced green onions
1 cup crumbled Cotija cheese
¼ cup panko
2 tsp. vegetable oil

1. Preheat oven to 350°F. Butter a 2-qt. gratin or rectangular baking dish.
2. Halve pineapple lengthwise; thinly slice one half (Reserve remaining half for another use.) Heat a small saucepan over medium. Add cumin seeds; heat 1 to 2 minutes or until toasted. Add heavy cream, poblano, garlic, salt, and black pepper. Heat through; remove from heat.
3. Layer half the potatoes, pineapple, and green onions in prepared dish. Sprinkle with half the cheese. Repeat layers. Pour cream mixture over top. Bake, covered, 25 minutes.
4. In a small bowl combine panko and oil. Sprinkle over top. Bake, uncovered, 55 minutes more or until potatoes are tender and top is golden. Let stand 10 minutes. Makes 6 to 8 servings.
PER SERVING *361 cal, 22 g fat, 65 mg chol, 752 mg sodium, 34 g carb, 4 g fiber, 10 g sugars, 8 g pro.*

POMEGRANATE-GLAZED SWEET POTATOES

Photo on page 261.

If you thought the spiralizer was a zucchini game changer, check out what it can do for orange and purple sweet potatoes. Toss the barely cooked curls in a cardamom- and nutmeg-spiced sauce for this irresistible warm side dish.

TOTAL TIME 25 minutes

1½ lb. orange and/or purple sweet potatoes, peeled and spiralized* (6 cups)
⅓ cup pomegranate juice or orange juice
⅓ cup honey
3 Tbsp. butter
½ tsp. salt
¼ tsp. black pepper
½ tsp. ground cardamom
⅛ tsp. freshly grated nutmeg or ¼ tsp. ground nutmeg
¼ cup chopped fresh Italian parsley
¼ cup chopped fresh mint
½ cup pomegranate seeds

1. In a 6-qt. pot bring lightly salted water to boiling. Add sweet potato spirals. Cook, uncovered, 2 minutes (cook purple sweet potatoes only 1 minute). Drain.
2. In the same pot stir together pomegranate juice, honey, butter, salt, black pepper, cardamom, and nutmeg over high. Bring to boiling, stirring to melt butter; reduce heat. Simmer, uncovered, 5 minutes or until glazing consistency. Add sweet potatoes; gently toss to glaze. Heat through, then remove from heat and stir in fresh herbs. Top with pomegranate seeds before serving. Makes 6 to 8 servings.
*Tip If you do not have a spiralizer, thinly slice potatoes, then cut into ⅛- to ¼-inch-wide matchsticks.
PER SERVING *246 cal, 6 g fat, 15 mg chol, 317 mg sodium, 47 g carb, 5 g fiber, 25 g sugars, 3 g pro.*

ASIAN-STYLE SWEET POTATOES

The dressing of ginger, lemon, and soy, plus toasted almonds and coconut, make this dish exceptional.

HANDS-ON TIME 20 minutes
TOTAL TIME 50 minutes

2 to 2½ lb. sweet potatoes, peeled and cut into ½-inch cubes (6 cups)
1½ cups sliced onion
3 Tbsp. vegetable oil
½ tsp. salt
¼ tsp. black pepper
3 cups broccoli florets
⅓ cup almond butter
3 Tbsp. lemon juice
3 Tbsp. soy sauce
1 Tbsp. minced garlic
1 Tbsp. grated fresh ginger
¼ tsp. crushed red pepper
¼ cup unsweetened flaked coconut, toasted*
¼ cup chopped almonds or pecans, toasted (tip, page 27)

1. Preheat oven to 425°F. In a large bowl combine sweet potatoes, onion, oil, salt, and black pepper. Divide among two 15×10-inch baking pans. Roast on two racks 15 minutes. Add broccoli. Roast 10 minutes more or until potatoes and broccoli are browned and tender.
2. Meanwhile, for dressing, in a bowl whisk together ⅓ cup water, the almond butter, lemon juice, soy sauce, garlic, ginger, and crushed red pepper until smooth.
3. Transfer vegetables to a platter. Drizzle with dressing. Top with coconut and nuts. Makes 6 servings.
*Tip To toast coconut, preheat oven to 350°F. Spread in a shallow baking pan. Bake 5 to 6 minutes or until lightly browned, shaking pan once or twice.
PER SERVING *345 cal, 19 g fat, 812 mg sodium, 39 g carb, 8 g fiber, 10 g sugars, 9 g pro.*

ASIAN-STYLE
SWEET POTATOES

TURKEY TIME

For the past 90 years, the BH&G® Test Kitchen has turned out hundreds of turkeys to make sure yours turns out golden on the outside and juicy on the inside. Follow these helpful tips for buying, stuffing, carving, making gravy, and more.

LET IT THAW

It's best to thaw turkey in the refrigerator because cold prevents bacteria from growing. You need to plan ahead: Allow one day for each 4 pounds of turkey plus one day extra.

If you're short on time, there's still hope. To speed the process, place the bird in a leakproof plastic bag and immerse in a sink of cold water. Change water every half hour, turning turkey occasionally. Totally out of time? You can roast still frozen, but it will take about 50 percent longer to cook.

PICK A PAN

The ideal pan for roasting a turkey is large and sturdy with strong handles for safe lifting and a rack to allow for airflow around the bird. If you don't have a roasting pan, use a 13×9-inch baking pan and place vegetables under the turkey to serve as a rack. In a pinch, a large foil roasting pan (19½×11½ inches) placed on a shallow baking pan is stable.

TIME IT RIGHT

Although a turkey is safe to eat at 165°F, the Test Kitchen believes the meat looks and tastes better at 175°F. (Dark meat is cooked to a better doneness and juices run clear.) However, getting to this temp while avoiding dry meat can be tricky. Here's what we do: Insert an oven-going thermometer into the thigh, making sure the probe doesn't touch bone. And tent foil loosely over the breasts (allow for some air circulation) to deflect heat, which slows the cooking rate so they aren't overdone by the time the thighs are done.

COOK TIME AT 325°F	
8 to 12 lb.	2¾ to 3 hr.
12 to 14 lb.	3 to 3¾ hr.
14 to 18 lb.	3¾ to 4¼ hr.
18 to 20 lb.	4¼ to 4½ hr.
20 to 24 lb.	4½ to 5 hr.

What about stuffed birds? They generally require 15 to 45 minutes more roasting time than unstuffed birds. If you go the stuffed-bird route, verify that the center of stuffing reaches 165°F, too.

STUFFING THE BIRD

If you choose to stuff, do so just before roasting to keep bacteria from multiplying. Any stuffing that doesn't fit inside the turkey can bake in a dish alongside.

STUFF LOOSELY Wipe out the cavity with paper towels and loosely spoon in stuffing. Leave some space for air to circulate so the stuffing cooks evenly and reaches a safe temperature at the same time as the turkey.

TIE THE LEGS The more uniform the turkey shape, the more evenly it will roast. First, use kitchen string to tie the legs together, then to the tail (if it is still on the turkey). Second, tuck the wing tips behind the back to prevent them from burning.

STUMPED BY HOW MUCH TURKEY TO BUY? IT'S SIMPLE: PLAN ON 1 LB. PER PERSON. IF LEFTOVERS ARE A MUST (AND AREN'T THEY ALWAYS?) MAKE IT 1½ LB.

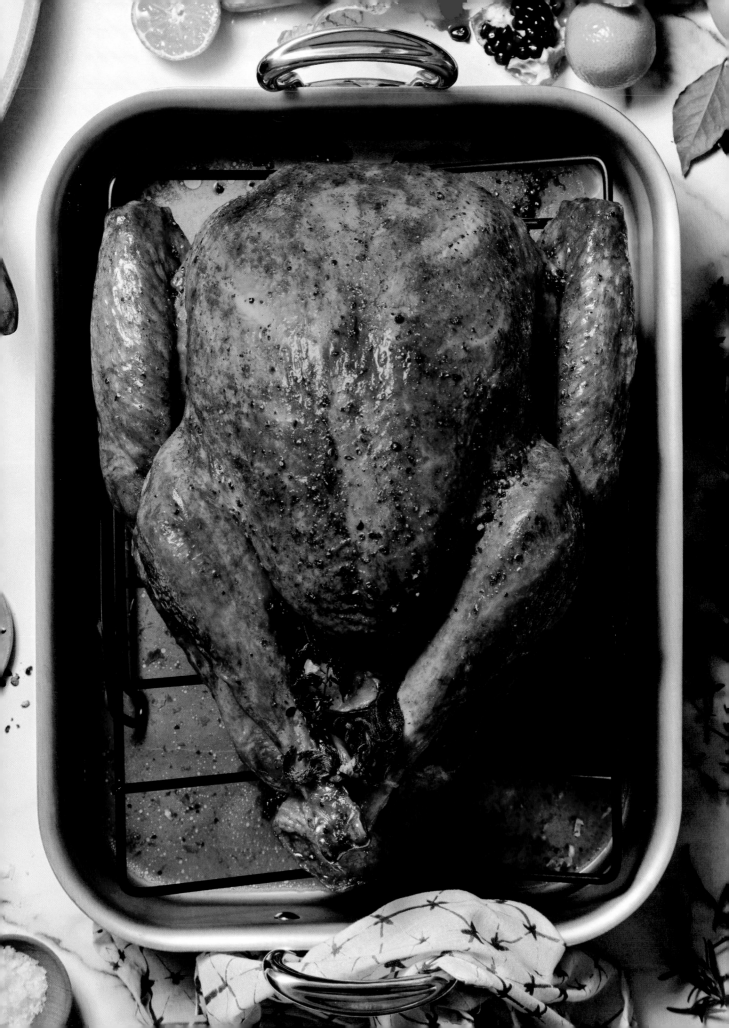

FLAVOR **PERSONALITIES** If turkey is the only food on your menu that never changes, try one of these low-risk, high-reward enhancers.

BRINES

Meat traps some of the salty solution to render a moist, tender turkey. Prepare one, below, in a 10-qt. pot, cool, then add 12 cups ice. Add turkey, cover, and refrigerate 12 hours.

THYME-PEPPERCORN

Heat 12 cups water, 1½ cups each kosher salt and sugar, 8 sprigs thyme, 5 bay leaves, and 1 Tbsp. peppercorns.

CIDER-GINGER

Heat 8 cups water; 4 cups apple cider; ½ cup each sliced fresh ginger, kosher salt, and packed brown sugar; 4 strips orange zest; and 1 Tbsp. peppercorns.

ROSEMARY-MAPLE

Heat 12 cups water, 1½ cups kosher salt, 1 cup maple syrup, ½ cup packed brown sugar, 8 rosemary sprigs, 8 cloves peeled garlic, and 1 Tbsp. peppercorns.

DRY RUBS

Liberally seasoning with spices and salt draws some moisture from the flesh and creates crispy skin. Spread half the rub under the breast skin and the other half over all the skin.

SMOKY HERBES DE PROVENCE

Combine 1 Tbsp. herbes de Provence, 2 tsp. smoked salt, 1½ tsp. crushed red pepper, and 1 tsp. garlic powder.

SWEET CORIANDER

Combine 1 Tbsp. packed brown sugar, ½ tsp. coarsely ground black pepper, 1 tsp. ground coriander, ½ tsp. onion powder, ½ tsp. dried thyme, and ½ tsp. kosher salt.

WARM AND SPICY

Combine 1 tsp. sweet paprika; ½ tsp. each garlic powder, dried thyme, ground ginger, and kosher salt; ¼ tsp. each ground turmeric, ground cinnamon, and ground black pepper; and a dash ground allspice.

GLAZES

The sugars in a glaze caramelize the skin and create a lacquered finish. Brush with half the glaze every 15 minutes the last hour of roasting; serve the other half alongside.

BUTTERY HERB

In a saucepan melt ¼ cup butter. Stir in ⅓ cup honey, 1 tsp. chopped fresh sage, 1 tsp. chopped fresh thyme, and ½ tsp. orange zest.

DOUBLE-CRANBERRY

In a saucepan bring 1 cup fresh cranberries, ½ cup maple syrup, ¼ cup cranberry juice, and ¼ tsp. cayenne pepper to boiling. Simmer 15 minutes; stir in ¼ cup butter.

PEACH-VINEGAR

In a saucepan combine 1 cup peach preserves, 2 Tbsp. cider vinegar, and 1 tsp. dry mustard; heat through.

BROWN SUGAR-MUSTARD

In a saucepan bring 1½ cups packed brown sugar, 1 cup red wine vinegar, and 2 Tbsp. spicy brown mustard to boiling. Boil 5 minutes.

AROMATICS

As they heat, these ingredients release flavored steam into the turkey cavity, flavoring the meat from within. Aromatics aren't eaten, so no need to remove the stems and peels.

ORANGE-SAGE

Stuff cavity with 1 orange, cut into wedges; 1 small shallot, halved; and 1 bunch sage sprigs.

LEMON-THYME

Stuff cavity with 1 lemon, cut into wedges; 1 medium onion, cut into wedges; 3 cloves garlic; and 1 bunch thyme sprigs.

APPLE-ROSEMARY

Stuff cavity with 1 medium apple, cored and cut into wedges; 1 medium red onion, cut into wedges; 1 bunch rosemary sprigs.

CARVE LIKE A PRO

Patience is key. Let the roasted turkey stand
15 to 20 minutes before carving (the temp will rise
5°F to 10°F) to allow the meat to firm so it's easier
to slice and to give juices time to redistribute
through the meat.

1. Pull the legs away from the body and cut joints
attaching the thighs.
2. Cut the joints connecting the drumsticks
and thighs.
3. Slice the thigh meat.
4. Cut off the wings.
5. Cut breast meat from the bone, following as close
to the rib cage as possible.
6. Slice the breast halves crosswise into slices.

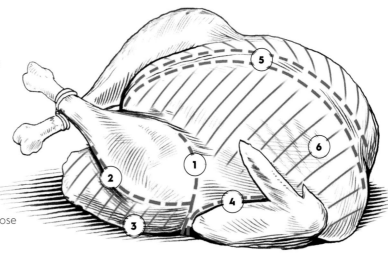

A TALE OF TWO GARNISHES

You've spent hours roasting a delicious turkey and carved it like a champion.
Now finish it with a few colorful additions. Cook some vegetables along with the
bird or embellish the platter with fresh fruits and herbs.

ROASTED CARROTS AND LEMONS
Add halved rainbow carrots and halved
lemons to the roasting pan the last
45 minutes of cooking. Add to the platter
along with the carved turkey. Sprinkle
with fresh sage leaves before serving.

FRESH POMEGRANATE AND
ORANGES After carving, garnish
the platter with fresh orange slices,
a pomegranate torn into pieces,
and fresh cranberries. Finish with
sprigs of fresh thyme.

GRAVY TRAIN

USE THE DRIPPINGS The drippings
in the roasting pan are loaded with
flavor, as are the browned bits stuck
to the bottom of the pan. Place the
pan on the stove top over medium
heat, add 1 cup chicken broth, and
use a wooden spatula to scrape up
the bits.

SEPARATE THE FAT Pour the broth
mixture into a glass measuring
cup. Skim the fat with a spoon and
reserve; you'll need ¼ cup. If you
didn't get that much, add melted
butter. If you don't have 2 cups liquid
in the cup, add morel broth.

MAKE A ROUX A lump-free gravy
starts with a smooth roux (a thickener
made by cooking flour and fat).
For that, you need equal portions
of each. In a saucepan heat the
reserved ¼ cup fat over medium and
whisk in ¼ cup flour until smooth.

COOK Continue to whisk the roux
while gradually adding the 2 cups
broth. Cook and stir until thickened
and bubbly. Season to taste with salt
and black pepper.

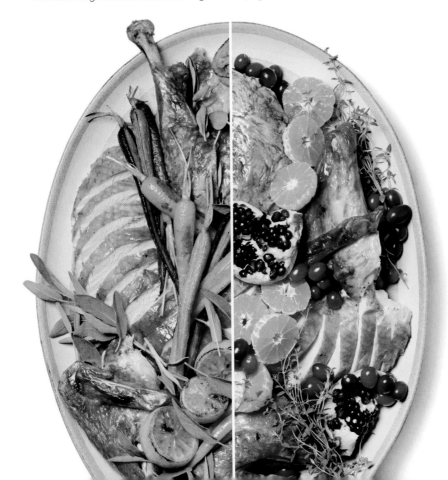

SILVER AND GOLD
YULE LOG
Recipe on page 291

december

Entertain with confidence and ease this holiday season: Breakfast casseroles—both sweet and savory—no-fuss one-pan dinners, and cakes and cookies all add up to a delicious table.

275

277

294

rise and
DINE

The halls are decked, the gifts are wrapped, and the house is full of holiday guests—whom you need to feed. With just 30 minutes of prep time, you'll have a delicious make-ahead brunch casserole, so all you have to do is wake up, pop it in the oven, and open the bubbly.

MONTE CRISTO BREAKFAST CASSEROLE

The Monte Cristo (a cross between a ham-and-Swiss and French toast) often comes with a side of jam for dipping. If you like, between sandwich layers smear on a little of your favorite strawberry or raspberry jam along with the butter. Or add a few thin slices of apple or pear for crunch and sweetness.

HANDS-ON TIME 30 minutes
TOTAL TIME 1 hour 15 minutes, plus overnight chilling

2½   cups milk
8   eggs
3   cloves garlic, minced
½   tsp. salt
¼   tsp. black pepper
1   1- to 1½-lb. round loaf country Italian bread, cut into ten ½-inch thick slices
¼   cup Dijon-style mustard
8   oz. thinly sliced cooked ham
6   oz. Gruyère or Swiss cheese, shredded (1½ cups)
¼   cup butter, softened
     Powdered sugar

1. Grease a 3-qt. baking dish. In a large bowl whisk together milk, eggs, garlic, salt, and pepper.
2. Spread half the bread slices with mustard then top with ham and half the cheese. Spread remaining bread slices with butter, then place buttered sides down on cheese. Cut each sandwich diagonally into four triangles. Arrange points up in prepared baking dish. Pour egg mixture over sandwiches. Sprinkle with remaining cheese. Cover; chill overnight.
3. Preheat oven to 350°F. Uncover dish. Bake 35 minutes or until golden and egg mixture is set. Remove. Let cool 10 minutes. Sprinkle with powdered sugar. Makes 12 servings.
PER SERVING *319 cal, 17 g fat, 170 mg chol, 804 mg sodium, 23 g carb, 1 g fiber, 5 g sugars, 17 g pro.*

IN THIS CASSEROLE TWIST ON THE CLASSIC DINER SANDWICH, THE MONTE CRISTO, A LAYER OF RICH EGG-SOAKED BREAD CONTRASTS THE CRISPY BROWN TOP, AND POWDERED SUGAR IS A SWEET FOIL TO SALTY HAM AND CHEESE.

THE SMOKY CHIPOTLE SAUCE COATS SHREDDED CHICKEN AND CRISPY TORTILLAS IN THIS MEXICAN FAVORITE MADE FOR A CROWD. DAY-OF DUTIES REQUIRE LITTLE MORE THAN CRACKING A FEW EGGS.

BRING ON THE BUBBLES

When you set up a make-your-own bubbly bar of juices, liqueurs, and garnishes, each guest plays bartender. Here are a few of our favorite combinations:

POMEGRANATE

Combine 2 Tbsp. pomegranate juice and 1 Tbsp. orange liqueur. Top with Champagne. Garnish with pomegranate seeds and an orange twist.

BLOOD ORANGE

Combine 2 Tbsp. blood orange juice and 1 Tbsp. vodka. Top with Champagne. Garnish with an orange slice and a rosemary sprig.

CRANBERRY-PEAR

Combine 1 Tbsp. each cranberry juice and pear nectar. Top with Champagne. Garnish with a fresh pear slice and cranberries.

CHILAQUILES BREAKFAST CASSEROLE

HANDS-ON TIME 35 minutes
TOTAL TIME 1 hour 30 minutes, plus overnight chilling

12	6-inch corn tortillas, quartered
1	Tbsp. vegetable oil
1	cup chopped onion
4	cloves garlic, minced
2	tsp. dried oregano, crushed
1	28-oz. can crushed tomatoes, undrained
1	cup reduced-sodium chicken broth
2	chipotle peppers in adobo sauce, finely chopped
2	cups shredded cooked chicken
8	eggs
¼	tsp. black pepper
	Toppings such as avocado, Cotija or feta cheese, tortilla strips, and/or cilantro

1. Preheat oven to 350°F. Grease a 3-qt. baking dish. Spread tortillas evenly on two baking sheets. Bake on separate oven racks 15 minutes. Remove; let cool.
2. Meanwhile, in a large skillet heat oil over medium-high. Add onion, garlic, and oregano. Cook and stir 2 minutes. Add tomatoes, broth, and chipotle peppers. Bring to boiling; reduce heat. Simmer, uncovered, 10 minutes, stirring occasionally. Stir in chicken.
3. Cover bottom of prepared baking dish with the tortillas. Top with chicken mixture; let cool. Cover; chill overnight.
4. Preheat oven to 350°F. Bake casserole, covered, 35 minutes. Remove from oven. Make eight indents in chicken mixture with the back of a spoon. Crack an egg into a custard cup; slip egg into an indent. Repeat with remaining eggs. Sprinkle with pepper. Bake, uncovered, 10 to 15 minutes or until whites are set and yolks are thickened. Remove. Let stand 10 minutes. Serve with toppings. Makes 8 servings.
PER SERVING 303 cal, 15 g fat, 225 mg chol, 464 mg sodium, 22 g carb, 4 g fiber, 6 g sugars, 22 g pro.

BLUEBERRY AND
MASCARPONE-
STUFFED FRENCH
TOAST CASSEROLE

BLUEBERRY AND MASCARPONE-STUFFED FRENCH TOAST CASSEROLE

HANDS-ON TIME 20 minutes
TOTAL TIME 1 hour 20 minutes, plus overnight chilling

3	8-oz. French baguettes
8	oz. mascarpone or cream cheese, room temperature
2	tsp. vanilla
2	cups powdered sugar
2	cups fresh blueberries
6	eggs
2	cups milk
¾	cup granulated sugar
1½	tsp. ground cinnamon

1. Grease a 3-qt. baking dish. Cut each baguette into 1-inch slices, cutting to but not through bottom of loaf. For filling: In a medium bowl beat mascarpone and 1 tsp. vanilla until smooth. Beat in powdered sugar until combined. Fold in blueberries. Spoon filling between baguette slices; arrange baguettes side by side in prepared dish.

2. In a large bowl whisk together eggs, milk, ½ cup granulated sugar, remaining vanilla, and ½ tsp. cinnamon. Pour over bread. Cover; chill overnight.

3. Preheat oven to 350°F. Uncover dish. In a small bowl stir together remaining ¼ cup granulated sugar and 1 tsp. cinnamon. Sprinkle over bread. Bake, uncovered, 40 to 45 minutes or until egg mixture is set, covering with foil the last 15 minutes, if necessary, to prevent overbrowning. Remove. Cool slightly. Makes 12 servings.

PER SERVING *434 cal, 13 g fat, 123 mg chol, 404 mg sodium, 68 g carb, 2 g fiber, 39 g sugars, 11 g pro.*

MINI BACON AND EGG BAKES

MINI BACON AND EGG BAKES

These individual quiches are also a convenient grab-and-go breakfast.

HANDS-ON TIME 25 minutes
TOTAL TIME 55 minutes, plus overnight chilling

	Nonstick cooking spray
12	slices bacon
9	eggs
⅓	cup milk
2	to 3 cups chopped fresh spinach
2	cloves garlic, minced
¾	cup shredded white cheddar cheese (3 oz.)
½	tsp. salt
¼	tsp. black pepper
1	roma tomato, cut into 12 slices

1. Coat twelve 2½-inch muffin cups with nonstick cooking spray. In a large skillet cook bacon 5 to 7 minutes or until cooked through but still pliable and just starting to brown, turning occasionally. Drain on paper towels; let cool until easy to handle.

2. Wrap one slice of bacon around the inside of each muffin cup. In a large bowl whisk together eggs, milk, spinach, garlic, cheese, salt, and pepper. Divide egg mixture among cups. Cover; chill overnight.

3. Preheat oven to 375°F. Uncover muffin cups. Top each with a tomato slice. Bake 25 minutes or until eggs are puffed and set. Let cool in cups 5 minutes. (Eggs may fall slightly during cooling.) Loosen sides; remove from cups. Serve warm. Makes 12 servings.

PER SERVING *126 cal, 9 g fat, 155 mg chol, 335 mg sodium, 1 g carb, 1 g sugars, 10 g pro.*

HERB-RUBBED PORK
WITH SQUASH
AND GRAPES

FAST & FRESH

Easy, delicious recipes for a better dinner tonight.

HERB-RUBBED PORK WITH SQUASH AND GRAPES

Roasting grapes caramelizes the sugars and concentrates the flavor for a sweet contrast to savory pork or chicken. Grapes also make a delicious appetizer. Roast a bunch to serve with goat cheese and crusty bread.

HANDS-ON TIME 15 minutes
TOTAL TIME 40 minutes

2	tsp. dried herbs, such as thyme, oregano, basil, and/or rosemary
½	tsp. chili powder
2	cloves garlic, minced
½	tsp. salt
½	tsp. black pepper
1	to 1½ lb. pork tenderloin
½	2 lb. butternut squash, peeled, seeded, and cut into 1- to 2-inch pieces
½	red onion, cut into wedges
2	Tbsp. olive oil
1	cup seedless red grapes

1. Preheat oven to 425°F. Line a 15×10×1-inch baking pan with foil. In a small bowl combine herbs, chili powder, garlic, ¼ tsp. salt, and ¼ tsp. black pepper. Rub all over pork. Place pork on one side of prepared pan. Add squash and onion to opposite side of pan; sprinkle with remaining ¼ tsp. each salt and pepper. Drizzle pork, squash, and onion with olive oil.
2. Roast 15 minutes. Stir squash and onion; add grapes. Roast 10 to 15 minutes more or until pork is done (145°F). Let stand 5 minutes before serving. Makes 4 servings.
PER SERVING *297 cal, 9 g fat, 73 mg chol, 357 mg sodium, 29 g carb, 4 g fiber, 14 g sugars, 26 g pro.*

GINGER SHRIMP AND VEGETABLES

Photo on page 278.

While the shrimp and vegetables cook, boil rice noodles for a quick side. After draining the noodles, toss them with a little sesame oil and a squeeze of orange juice.

HANDS-ON TIME 15 minutes
TOTAL TIME 25 minutes

1	lb. medium shrimp in shells, peeled, deveined, and patted dry
3	carrots, thinly bias-sliced
3	cups broccoli florets
1	cup snow peas, trimmed
2	Tbsp. canola oil
2	Tbsp. reduced-sodium soy sauce
1	Tbsp. fish sauce
1	Tbsp. orange juice
1	Tbsp. fresh ginger, grated
2	cloves garlic, minced
¼	tsp. black pepper
¼	tsp. crushed red pepper
1	small orange, peeled, sliced, and halved (optional)
	Fresh cilantro (optional)

1. Preheat oven to 400°F. In a 15×10×1-inch baking pan combine shrimp, carrots, broccoli, and snow peas.
2. In a small bowl whisk oil, soy sauce, fish sauce, orange juice, ginger, garlic, black pepper, and crushed red pepper. Pour over shrimp and vegetables; toss to coat.
3. Roast 10 to 15 minutes or until vegetables are crisp-tender and shrimp is opaque. If desired, top with oranges and cilantro. Makes 4 servings.
PER SERVING *234 cal, 8 g fat, 183 mg chol, 760 mg sodium, 16 g carb, 4 g fiber, 8 g sugars, 27 g pro.*

ROASTED CURRY CHICKEN AND CAULIFLOWER

Photo on page 279.

A cool cucumber and yogurt sauce tempers the chicken's spice. Another night, spoon the stir-together sauce over spice-rubbed lamb or steak.

HANDS-ON TIME 10 minutes
TOTAL TIME 35 minutes

¾	cup plain Greek yogurt
2	Tbsp. olive oil
2	tsp. curry powder
¾	tsp. salt
¼	tsp. black pepper
4	bone-in, skin-on chicken thighs
1	small head cauliflower, cut into florets
½	cup cucumber, chopped
1	clove garlic, minced
2	Tbsp. mint leaves

1. Preheat oven to 450°F. In a large resealable plastic bag combine ¼ cup yogurt, the olive oil, curry powder, ½ tsp. salt, and ⅛ tsp. black pepper. Add chicken and cauliflower; shake to coat. Arrange in a 15×10×1-inch baking pan. Bake 25 to 30 minutes or until chicken is done (175°F), turning chicken and stirring cauliflower halfway through.
2. Meanwhile, in a small bowl stir together remaining yogurt, the cucumber, garlic, remaining ¼ tsp. salt, and ⅛ tsp. black pepper. Serve chicken and cauliflower with sauce and a sprinkle of mint. Makes 4 servings.
PER SERVING *327 cal, 15 g fat, 163 mg chol, 611 mg sodium, 8 g carb, 3 g fiber, 4 g sugars, 40 g pro.*

**GINGER SHRIMP
AND VEGETABLES**
Recipe on page 277

ROASTED CURRY CHICKEN AND CAULIFLOWER
Recipe on page 277

retro
THUMBPRINTS

This is the kind of classic made to be messed with. We transformed one foolproof dough into a colorful collection ready to rock the cookie tin.

BASIC THUMBPRINTS

HANDS-ON TIME 40 minutes
TOTAL TIME 2 hours

- ⅔ cup butter, softened
- ½ cup sugar
- 2 egg yolks
- 1 tsp. vanilla
- 1½ cups all-purpose flour
  Desired coating (opposite)
  Desired filling (opposite)

1. In a large bowl beat butter with a mixer on medium 30 seconds. Add sugar. Beat until combined, scraping sides of bowl as needed. Beat in egg yolks and vanilla until combined. Beat in flour. Chill, covered, 1 hour or until dough is easy to handle.

2. Preheat oven to 375°F. Grease a cookie sheet. Shape dough into 1-inch balls. Roll in desired coating. Place balls 1 inch apart on prepared cookie sheet. Using your thumb, make an indent in the center of each ball.

3. Bake 10 to 12 minutes or until bottoms are light brown. If centers puff up during baking, repress with the round side of a measuring teaspoon. Remove cookies; let cool on a wire rack. Before serving, fill centers with desired filling. Makes 30 cookies.

THERE ARE AS MANY WAYS TO DRESS UP A THUMBPRINT AS THERE ARE WAYS TO TRIM A TREE. LET THESE VARIATIONS BE A JUMPING-OFF POINT FOR YOUR OWN COOKIE CREATIVITY.

Lemon-Coconut
Prepare dough as directed, except add 1 tsp. lemon, lime, or orange zest with the egg yolks. Roll balls in egg whites then in 1 cup shredded coconut. Bake and let cool as directed. Fill each with ½ tsp. lemon or lime curd.

Triple-Chocolate
Prepare dough as directed, except reduce flour to 1¼ cups and add ¼ cup unsweetened cocoa powder with the flour. Roll balls in two lightly beaten egg whites then in 1 cup chocolate sprinkles. Bake as directed. Immediately press a chocolate Kiss into each.

Almond-Cherry
Prepare dough as directed, except add ½ tsp. almond extract with the egg yolks. Roll balls in 2 lightly beaten egg whites then in 1 cup finely chopped slivered almonds. Bake and let cool as directed. Fill each with 1 tsp. cherry pie filling, placing a cherry on top.

Mint Sparklers
Prepare dough as directed, except add ½ tsp. mint extract with the egg yolks. Do not grease cookie sheet. Roll balls in coarse red or green sugar. Bake as directed. Immediately place a red or green candy coating disk* in the center of each cookie. Bake 1 minute more. If desired, use a toothpick to swirl melted disks slightly.
*Tip Look for red and green candy coating disks in the cake-decorating department of hobby and crafts stores.

Linzer
Prepare dough, bake, and let cool as directed. Once cool, place ⅔ cup powdered sugar in a large plastic bag. Add cookies, a few at a time, shaking to coat. Fill each with ½ tsp. raspberry preserves. Top with toasted sliced almonds.

Walnuts and Jam
Prepare dough as directed, except roll balls in two lightly beaten egg whites then in 1 cup finely chopped walnuts. Bake and let cool as directed. Fill each with ½ tsp. apricot or strawberry preserves.

Sprinkle Stars
Prepare dough as directed, except do not grease cookie sheet. Roll balls in assorted nonpareils. Bake and cool as directed. Spoon ¾ cup canned or homemade vanilla frosting into a decorating bag fitted with a small star tip. Pipe frosting into each center.

PB&J
Prepare dough as directed, except roll balls in two lightly beaten egg whites then in 1 cup finely chopped peanuts. Bake and let cool as directed. Fill with ½ tsp. creamy peanut butter and ½ tsp. grape jelly. Sprinkle with chopped peanuts.

COOKIE STORAGE Layer filled Mint Sparklers and Triple-Chocolate between waxed paper in an airtight container. Layer and store all others unfilled. Store at room temperature up to 3 days or freeze up to 3 months. To serve, thaw (if frozen) and fill as directed.

sweet WONDERLAND

The season calls for an over-the-top dessert. Your mounting to-do list says otherwise. Enter pastry chef Zoë François, who shares five spectacular sweets that are easier than they look.

"For me baking is all joy, but I get that a lot of people are daunted by it," says pastry chef and cookbook author Zoë François. "I try to take the intimidation out of making dessert." Since starting her blog in 2007, Zoë has become known for her spectacular creations, which tend to generate thousands of likes on Instagram (@zoebakes), and for how she walks readers through her recipes with easy-to-follow instructions and videos.

That's why she's just the person to help home bakers during the holiday season. "It's a time of year when we all want to bake something festive, but there's not a lot of time or room for error," says Zoë, who lives in Minneapolis with her husband and two sons. The five festive desserts she created for BH&G® don't require any hard-to-master skills or obscure ingredients and can be made in part or entirely in advance. In other words, "Even a beginner can pull them off," Zoë says. "But they'll look like you've been baking all day."

Lightly press and lift a spoon to create swirls and peaks in meringue. Ridges and edges will toast quickly under a culinary torch or the broiler.

EGGNOG BAKED ALASKA

HANDS-ON TIME 20 minutes
TOTAL TIME 4 hours 20 minutes, includes freezing

RED VELVET CAKE

1   cup plus 2 Tbsp. all-purpose flour
2   Tbsp. unsweetened cocoa powder
¾   tsp. baking soda
¼   tsp. salt
½   cup whole milk
1   egg
1½   tsp. distilled white vinegar
1½   tsp. vanilla
⅓   cup vegetable oil
¾   cup sugar
1   Tbsp. red food coloring

ICE CREAM

½   gallon eggnog ice cream (or vanilla ice cream, softened
1 Tbsp. freshly grated nutmeg
2 Tbsp. bourbon

MERINGUE

1   cup egg whites (8 eggs), at room temperature
2   cups sugar

1. Preheat oven to 350°F. Butter a 9-inch square cake pan, line with parchment paper, then butter paper.
2. For Cake: In a medium bowl whisk together flour, cocoa, baking soda, and salt. In a separate bowl whisk together milk, egg, vinegar, and vanilla.
3. In a large bowl beat oil and sugar with a mixer on medium until combined. Beat in one-third of the flour mixture just until combined. Scrape sides of bowl; add half the milk mixture and mix just to combine. Add half the remaining flour mixture, then the remaining milk mixture and food coloring, scraping sides of bowl and mixing just to combine between additions. Beat in remaining flour mixture until batter is combined and uniform.

4. Pour into prepared pan. Bake 20 to 25 minutes or until a skewer inserted near center comes out with a few crumbs. Cool in pan 10 minutes. Remove from pan and let cool completely.
5. For Ice Cream, in a large bowl stir together softened ice cream, nutmeg, and bourbon.
6. To assemble: Line a 9×4-inch Pullman pan (or 9×5-inch loaf pan) with plastic wrap. Spoon ice cream to within 1 inch of the top of the pan.
7. Cut cake in half. Place half on ice cream in pan. Cover and freeze several hours or up to 1 month. (Wrap and freeze remaining cake up to 2 months.)
8. For Meringue: In a large heatproof bowl whisk together egg whites and sugar. (Mixture will be thick and grainy.) (For a 9×5-inch pan, reduce egg whites to ¾ cup [6 eggs] and sugar to 1½ cups.)
9. Place bowl over a saucepan of simmering water, being careful that bowl doesn't touch water. Whisk egg white mixture 10 minutes or until 160°F, sugar is completely dissolved, and mixture is smooth. Remove bowl from saucepan.
10. Beat meringue with a mixer on medium-high 6 minutes or until light, fluffy, glossy, and stiff peaks form.
11. To finish: Invert and unmold cake onto a chilled serving plate. Remove plastic wrap. Cover with meringue, creating peaks with the back of a spoon (see photo, left). Return to the freezer 1 hour or up to 4 hours. Immediately before serving, toast meringue using a culinary torch. (Or unmold cake onto a baking sheet lined with foil. Cover with meringue as directed; freeze at least 1 hour. Place oven rack 4 to 5 inches away from broiler; preheat broiler. Broil 2 to 3 minutes or until peaks are golden brown. Transfer to a chilled serving plate.) Serve immediately. Makes 12 servings.
PER SERVING *377 cal, 12 g fat, 49 mg chol, 154 mg sodium, 64 g carb, 1 g fiber, 56 g sugars, 6 g pro.*

ZOË REINVENTED CHEESECAKE, STARTING WITH THE FLAVORS: GINGER AND WHITE CHOCOLATE IN THE CAKE, HAZELNUT IN THE CRUST. THE DOME SHAPE, WHICH WAS INSPIRED BY SNOW GLOBES, IS CREATED BY BAKING THE CAKE IN A BOWL. A GLOSSY GANACHE AND WHITE CHOCOLATE SHAVINGS HIDE ANY IMPERFECTIONS. "THINK OF THEM AS INSURANCE," ZOË SAYS.

WHITE CHOCOLATE CHEESECAKE BOMBE

Crêpes dentelles are crunchy caramelized crepes. When you break the delicate rolled cookies into small flakes, you get feuilletine.

HANDS-ON TIME 45 minutes
TOTAL TIME 2 hours 30 minutes, plus chilling

CHEESECAKE
- ¾ cup heavy cream
- 12 oz. white baking chocolate, finely chopped
- 2 tsp. freshly grated ginger
- ½ cup sour cream
- 2 8-oz. pkg. cream cheese, softened
- ⅔ cup sugar
- 3 eggs, at room temperature
- 2 tsp. vanilla
- Pinch of salt

CRUST
- 2 oz. white baking chocolate, chopped
- 3 Tbsp. chocolate-hazelnut spread
- 2 oz. feuilletine or 1 cup crisp rice cereal or crushed rolled sugar ice cream cones

WHITE CHOCOLATE GANACHE
- ¾ cup heavy cream
- 12 oz. white baking chocolate, chopped

GARNISH
- White chocolate bar

1. Preheat oven to 325°F. Lightly butter a 2-qt. stainless-steel or tempered glass bowl (8-inch diameter across the top).
2. For Cheesecake: In a medium saucepan heat cream just until simmering. Turn off heat; add 12 oz. white chocolate and the ginger. Let stand 3 minutes; gently stir until smooth. Gently whisk in sour cream.

3. In a large bowl beat cream cheese with a mixer on medium 1 minute; scrape sides of bowl and beat 30 seconds more or until smooth. Add sugar; beat 1 minute more. Add eggs one at a time, scraping sides of bowl after each addition. Add vanilla and salt; beat 30 seconds or until smooth. Add white chocolate mixture; beat until combined.
4. Pour batter into prepared bowl. Set bowl in a roasting pan and fill about one-quarter of the way up the sides of the bowl with boiling water. (A water bath helps the cheesecake bake evenly and results in silky texture.) Loosely tent bowl with foil to prevent overbrowning. Bake 1 hour 45 minutes or until cheesecake is just set in the middle and temperature reads 175°F.
5. Remove bowl from water bath. Let cool completely in bowl on a wire rack (about 2 hours). Refrigerate at least 4 hours or overnight.
6. For Crust: In a small saucepan or double boiler melt 2 oz. white chocolate over low heat. Stir in chocolate-hazelnut spread and feuilletine. Crumble mixture over cheesecake; press gently. Chill 30 minutes.
7. Dip bottom of the bowl in a large pot of hot water several seconds. Using a rubber spatula, slowly press on crust edges to release from bowl. Working around crust edges, dip bowl in hot water as needed to loosen cheesecake from the bowl. Invert a small plate onto the crust. Gently press down on one side of the plate to slide the dome up the other side of the bowl. Invert the cheesecake and transfer crust side down onto a wire rack set in a baking pan lined with parchment paper.
8. For White Chocolate Ganache: In a medium saucepan heat cream just until simmering. Turn off heat; add white

chocolate. Let stand 3 minutes then gently stir until smooth. Cool to room temperature, stirring often.
9. Pour half the ganache over the cheesecake in an even layer. Return cheesecake to refrigerator 30 minutes to set. Repeat with remaining ganache, if necessary rewarming to a pourable consistency. Chill cheesecake loosely covered 30 minutes or up to 2 days.
10. To Garnish: Transfer cheesecake to a serving platter. Scrape the blade of a vegetable peeler over white chocolate bar to create curls. Cover cake top with curls. Serve immediately. Makes 12 servings.
PER SERVING *520 cal, 36 g fat, 102 mg chol, 172 mg sodium, 44 g carb, 41 g sugars, 7 g pro.*

After adding the crust and chilling, work your way around the bowl with a rubber spatula to loosen the domed cheesecake.

**TRIPLE-LAYER
HAZELNUT
SPICE CAKE**
Recipe on page 288

HOLIDAY PAVLOVA PARFAITS
Recipe on page 289

CANDIED HAZELNUTS

READY TO DIP Caramel thickens as it cools. It's ready to use when it coats and drips. If it runs off the hazelnut, wait 1 minute then try again.

DRIP-DRY Place skewers under a cutting board and let gravity do the rest. As the caramel drips, it creates dramatic strands.

SPUN SUGAR For an alternative, prepare caramel as in Step 11. Dip a fork into slightly cooled caramel and carefully drizzle in a circle onto greased foil from 2 feet above. Serve immediately.

TRIPLE-LAYER HAZELNUT SPICE CAKE

Photo on page 286.

If you were a contestant on The Great British Baking Show, *this might be your showstopper entry. Made with rum-soaked dried fruits and warm spices, this fruitcake is a world away from the one that's been circulating since the 1960s. The cake is so straightforward to make that you'll have time to create the dramatic candied hazelnut crown.*

HANDS-ON TIME 30 minutes
TOTAL TIME 4 hours 25 minutes, includes cooling

CAKE
2½   cups dried fruit, such as raisins or apricots and/or cherries chopped to the size of raisins
1   cup rum or apple juice
2¾   cups all-purpose flour
2   Tbsp. unsweetened cocoa powder
1   Tbsp. ground cinnamon
1   tsp. kosher salt
1   tsp. baking powder
1   tsp. ground ginger
1   tsp. ground nutmeg
1   tsp. ground allspice
¼   tsp. ground cloves
2¼   cups sugar
1   cup vegetable oil
¼   cup sour cream
2   Tbsp. molasses
3   eggs
1   cup milk
6   oz. hazelnuts (1¼ cups), toasted* and finely chopped

BUTTERCREAM
1½   cups unsalted butter (3 sticks), softened
6   cups powdered sugar
1   Tbsp. vanilla
     Homemade Lemon Curd (recipe, opposite page) or ½ cup purchased lemon curd and 1 tsp. lemon zest

CANDIED HAZELNUTS (OPTIONAL)
16   hazelnuts
1   cup sugar
¼   cup water
1   Tbsp. light-color corn syrup

1. For Cake: In a medium bowl soak dried fruit in rum at least an hour or overnight.
2. Preheat oven to 375°F. Butter three 8-inch cake pans, line with parchment paper, then butter paper.

3. In a medium bowl whisk together flour, cocoa powder, cinnamon, salt, baking powder, ginger, nutmeg, allspice, and cloves.
4. In a large bowl beat sugar, oil, sour cream, and molasses with a mixer on medium-high just until combined. Add eggs one at a time, beating until combined after each. Strain fruit. Add liquid to batter. Set aside fruit.
5. Beat in one-third of the flour mixture just until combined. Scrape sides of bowl; add half the milk and mix to combine. Add half the remaining flour mixture then remaining milk, scraping sides of bowl and mixing just to combine between additions. Beat in remaining flour until batter is combined and uniform. Fold in hazelnuts and soaked fruit. Pour batter into prepared pans.
6. Bake 35 to 40 minutes or until a skewer inserted near center comes out with moist crumbs. Cool completely in pans on wire racks. Remove from pans. If desired, wrap and freeze cakes up to 1 month.
7. For Buttercream: In an extra-large bowl beat unsalted butter and powdered sugar with a mixer on medium 3 to 4 minutes or until fluffy (mixture may appear crumbly at first but will come together). Beat in vanilla.
8. In a large bowl fold together buttercream and Homemade Lemon or Lime Curd. Spread a thick layer between cake layers, then frost cake with remaining. Secure cake layers with skewers, if necessary, until set. Loosely cover and refrigerate up to 1 day. Let stand 1 hour before serving.
9. For Candied Hazelnuts:* Set a heavy cutting board or 15×11-inch baking pan along the edge of the counter. (Skewers will wedge under the cutting board while candied hazelnuts set.) Place parchment paper on floor below to catch caramel drips.
10. Preheat oven to 350°F. Place hazelnuts in a shallow baking pan. Bake 5 to 8 minutes or until toasted. Transfer to a towel; rub to remove loose skins. Gently twist a wood skewer into each hazelnut while warm; set aside.
11. In a medium saucepan stir together sugar, the water, and corn syrup. Use a pastry brush dipped in water to brush down any sugar crystals on sides of saucepan as mixture comes to boil. Bring to boiling over medium-high without stirring. Reduce heat to medium. Once

mixture starts to caramelize (about 15 minutes), remove from heat and let stand 5 minutes, stirring occasionally.

12. Dip a skewered hazelnut into caramel and lift to see if caramel is ready. When caramel coats hazelnut and drips off in long strands, secure end of skewer under cutting board, letting caramel drip onto the parchment paper below. Repeat with remaining hazelnuts. Let stand until caramel is set, about 15 minutes.

13. Gently twist skewers to release hazelnuts; arrange on cake.

14. To finish: If desired, arrange Candied Hazelnuts or spun sugar (see sidebar, opposite) on cake. Makes 18 servings.

PER SERVING *814 cal, 39 g fat, 123 mg chol, 122 mg sodium, 108 g carb, 2 g fiber, 86 g sugars, 7 g pro.*

*Note Save these until an hour or two before you're ready to top and serve the cake. Humidity and temperature can wilt the caramel strands.

HOMEMADE LEMON OR LIME CURD

TOTAL TIME 45 minutes

- 2   lemons or limes (1½ tsp. zest; ⅓ cup juice)
- 4   egg yolks
- ⅔   cup sugar
     Pinch salt
- ⅓   cup unsalted butter, cut up

1. In a large heatproof bowl whisk together zest, juice, egg yolks, sugar, and salt.

2. Place the bowl over a saucepan of simmering water, being careful that the bowl doesn't touch the water. Cook until curd mixture begins to thicken (160°F), about 15 to 20 minutes, stirring constantly with a rubber spatula. Add butter; cook and stir 10 to 15 minutes more or until butter is melted and curd is the consistency of thick pudding and coats the back of a metal spoon.

3. If there are any lumps, press curd through a fine-mesh sieve. Place plastic wrap on curd surface; chill 30 minutes or up to 3 days. Makes 1 cup.

HOLIDAY PAVLOVA PARFAITS

Photo on page 287.

HANDS-ON TIME 1 hour
TOTAL TIME 2 hours 15 minutes

"This dessert looks really elegant even though you just throw it together," Zoë says. "You can't mess it up." Most of the components—sugared cranberries, lime curd, raspberry sauce, and meringues—can be made days ahead of time. On the night of the party, simply layer everything in your prettiest glassware.

MERINGUE
- ¼   cup egg whites (2 eggs), at room temperature
- ½   cup granulated sugar

CRANBERRY-RASPBERRY SAUCE
- 2   cups fresh or frozen cranberries, thawed
- ½   cup granulated sugar
- 2   cups frozen or fresh raspberries

SUGARED CRANBERRIES
- ½   cup granulated sugar
- ⅔   cup fresh or frozen cranberries, thawed
- 1   Tbsp. pasteurized egg whites or refrigerated egg whites

LIME CREAM
- 2   cups heavy cream
- 1   Tbsp. powdered sugar
- ⅔   cup purchased lime curd or Homemade Lime Curd (recipe, left)
- 1   tsp. lime zest

1. For Meringue: Preheat oven to 250°F. In a large heatproof bowl whisk together egg whites and sugar (mixture will be thick and grainy). Place bowl over a saucepan of simmering water, being careful that bowl doesn't touch water. Whisk egg mixture 3 to 5 minutes or until sugar is completely dissolved and mixture is smooth. Remove bowl.

2. Beat mixture on medium-high 3 to 5 minutes or until light, fluffy, glossy, and stiff peaks form.

3. Transfer meringue to a pastry bag fitted with a star tip. Pipe quarter-size rosettes on a baking sheet lined with parchment paper.

4. Bake 30 minutes. Turn off oven; let meringues stand in cooling oven 1 hour. Meringues can be made one day ahead and stored in an airtight container at room temperature.

5. For Cranberry-Raspberry sauce: (Whether you use frozen or fresh raspberries determines when you add them.) In a medium saucepan combine cranberries, sugar, and raspberries if using frozen. Bring to boiling, stirring frequently; reduce heat. Simmer, uncovered, 10 minutes or until cranberries are soft and juices are thick. (If using fresh raspberries, fold in now.) Let cool. Chill, covered, up to 1 week.

6. For Sugared Cranberries: Pour sugar into a shallow pie plate. Working in batches, roll cranberries in pasteurized egg whites then in sugar to coat. Allow to dry on a baking sheet lined with parchment paper.

7. For Lime Cream: In a large bowl beat cream and powdered sugar until soft peaks form. Beat in lime curd and zest.

8. To assemble: Layer Lime Cream, Cranberry-Raspberry Sauce, and Meringues in eight glasses; repeating layers. Garnish with Sugared Cranberries. Serve immediately or within 2 hours. Makes 8 servings.

PER SERVING *452 cal, 23 g fat, 88 mg chol, 47 mg sodium, 58 g carb, 4 g fiber, 52 g sugars, 3 g pro.*

THIS BEJEWELED YULE LOG MAY LOOK ALMOST TOO AMBITIOUS TO ATTEMPT. IN REALITY, "EACH STEP IS SUPER SIMPLE," ZOË SAYS.

SILVER AND GOLD YULE LOG

Most tasks can also be done in advance, which eases the pressure on Christmas Day. The only key bit of timing: To avoid cracks, be sure to roll the cake while it's warm out of the oven.

HANDS-ON TIME 50 minutes
TOTAL TIME 4 hours 50 minutes, including cooling

ALMOND SPONGE CAKE

4 large eggs, at room temperature
⅓ cup sugar
½ tsp. vanilla
1 cup almond flour (almond meal)
½ cup all-purpose flour
¼ tsp. baking powder

ALMOND PRALINE

½ cup sugar
1 tsp. light-color corn syrup
½ cup slivered almonds, lightly toasted (tip, page 27)

SWISS BUTTERCREAM

⅔ cup egg whites (5 eggs), at room temperature
2 cups sugar
1 lb. unsalted butter (4 sticks), cut into 2-Tbsp. pieces, at room temperature
1 tsp. vanilla

GARNISH

2 Tbsp. oz. white chocolate, melted
   Gold edible luster dust (optional)
   Silver, gold, and white dragées and/or large nonpareils

1. For Almond-Sponge Cake: Preheat oven to 375°F. Butter a 15×10-inch baking pan, line with parchment paper, then butter paper.
2. In a large mixing bowl beat eggs, sugar, and vanilla with a mixer on high 7 to 9 minutes or until light, fluffy, and tripled in volume.

3. In a small bowl whisk together flours and baking powder. Gently fold half the flour mixture into the egg mixture; repeat with remaining flour mixture. Spread batter evenly into prepared pan.
4. Bake 12 minutes or until cake is set and lightly golden. Use a small knife to loosen edges of the cake.
5. Lay a clean kitchen towel on a work surface; generously dust with powdered sugar. Quickly invert hot cake onto towel. Peel off parchment paper and starting at a short end roll hot cake and towel into a log (see how-tos, page 292). Let cool completely on a wire rack.
6. For Almond Praline: In a large skillet cook sugar, 2 Tbsp. water, and the corn syrup over medium-high, without stirring, 2 minutes or until melted and showing signs of caramelizing (beginning to brown). Stir; cook 3 to 4 minutes more or until evenly dark and starting to smoke. Remove from heat; stir in almonds and a pinch of salt. Pour mixture onto a silicone baking mat or lightly buttered parchment paper; let cool.
7. Break into pieces and place in a food processor; pulse until chopped into pieces no larger than pine nuts. Store in an airtight container in a cool, dry place up to 1 day.
8. For Swiss Buttercream: In a large heatproof bowl whisk together egg whites and sugar (mixture will be thick and grainy). Place bowl over a saucepan of simmering water, being careful that bowl doesn't touch water. Whisk 10 minutes or until 160°F, sugar is completely dissolved, and mixture is smooth. Remove bowl from saucepan.
9. Beat meringue on medium-high 8 to 12 minutes or until light, fluffy, glossy, and stiff peaks form.
10. Transfer ½ cup meringue to a pastry bag fitted with a ¼-inch round tip (to pipe mushrooms); set aside.
11. Let bowl with remaining meringue sit at room temperature 10 minutes. Beat

in butter, 2 Tbsp. at a time, on medium 10 minutes or until fluffy. After all the butter is added, beat 1 minute more or until buttercream is creamy and glossy. Beat in vanilla and a pinch of salt.
12. Divide buttercream in half. Stir almond praline mixture into one half. (Chill remaining buttercream until needed, up to 2 days. To soften, stand at room temperature 2 hours, then place bowl over saucepan of simmering water and heat 1 minute. Beat on medium-high until creamy.)
13. For meringue mushrooms: Preheat oven to 250°F. On a baking sheet lined with parchment paper, pipe half the meringue in the pastry bag into ¾- to 1-inch mounds (about 20 mushroom caps). Pipe remaining meringue into squat stems that come to a point (about 20). Bake 30 minutes. Turn off oven; let meringues stand in cooling oven 1 hour. (Meringues can be made 1 day ahead. Store in an airtight container at room temperature.)
14. Using a paring knife or wooden skewer, poke a small hole into center of flat side of caps. Dip stem tips in melted white chocolate, then insert into caps for mushrooms. If desired, brush tops of mushrooms with luster dust.
15. To assemble: Unroll cooled cake. Spread praline buttercream in an even layer over cake. Reroll cake into a log, lifting towel to guide roll.
16. Cut off a few inches from the end of roll at an angle to resemble a branch. Transfer log portion to a serving platter. Frost one end of branch with enough buttercream to stick to log; gently press branch onto the top of log. Frost entire cake, dragging a spatula for texture. Decorate with dragées and meringue mushrooms. Makes 12 servings.
PER SERVING *612 cal, 40 g fat, 143 mg chol, 81 mg sodium, 60 g carb, 2 g fiber, 53 g sugars, 7 g pro.*

YULE LOG HOW-TOS

BUTTERCREAM

ZOË'S EASY-TO-HANDLE STEPS FOR HER FESTIVE YULE LOG ENSURE YOURS WILL TURN OUT BEAUTIFULLY.

1 The meringue mixture may look curdled and runny as you add butter. Keep adding butter and mixing.

2 After all the butter has been added, the mixture will come back to a smooth buttercream.

MERINGUE MUSHROOMS

1 Pipe meringue into two shapes: small round mounds (caps) and tall pointed peaks (stems).

2 After meringues have baked and cooled, make divots in the flat sides of caps. Insert stems.

3 Dip a clean small paintbrush into edible gold luster dust and tap the brush over the mushrooms.

CAKE ROLL

1 A hot cake is pliable enough to roll without cracking, and a towel keeps the cake from sticking.

2 After the cake cools, unroll it, add buttercream, and reroll using the towel to lift and guide the cake.

3 Use a serrated knife to cut off one end of the roll. Then attach the piece to the top with buttercream.

EDIBLE TERRARIUM

If the sugarplum fairies aren't already dancing, this sweet and snowy scene will set them twirling.

FILL A LARGE GLASS COOKIE JAR WITH A COUPLE INCHES OF GRANULATED SUGAR TO SET THE SCENE FOR A WHIMSICAL FOREST. ADD A FEW FRESH ROSEMARY "BUSHES" THEN TIE TWINE AROUND THE LID TO COMPLETE THE COOKIE JAR TERRARIUM.

GINGERBREAD CUTOUTS

HANDS-ON TIME 50 minutes
TOTAL TIME 2 hours, including chilling

½   cup shortening
¼   cup butter, softened
½   cup granulated sugar
1   tsp. baking powder
1   tsp. ground ginger
½   tsp. baking soda
½   tsp. ground cinnamon
½   tsp. ground cloves
¼   tsp. salt
1   egg
½   cup molasses
1   Tbsp. cider vinegar
3   cups all-purpose flour

1. In a large bowl beat shortening and butter with a mixer on medium to high 30 seconds. Add the next seven ingredients (through salt). Beat until combined, scraping bowl as needed. Beat in egg, molasses, and vinegar. Beat in as much of the flour as you can with the mixer. Stir in any remaining flour. Divide dough in half. Cover and chill 1 hour or until dough is easy to handle.
2. Preheat oven to 375°F. On a lightly floured surface, roll out one dough portion at a time and cut out shapes, rerolling scraps as needed. Place cutouts 1 inch apart on ungreased cookie sheets.
3. Bake 6 to 8 minutes or until edges are firm. Cool on cookie sheet 1 minute. Remove; cool on wire rack. Makes 24 to 48 cookies.
To Store Place between sheets of waxed paper in an airtight container. Store at room temperature up to 3 days or freeze undecorated cookies up to 3 months. Thaw cookies; decorate, if desired.
PER SMALL COOKIE *151 cal, 7 g fat, 13 mg chol, 92 mg sodium, 21 g carb, 9 g sugars, 2 g pro.*

SUGAR COOKIE CUTOUTS

HANDS-ON TIME 40 minutes
TOTAL TIME 1 hour 20 minutes, including chilling

⅔   cup butter, softened
¾   cup sugar
1   tsp. baking powder
¼   tsp. salt
1   egg
1   Tbsp. milk
1   tsp. vanilla
2   cups all-purpose flour

1. In a large bowl beat butter with a mixer on medium to high 30 seconds. Add sugar, baking powder, and salt. Beat until combined, scraping bowl as needed. Beat in egg, milk, and vanilla until combined. Beat in as much of the flour as you can with the mixer. Stir in any remaining flour. Divide dough in half. Cover and chill dough 30 minutes or until easy to handle.
2. Preheat oven to 375°F. On a floured surface, roll one portion of dough at a time to ⅛- to ¼-inch thickness. Using cookie cutters, cut into shapes. Place 1 inch apart on ungreased cookie sheets.
3. Bake 7 to 10 minutes or until edges are firm and bottoms are very light brown. Transfer to wire racks and let cool. Makes 36 to 48 cookies.
PER SMALL COOKIE *74 cal, 4 g fat, 15 mg chol, 49 mg sodium, 10 g carb, 4 g sugars, 1 g pro.*

ROYAL ICING

TOTAL TIME 15 minutes

1   16-oz. pkg. powdered sugar
3   Tbsp. meringue powder*
½   tsp. cream of tartar
½   cup warm water
1   tsp. vanilla

1. In a large bowl stir together powdered sugar, meringue powder, and cream of tartar. Add the water and vanilla. Beat with a mixer on low until combined. Beat on high 7 to 10 minutes or until icing is very stiff. If not using immediately, cover bowl with a damp paper towel then cover tightly with plastic wrap (icing will dry out quickly when exposed to air). Chill up to 48 hours. Stir before using. Makes 3 cups.
*Note Meringue powder is a mixture of pasteurized egg whites, sugar, and edible gums. It is the crucial ingredient to make Royal Icing dry quickly with a smooth, hard finish. Look for it in the baking aisle of supermarkets or the cake decorating department of hobby and crafts stores.

SIMPLE WOODLAND DECORATING

You can be a novice cookie decorator and achieve cuteness. Simply use white Royal Icing and a piping bag fit with a small round tip to pipe dots and lines on fauna and florals.

PAIR OF BUNNIES

FAWN

MUSHROOM

TALL GREEN TREE

COOKIE STAND

To prop up cookies for display, cut triangles from dough scraps, bake, then attach the stands to the backs of cookies using Royal Icing.

BUILD A GINGERBREAD HOUSE

Create freehand templates using parchment paper, a ruler, and a pencil to cut out the front, back, sides, and roof pieces (six pieces total).

1 Place template on rolled-out dough. Using a sharp knife, trace around templates. Bake as directed. Pipe thin lines of icing for door, siding, and/or windows on cooled cookies.

2 Pipe icing along the edge of one side piece. Press on the back of the front piece to form a corner, holding pieces together to set. Repeat with remaining pieces.

3 Once sides are set, add the roof. Pipe icing along the triangular edges of the front and back pieces. Attach the roof, holding each piece in place to set.

RECIPE INDEX

METRIC INFORMATION

PRODUCT DIFFERENCES

Most of the ingredients called for in the recipes in this book are available in most countries. However, some are known by different names. Here are some common American ingredients and their possible counterparts:

SUGAR (white) is granulated, fine granulated, or castor sugar.

POWDERED SUGAR is icing sugar.

ALL-PURPOSE FLOUR is enriched, bleached or unbleached white household flour. When self-rising flour is used in place of all-purpose flour in a recipe that calls for leavening, omit the leavening agent (baking soda or baking powder) and salt.

LIGHT-COLOR CORN SYRUP is golden syrup.

CORNSTARCH is cornflour.

BAKING SODA is bicarbonate of soda.

VANILLA OR VANILLA EXTRACT is vanilla essence.

GREEN, RED, OR YELLOW SWEET PEPPERS are capsicums or bell peppers.

GOLDEN RAISINS are sultanas.

SHORTENING is solid vegetable oil (substitute Copha or lard).

MEASUREMENT ABBREVIATIONS

MEASUREMENT	ABBREVIATIONS
fluid ounce	fl. oz.
gallon	gal.
gram	g
liter	L
milliliter	ml
ounce	oz.
package	pkg.
pint	pt.

COMMON WEIGHT EQUIVALENTS

IMPERIAL / U.S.	METRIC
½ ounce	14.18 g
1 ounce	28.35 g
4 ounces (¼ pound)	113.4 g
8 ounces (½ pound)	226.8 g
16 ounces (1 pound)	453.6 g
1¼ pounds	567 g
1½ pounds	680.4 g
2 pounds	907.2 g

OVEN TEMPERATURE EQUIVALENTS

FAHRENHEIT SETTING	CELSIUS SETTING
300°F	150°C
325°F	160°C
350°F	180°C
375°F	190°C
400°F	200°C
425°F	220°C
450°F	230°C
475°F	240°C
500°F	260°C
Broil	Broil

*For convection or forced air ovens (gas or electric), lower the temperature setting 25°F/10°C when cooking at all heat levels.

APPROXIMATE STANDARD METRIC EQUIVALENTS

MEASUREMENT	OUNCES	METRIC
⅛ tsp.		0.5 ml
¼ tsp.		1 ml
½ tsp.		2.5 ml
1 tsp.		5 ml
1 Tbsp.		15 ml
2 Tbsp.	1 fl. oz.	30 ml
¼ cup	2 fl. oz.	60 ml
⅓ cup	3 fl. oz.	80 ml
½ cup	4 fl. oz.	120 ml
⅔ cup	5 fl. oz.	160 ml
¾ cup	6 fl. oz.	180 ml
1 cup	8 fl. oz.	240 ml
2 cups	16 fl. oz. (1 pt.)	480 ml
1 qt.	64 fl. oz. (2 pt.)	0.95 L

CONVERTING TO METRIC

centimeters to inches	divide centimeters by 2.54
cups to liters	multiply cups by 0.236
cups to milliliters	multiply cups by 236.59
gallons to liters	multiply gallons by 3.785
grams to ounces	divide grams by 28.35
inches to centimeters	multiply inches by 2.54
kilograms to pounds	divide kilograms by 0.454
liters to cups	divide liters by 0.236
liters to gallons	divide liters by 3.785
liters to pints	divide liters by 0.473
liters to quarts	divide liters by 0.946
milliliters to cups	divide milliliters by 236.59
milliliters to fluid ounces	divide milliliters by 29.57
milliliters to tablespoons	divide milliliters by 14.79
milliliters to teaspoons	divide milliliters by 4.93
ounces to grams	multiply ounces by 28.35
ounces to milliliters	multiply ounces by 29.57
pints to liters	multiply pints by 0.473
pounds to kilograms	multiply pounds by 0.454
quarts to liters	multiply quarts by 0.946
tablespoons to milliliters	multiply tablespoons by 14.79
teaspoons to milliliters	multiply teaspoons by 4.93